The World Atlas of
PIRATES

The World Atlas of
PIRATES

*Treasures and Treachery on the Seven Seas,
in Maps, Tall Tales, and Pictures*

ANGUS KONSTAM

The Lyons Press
Guilford, Connecticut
An imprint of Globe Pequot Press

First Lyons Press edition, 2010

Packaged for AA Media Limited by Hunkydory Publishing Ltd.
www.hunkydorypublishing.com

The maps in this book are for historical reference only
and should not be used for navigational purposes.

The Lyons Press is an imprint of Globe Pequot Press.

Library of Congress Cataloging-in-Publication Data is available on file.

ISBN 978-1-59921-474-0

Printed in China

10 9 8 7 6 5 4 3 2 1

Contents

Right: A 17th-century painting by Willem van de Velde the Younger, showing pirates attacking a British Navy warship of the time. A daring act, as pirates usually attacked only smaller, less well-defended craft.

Introduction

The aim of this book is to set the record straight—to expose the romantic myths about pirates that have existed for centuries. In fact, piracy was a brutal business, far removed from the rose-tinted world of captain Jack Sparrow.

One of many depictions of Blackbeard—the most notorious pirate—in his final battle with Maynard.

Piracy is neither the invention of Hollywood, nor something from a bygone age. You only have to pick up a newspaper or watch the news to be reminded that pirates are very real, and in deadly earnest. This might surprise many who see piracy as something more benign—a theme for costume parties or the actions of romantic swashbucklers.

The unvarnished truth is that piracy is a crime. According to the dictionary it involves an act of robbery, committed on the high seas. If that doesn't sound particularly exotic or romantic, it shouldn't. Piracy has been known to encompass assault, murder, kidnapping, and torture, none of which sit comfortably with the popular view of piracy.

Piracy has existed since the dawn of recorded history and is still happening today. The first pirates used oared galleys; those from the so-called "Golden Age of Piracy" in the early 18th century operated in small fast-sailing craft. Instead of sailing ships and cutlasses, modern pirates use speedboats and assault rifles. Piracy flourishes in waters that are inadequately policed or along coasts where there is little law and order. This was true in the waters of the Aegean Sea during the ancient Greek era and in the Caribbean of the mid-17th century, and it is true in the Red Sea today, where Somali pirates prey on passing supertankers and container ships.

As a historian, I first became interested in piracy when I was asked to curate a piracy exhibition for a maritime museum based in Key West, Florida. We managed to find plenty of objects to display from shipwrecks or borrowed from other museums. However, what we seemed to lack were hard facts—the bare bones of the story. While a lot had been written about pirates over the years, most of this literature seemed to perpetuate the same pirate myths. It was hard to sort out the fact from the fiction. This job was made harder by Hollywood,

Modern pirates based at Riau Islands, Indonesia. Piracy is a big problem in the South China Sea.

and before that by fiction writers, both of whom consistently portrayed pirates as romantic figures inhabiting a world of cruel governors, richly laden treasure ships, and pretty but wayward daughters. I decided I had to try and cut away the myth from the reality. Little did I know, but the job was to take the best part of a decade.

The problem was that the truth about pirates was very hard to find, buried deep in dusty court records, newspapers, letters, and reports. What emerged was a very different kind of pirate from those we had become accustomed to. Most of these pirates were men who were driven to a life of crime by circumstance. These included mutiny against an unpopular captain, being cast ashore in port without any prospects of gainful work, or being captured by pirates and then forced to join their crew. If captured, these men often railed against the injustices of society and the way seamen were treated by ship owners and captains. While much of this was just gallows rhetoric, it had its roots in the realities of life at sea during the Age of Sail.

This is strangely similar to accounts of modern pirates. Those who attack oil rigs off the coast of West Africa claim they are protesting against the harsh conditions of life in the region, where oil companies are seen as all-powerful, exploitative, and unsympathetic. In the waters of Indonesia and the Philippines, pirates often claim they attack passing ships in order to steal the food, weapons, and money they need to survive. For them, piracy is seen as a necessary means to an end. Then there are the Somali pirates, who capture ships and their crews and hold them for ransom. In interviews, they speak of themselves as coastguards, protecting their coasts and fishing stocks from rapacious interlopers. In all these cases, the excuses are pretty similar to those given in the early 18th century. For these people, piracy is a way of fighting back.

We know how these modern pirates justify their actions because most pirate groups around the world have given press interviews. This in turn reflects our enduring fascination with piracy. We seem determined to continue surrounding the crime with a cocoon of romanticism, regardless of how brutal the truth can be. This was the same in the days of Blackbeard, "Black Bart" Roberts, and William Kidd. Back in 1724, a London company published a bestseller—a lurid exposé of the business of piracy called A General History of the Robberies and Murders of the Most Notorious Pyrates. It revealed a world of brutal attacks and acts of depravity, but also offered readers an escapist look at a life which existed beyond the rigid confines of polite 18th-century society.

By reading about pirates, people were transported into a world very different from their own, set amid an exotic backdrop of palm-fringed beaches and warm tropical seas.

My hope is that this book, The World Atlas of Pirates, will offer you

Jack Sparrow captured the imagination of millions, but he represents Hollywood's romanticized view of pirates.

that same opportunity to read about pirates and their lives from the safety of your armchair, but these are "real" pirates, whose stories may not be quite so romantic. You can follow their journeys of wealth and fortune, as well as murder and betrayal.

I have made every attempt to add exact dates to their raiding maps, but do remember, these rascals had little time to keep diaries.

Angus Konstam

What's in a Name?

One of the problems with historical pirates is trying to determine if they were pirates at all. A pirate in one country could have been an explorer or hero in another, commissioned by a monarch to "conquer" new lands or seas.

Correctly applied, someone who is a "pirate" would attack ships without worrying which national flag they flew. Even then, some pirates operated under self-applied restrictions, hoping that if they avoided attacks on the shipping of their home country, they might earn a pardon.

The line between legal "privateer" and illegal "pirate" was often all to easy to cross, as Captain Kidd (see pages 115-118) discovered to his cost. Other names keep cropping up throughout history—"corsair," "freebooter," "swashbuckler," "buccaneer," and several others, all of which have their own meaning. Often these people weren't pirates at all, and the words are used without too much care. Clearly we need to define exactly what a pirate is—and what he isn't.

First of all, a pirate isn't a privateer, buccaneer, filibuster, corsair, freebooter, or swashbuckler. All these terms have their own meanings, and none of them really say pirate. While we'll look at most of these in more detail later on, we need to say a little about

Right: Edward Teach, better known as "Blackbeard," was one of the most notorious pirates in history.

Left: The pirate Henry Every, notable for being one of the few who managed to retire with his plunder.

itself, many of which were purpose-built for the job. What the word didn't mean was a pirate. Even the people who were attacked knew the difference between the two. Put simply, privateers operated under fairly strict rules; pirates wrote their own.

As for real pirates, they were the people who didn't hide behind laws as privateers did, or limit their attacks to the Spanish, as the "buccaneers" did. They attacked anyone, regardless of nationality. And unlike the buccaneers, who tended to land and raid towns, the pirates we encounter in the early 18th century—the pirates' heyday—rarely set foot ashore outside a few pirate havens such as New Providence in the Bahamas, St. Mary's Island off Madagascar, or Ocracoke Island in North Carolina's Outer Banks. These and other bases provided bolt-holes, where the pirates could sell their plunder, spend their ill-gotten gains, and were protected by the local populace who often provided an infrastructure designed to support piratical activities. This was just as true

some of them before we go any further. A "privateer" was a captain who belonged to a country that was at war, and was given permission to attack enemy shipping. He was given a contract—a "letter of marque," which meant that as a privateer he was legally permitted to hunt down and capture enemy ships as long as his country remained at war with the enemy. Once peace was declared, the whole agreement was canceled. In effect, a privateer was a licensed pirate who didn't attack his own countrymen. The French often called privateers "corsairs," although the term later became associated with Mediterranean pirates rather than just privateers, which of course muddies the waters even more!

What the government who issued the "letter of marque" gained from the deal was a free warship—or at least one that would go off and attack enemy merchant ships. It also got a share of the spoils—usually

20 percent of the value of any captured ship and its cargo. This meant that privateering was a worthwhile business in the Age of Sail, and most of the major maritime powers made use of them. Of course, the term privateer was often used to refer to a seaman as well as a ship's captain or ship owner, and it was even used when speaking about the vessel

Buccaneers, Filibusters, and Swashbucklers

Another confusing term is "buccaneer," which— if used properly—should only be applied to the men who fought against the Spanish in the Caribbean of the later 17th century. The word had its roots in the French word *boucan*, the smoked meat produced by the hunters of Hispaniola. The term eventually came to be applied to the English, French, and Dutch raiders who preyed on the Spanish Main, capturing Spanish ships and sacking Spanish cities. The French confused things by using the term "filibuster" for the same people, a word

that was later anglicized to "freebooter."

Another confusing term is "swashbuckler," which was a 16th-century word meaning an armed brigand or outlaw. By the following century it meant "swordsman," and in the 20th century was adopted by pirate novelists and then by Hollywood to refer to dashing pirates. In other words, the term is a modern invention, and has nothing to do with the pirates of history.

Left: Unlike earlier pirates, the buccaneers of the 17th century frequently operated in large groups. For his attack on Panama in 1671, Henry Morgan commanded a force of more than 1,500 buccaneers.

PIRATE OR PRIVATEER?

The distinction between piracy and something less illegal isn't a new phenomenon. Captain William Kidd was a privateer who later turned to piracy when his privateering cruise proved unsuccessful. He then tried to claim that he had remained on the proper side of the law, but the evidence against him proved too damning. Blackbeard's mentor Benjamin Hornigold was a pirate who refused to attack English ships. By concentrating his efforts against the Spanish and the French he tried to maintain the illusion that he was a law-abiding privateer rather than a fully fledged pirate. Actually, this ploy worked for Hornigold because he eventually secured a royal pardon. Bizarrely, he then became a pirate-hunter, and helped Governor Woodes Rogers drive pirates from the waters of the Bahamas.

Sir Francis Drake, a man now viewed as a national hero, was in his time regarded either as a pirate or a privateer, depending on who was judging him. While he officially claimed he was a privateer, and this illusion was supported by Queen Elizabeth who also had a financial stake in his voyages, he was in fact a pirate. After all, for most of the time he operated, England and Spain were at peace, so he had little right to declare himself a law-abiding privateer. However, an obscure legal loophole allowed him to attack the Spanish to seek redress—to help right a wrongdoing. The wrongdoing mentioned in this less-than-legal "letter of redress" was the attack on the ships of Drake and his kinsman John Hawkins in a

Are Pirates Lone Wolves or Members of the Pack?

While the buccaneers tended to hunt in packs, with a few notable exceptions pirates tended to operate on their own—lone wolves who rarely teamed up with others. This really applied to the pirates of the so-called "Golden Age"—those who operated during the first decades of the 18th century. At other times and places—most notably in the Mediterranean of the ancient world or Chinese waters during the early 19th century—piracy was a much bigger operation, and whole pirate fleets tended to operate together. While this was potentially dangerous, these pirates usually offered protection, for a fee, of course. Most often, ship owners found it cheaper and less dangerous to pay protection money than to risk passing through pirate waters without striking a deal.

in the days of Blackbeard as it is today, on the coasts of West Africa or Somalia.

Some pirates offered protection to ensure the safe passage of ships whose owners had reached an agreement with them. It can be argued that these people weren't pirates at all, but protectors. This type of arrangement was as common in the waters of the ancient Mediterranean and early 19th-century China as it is today. When interviewed recently, Somali pirates claimed they were coast guards, protecting ships passing through their waters in return for the right to demand payment for their services. This argument is less impressive when the Somali pirates attack ships in international waters, or hijack them and hold their crews for ransom. In these cases, the pirates see themselves as law-abiding but their victims see them as criminals.

Above: Edward England was a Red Sea roundsman"
—a pirate who operated in the Red Sea and Indian
Ocean, preying on Indian merchantmen and ships
of the English East India Company.

port on the Mexican coast in 1568. The fact
that Drake and Hawkins were there illegally
was never mentioned. While Drake saw
himself as a privateer, the Spanish viewed him
as a pirate, and a bloodthirsty one at that.

Morgan's Duality

Another character whose role was difficult
to define was Sir Henry Morgan. At first,
Morgan operated as a law-abiding privateer,

attacking Spanish ships and settlements in the
Caribbean. However, when England and Spain
signed a peace treaty, Morgan continued to
attack the hapless Spaniards. Technically he
had become a pirate, but he still enjoyed
the protection of the Governor of Jamaica
who represented the English crown. In the
end he was arrested and shipped back to
London to stand trial. Morgan's triumph
was that he managed to earn the good
grace of King Charles II and returned to
Jamaica a free man. All this time the Spanish
saw Morgan as a criminal, even though he
ended up as Jamaica's Deputy
Governor, and one of the wealth-
iest and most respected land-
owners in the Caribbean.

Pirates of Fiction

Regardless of what they called
themselves, or how others saw
them, most pirates throughout
history operated the same way.
These principles—the basics of the
craft of piracy—were applied just as
much in the ancient Mediterranean
as they were in the Caribbean of
the 17th and 18th century, and
many any of these principles still
apply today. For a start, pirates like
to intimidate their victims, forcing
them to surrender without a fight.
Then they take what they came
for and make a fast getaway. The
fictional pirate adage "dead men

tell no tales" was based on harsh reality—
survivors could indentify their assailants.
Many pirates, particularly those who feared
retribution, would murder their victims in
order to protect themselves.

None bothered with the fictional piratical
favorite of walking the plank. It was much
easier to throw the victims overboard, and
watch them drown. Plank-walking was the
creation of JM Barrie, who wrote *Peter Pan.*
Many other examples of pirate lore can also
be linked to fiction—treasure maps were
the invention of Robert Louis Stevenson,

Right: Pirates never made their victims
walk the plank—this was the literary
invention of *Peter Pan* author, JM Barrie.

who created them for *Treasure Island*. He did the same with buried treasure and the "black spot," which was presented to a pirate to officially pronounce a verdict of guilt or judgment. What these pirate fiction writers did get right was the general atmosphere of piracy in its heyday.

So too did the screenwriters and directors of the movie *Pirates of the Caribbean*. What they all had at their fingertips was an excellent source, a reference book from which they took accurate information, fleshing out their characters and creating a feel for the period. It was Captain Johnson's *General History of the Robberies and Murders of the Most Notorious Pyrates*, a book written during the last years of the pirate heyday. Strangely, the real pirates portrayed in Johnson's almost 300-year-old book were often far more colorful and larger than life than any Long John Silver, Captain Hook, or Jack Sparrow.

A DEADLY BUSINESS

It is often very difficult to separate the truth about pirates from the myths and legends that have grown up around them. These days, pirates are everywhere. Advertisers use them to sell rum, food, hotel resorts, and even home insurance. Every time we play a DVD, we're reminded that piracy is a crime, even though these particular pirates probably never set foot on a ship in their lives. The word is misused, misapplied, and misunderstood. Pirates have become a pale parody of their original selves, watered down

Left: Contrary to popular belief, the only pirate known to ever bury treasure was Captain William Kidd, drawn here by U.S. illustrator Howard Pyle.

by a century or more of piratical nonsense.

The aim of this book is to untangle the truth from the fiction, to show the reality of life as a historical pirate and to explain what motivates pirates today. This journey will therefore take us far from the safe waters of fictional piracy, into the altogether more dangerous and murky seas infested by real pirates, the men—and a few women—who struck fear into the hearts of law-abiding mariners. For these people, piracy was not a light-hearted matter. There was nothing romantic about robbing people on the high seas in Blackbeard's day, any more than the Somali pirates of today can be seen as romantic figures when they take hostages at gunpoint and hold them for ransom.

For genuine pirates, the threat of a violent death, the risk of shipwreck or drowning, and the high chance of death through poverty, starvation, or disease were all too real. The only difference between the pirates

Right: Captain Scarfield, a fictional pirate created and drawn by Howard Pyle, is shown here at anchor in New York Harbor, around 1700.

Below: An Iraqi police boat patrols the port of Basra, Iraq, where modern pirates regularly attack and raid or hold to ransom visiting oil and food tankers.

of Blackbeard's day and those of today is that the tools they use now are more sophisticated, and more deadly. Pirates now have speedboats, satellite navigation systems, and rocket launchers. By the same token, pirate hunters no longer have to rely on cannons, pistols, and cutlasses. They have radar, satellite imagery, and jets capable of targeting a small boat in a vast, seemingly empty ocean. The risks are great, if not greater than before.

For all this new technology, though, the pirates themselves are remarkably similar to their historical forebears. This book will trace these similarities through the long and bloody history of piracy, from ancient times to the present day.

Piracy in the Ancient World

When we think of pirates we imagine characters like Blackbeard or "Black Bart" Roberts who were notorious during the early 18th century. Of course piracy is a much older profession, and has been around since the start of recorded history.

Piracy thrives in regions where there is a lack of central authority or proper law and order. That was as true in the ancient world as it was in the 18th century, and it still applies today.

Piracy can trace its roots back to the cradle of civilization—the ancient Mediterranean. It was in the *Mare Internum*—the "Inner Sea" as the Romans called it—that historical records reveal the first known instances of maritime trade. As merchants traveled further from home, they risked attacks from pirates or having their ship and cargo seized in unfriendly ports.

For more than 2,000 years, as ancient empires came and went, so too did the specter of piracy. At times when the ancient Egyptians, Greeks, Carthaginians, or Romans were unable to patrol the sea lanes, pirate communities grew. Most of them emerged in isolated, rocky coastlines, far from major ports but close to busy shipping lanes. It was only after the Roman Republic launched a major campaign against these piratical communities that the scourge of piracy was eradicated. From the mid-1st century BC until the collapse of the Roman Empire in the 5th century AD, the Romans considered the Mediterranean to be *Mare Nostrum*, "Our Sea," a safe place where maritime trade could flourish and piracy was a distant memory.

Below: The Romans used small, light galleys called *liburnians*—known for their speed and driven by two rows of oarsmen—to patrol the waters of the ancient Mediterranean and keep them free of pirates.

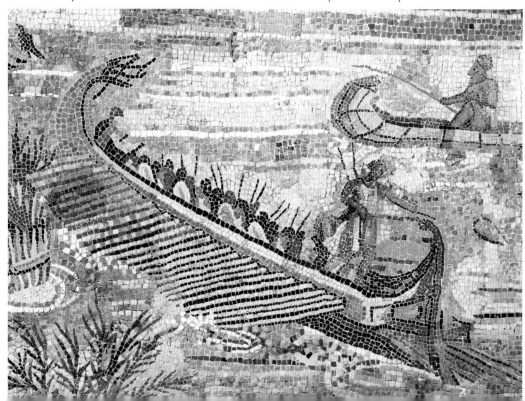

The Sea Peoples

The very early pirates sailed around the coastline of today's Turkey, making small sorties ashore. Then in the 12th century BC the "Sea Peoples" arrived, and they plundered on a far grander scale. Their goal was to ravage the richest civilization in the known world.

The first pirates in history roamed the waters of the eastern Mediterranean. Even before the building of the pyramids, ancient Egypt was beset by pirate raiders, who preyed on trading ships and coastal settlements.

THE FIRST PIRATES

The first people that history records as being pirates were the Lukka, a group of sea raiders who based themselves on the Mediterranean shores of Lycia in Asia Minor—now Turkey. In the 14th century BC they appear in the records of the port of Ugarit (on the coast of what is now Syria), and in the records of the Hittites, who ruled that part of the Mediterranean. Around 1340 BC Egyptian scribes recorded that the Lukkans raided the island of Cyprus. By the 13th century BC the Lukkans had formed an alliance with the Empire of the Hittites. The Hittites offered the Lukkans political autonomy and in return they gained a navy.

Before this alliance, Lukkan pirates were already preying on Egyptian merchant ships and coastal communities. This alliance with Egypt's great rival meant that these pirates became a major threat to the New Kingdom Egyptians and a political force of some considerable importance. That changed forever during the reign of the Pharaoh

Above: We know little about the appearance of the Sea Peoples, although this 3,200-year-old carving of a warrior is meant to depict one of them.

Ramses II "the Great" (ruled 1279–1213 BC). First, Ramses and his Egyptian army defeated the Hittites in a major battle fought in 1274 BC at Kadesh in modern-day Syria. Hittite military power was broken, and Ramses was able to divert Egypt's considerable resources to dealing with the Lukkans.

From that point on the Lukkans slowly disappear from the historic records, which could have been because their power was waning. On the walls of a temple in Thebes the Pharaoh Merneptah (ruled 1212–1202 BC) records a victory by his fleet over the sea raiders of Egyptian ports—almost certainly a rare reference to the pirates of Lukka.

After that the Lukkans are never mentioned again. Although evidence is scarce, most historians and archaeologists now believe that their disappearance as a people is most probably linked to the emergence of a group of maritime raiders of diverse origins known as the "Sea Peoples." It seems that the Lukkan pirates were simply assimilated into this new loose maritime confederation.

Therefore, as the power of the Lukkans declined, the pirate threat didn't actually disappear. In fact, it became even more serious—the size of the threat had quite literally grown tenfold.

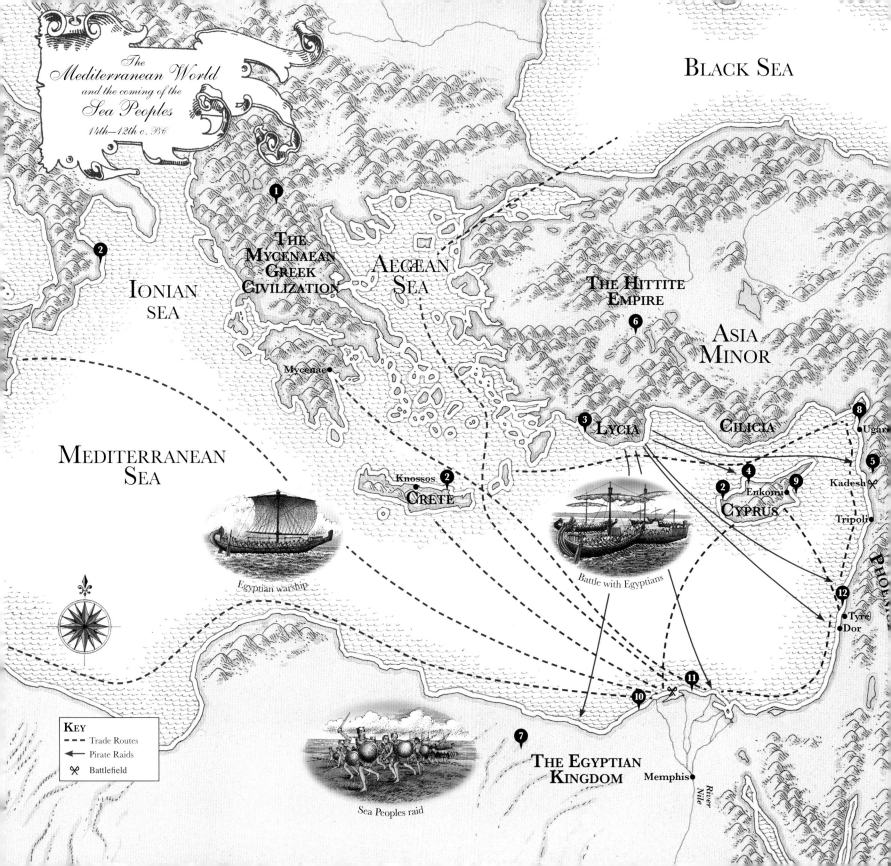

The Mediterranean World
and the coming of the
Sea Peoples
14th–12th c. BC

BLACK SEA

IONIAN SEA

THE MYCENAEAN GREEK CIVILIZATION

AEGEAN SEA

THE HITTITE EMPIRE

ASIA MINOR

Mycenae

MEDITERRANEAN SEA

Knossos
CRETE

LYCIA

CILICIA

Ugar

Enkomi
CYPRUS

Kadesh

Tripoli

Egyptian warship

Battle with Egyptians

PHO

Tyre
Dor

Sea Peoples raid

THE EGYPTIAN KINGDOM

Memphis

River Nile

KEY
- – – – Trade Routes
- ⟵ Pirate Raids
- ✕ Battlefield

The Coming of the Sea Peoples, 14–12th Centuries BC

By the 14th century BC trade had begun to develop in the Mediterranean, and Egyptian merchants ventured far afield in search of commerce. Then in the 13th and 12th centuries BC, the Sea Peoples arrived, ushering in a new era of instability and large-scale piracy.

1 Land attacks into **Mycenaean Greece** from "barbarians" in northern mountains took place around 1200 BC, and by 100 BC they had reached the southern tip of Greece.

2 Mycaenean Greek refugees flee to **Crete**, **Cyprus**, and **southern Italy**, as the Mycaenean civilization collapses, to be replaced by that of the "barbarian" Dorian Greeks.

3 The Lukkans (based on the coast of **Lycia**) develop a reputation as sea raiders. It is thought they were the forerunners of the Sea Peoples.

4 The Lukkans raid **Cyprus**, 1340 BC.

5 The **Battle of Kadesh**, 1285 BC—a major Egyptian victory over the Hittites. The border of the Hittite Empire and the New Kingdom of Egypt now ran just south of Ugarit and Tripoli, on the coast of Syria.

6 The **Hittite Empire** is invaded by barbarians from across the Bosphorus, 14th century BC.

7 Land-based people from deserts in the west, where modern-day Libya is, invade **Egypt**, but are repulsed, 1232 BC.

8 **Ugarit** and other cities destroyed by sea raiders, c.1200 BC.

9 **Enkomi** on Cyprus sacked and destroyed by either the Lukkans or the Sea Peoples. The Lukkans disappear from the historical records. This coincides with an Egyptian naval victory over these "pirates," c.1200 BC.

10 The Sea Peoples raid the **Egyptian coast**, and prey on shipping in the eastern Mediterranean during the early 12th century BC.

11 The Sea Peoples are defeated in a major sea battle, off the **Nile Delta**, 1183 BC.

12 The Sea Peoples conquer and settle the coastal areas of what is now **Israel**. By the 6th century BC this region has become **Phoenicia**. The city of **Dor** on what is now the coast of northern Israel has been linked to the Tjeker—a tribe of the Sea Peoples. The raiders had finally become settlers, merchants, and traders.

THE ELUSIVE SEA PEOPLES

Nobody really knows where the Sea Peoples first came from. The term is a collective one, used to cover the sea raiders who attacked the ships and ports of ancient Egypt in the 12th century BC. The name "Sea Peoples" (or *Hau-nebu*) was coined by Egyptian scribes, who recorded the names of six of their tribes: the Denyen, Peleset, Shardana, Shekelesh, Tjeker, and the Weshesh peoples. The Peleset, Shardana, and Shekelesh tribes may have come from the eastern coast of the Adriatic coast, although some scholars also think that the Shardana came from Sardinia. Wherever they hailed from, to the ancient Egyptians it was from beyond the western edge of the known world.

Later historians have added the names of two more tribes: the Tursha and Lycian peoples. They settled on the coast of Asia Minor—the Lycians occupying the Lukkans' ports. In fact, the Lukkans may have evolved into the Lycians—we simply don't know the details. However, neither of these peoples ever came into direct contact with the Egyptians, so the Egyptian scribes didn't record them alongside the other six tribes.

It appears that when the Sea Peoples were not engaged in piracy, they traded, developing their own sea routes throughout the eastern Mediterranean. This made sense. After all, the pirates had to sell the cargoes they had captured, and that meant finding a port where merchants were still willing to do business with them.

Egyptian warships such as this were flimsy affairs, but they were fast, stable, and capable of carrying a substantial complement of archers and spearmen. The craft used by their chief foes, the Sea Peoples, looked similar, but the raiders were less well armed than their Egyptian enemy.

Today, some historians claim that the arrival of the Sea Peoples led to the collapse of Bronze Age civilization in the eastern Mediterranean—bringing about the end of Mycenaean Greece and the Hittite Empire. In the process they plunged much of the known world into a "Dark Age." Only the Egyptians managed to survive the barbarian onslaught. So too did the inscriptions, which tell how the Sea Peoples formed an alliance with Egypt's enemies in Libya and Palestine. This meant that at the start of the 12th century BC, the Sea Peoples were poised to destroy the last great civilization in the known world.

THE FIRST GREAT SEA BATTLE

The temple of Medinet Habu stands on the west bank of the River Nile near Luxor. It was built as the mortuary temple of the Pharaoh Ramses III (ruled 1186–1155 BC), and its walls are inscribed with celebrations of his achievements. Pride of place is given to a record of an epic sea battle—the first recorded sea battle in history. It was fought in the Nile Delta in 1186 BC, between the Sea Peoples and the Egyptian navy. It tells of how the Sea Peoples were vanquished by the ships of Ramses III, and how the threat to the Egyptian Kingdom evaporated. This was a stunning victory, a triumph of civilization over darkness.

The scenes at Medinet Habu give us the first historical images of pirates in action, as well as showing us what their ships looked like, and how they fought. The ships of the Sea Peoples look smaller and flimsier than those used by the Egyptians, and while the

Left: Shipbuilding on the Mediterranean coast, a timeless scene painted by Pietro da Cortona.

Pharaoh's troops wear armor, or wield bows and arrows, the Sea Peoples appear unprotected and poorly equipped. But their ships may well have been lighter than those of the Egyptian fleet. That way they would have been better suited to raiding, where stealth and speed were more important than fighting ability. The impression of these carvings is of a fight against barbarians—after all, they were carved as a piece of propaganda. However, the truth might have been a little different, and the battle less one-sided than they suggest.

Just a few years later, the ancient Egyptians hired Sherden mercenaries for their army. These were fierce and well-armed warriors, who wore armor, and carried swords and shields. It has been suggested that the Sherden and the Shardana tribe were the same. A little earlier the Mycenaean Greeks

recorded that the Sea Peoples were great warriors and sailors, equipped with helmets and armed with long swords. It could also be argued that until they encountered the Egyptian fleet, they had defeated every enemy they ever encountered—on land or sea.

THE END OF THE SEA PEOPLES

The battle of 1186 BC marked a turning point. Until then, the Sea Peoples had managed to extend their control over most of the eastern Mediterranean. After the battle, they quickly disappear from the historical records. There is evidence that some settled in Palestine—the Peleset tribe have even been linked to the Philistines mentioned in the Bible. Settlements of the Tjeker people have been found near Dor in modern-day Israel, where they engaged in maritime trade. No doubt they also indulged in a little piracy too. It could be argued that their settlements are the oldest known pirate havens in the world.

The end of the Sea Peoples also coincided with the emergence of the Phoenicians—one of the great trading powers of the Mediterranean. It has already been suggested that the Tjeker people were amalgamated into Phoenicia by the 9th century BC. Could other survivors of the Sea Peoples have also turned their back on piracy and embraced trade? As usual, the evidence just isn't there to explain what happened. All we know is that by the end of the 12th century BC, the Sea Peoples had vanished from history.

Pirates of Ancient Greece

The demise of the Sea Peoples didn't mean an end to piracy in the waters of the Aegean and Adriatic Seas. Instead, the Greek city-states indulged in acts of piracy against one another.

While Greece emerged as a new center of civilization, some Greek states actively encouraged piracy. For centuries, whole communities made a good living from maritime plunder. Other states such as Athens tried to clear the pirates from the sea lanes and the many islands.

THE CRETANS

The collapse of the Mycenaean Greek civilization meant that no single state was powerful enough to patrol the sea lanes, or to protect isolated coastal settlements from attack. In fact, several city-states or semi-autonomous islands actively encouraged piracy as a means of generating income. Piracy continued to thrive, particularly after the 10th century BC and the collapse of the Minoan civilization in Crete. The island was a natural haven for pirates, with well-protected natural harbors that were close to the trade routes passing from the Aegean Sea into the Mediterranean.

This detail from a mosaic dating from the 11th century BC shows a bustling Cretan harbor scene. Crete later became a pirate haven.

Left: Captured Greek pirates are bound and keelhauled—dragged beneath a boat—a typical form of summary execution meted out by the pirate-hunters of the Athenian navy.

the enmity of Athens when they began preying on Athenian ships and raiding their coastline during the late 5th century BC.

The Athenians launched a campaign to clear the islands of the pirates. City-states which considered themselves friendly to Athens were forbidden to trade with the Samians, while anti-piracy patrols hunted the pirates down on the high seas. Eventually Mycale and Lemnos were captured and the pirate lairs destroyed. The historian Herodotus described these Athenian anti-

Below: In this Roman mosaic detail, the Greek god Dionysus is depicted turning pirates into sea creatures, by way of punishment.

The last remnants of the Minoan civilization on the island had been destroyed by the Dorian Greeks, who raided Crete in search of slaves. These Greek invaders then turned to piracy, attacking ships and conducting raids throughout the Aegean basin. The most profitable form of plunder was people—women and boys—who were then sold as slaves in Cretan ports such as Cydonia and Eleutherna, places that also became marketplaces for stolen plunder.

Homer regarded the names "Cretan" and "pirate" to be synonymous. In *The Odyssey*, he describes the island's inhabitants as being merciless pirates, while some of his other poems contain passing references to the Cretan slave-hunting raids. Crete remained a pirate haven for several centuries. It was not until the 5th century BC that anyone was able to counter their activities. By then the Athenian navy was powerful enough to protect its coastlines and trade routes from the Cretans, forcing the pirates to seek out

victims in less well-protected waters. The end came in the late 2nd century BC, when the island state of Rhodes finally eradicated the pirate menace by capturing all the pirate havens and razing them to the ground.

THE SAMIANS

In the northern Aegean Sea, several islands or settlements on the mainland also developed into small pirate havens. Mycale and the island of Lemnos were such places, occupied by the Samians who had been driven from their own island by Dorian invaders.

The historian Plutarch described how the Samians turned to piracy in the 6th century BC, and under the leadership of Polycrates they operated in the waters around the island city of Miletus. They also used the rivalry between Greece and Persia to their own advantage, offering their services or neutrality to both sides, in return for gold. They eventually incurred piracy operations in his writings, and he went on to describe the eradication of other pirate lairs on Kythnos (Thermia) and Mykonos.

THE AETOLIANS

The Aetolian League was formed in the 4th century BC as a confederation of small Greek city-states, sited to the north of the Gulf of Corinth. Its members regularly used piracy as a way of harming the economies of their rivals, and of generating income for their city-states. In other words, their small navies were regarded as little more than pirates.

The Aetolians extorted protection money from coastal communities in the Aegean and the Adriatic, and their galleys even ravaged the coastline of Asia Minor. The collapse of Athens as a naval power meant that there was no fleet in Greek waters that was powerful enough to stop them. Therefore these organized pirates continued to prey on ships and coastal towns until 192 BC, when the Aetolian League was defeated and conquered by the Romans. Deprived of their bases, many of these pirates simply moved east, and established a new pirate haven in Cilicia, on the southern coast of Asia Minor.

Cherubs in the guise of Graeco-Roman fisherman act as bait to attract pirates, in a detail from the mosaic shown on the opposite page. Fishermen were frequently captured, then coerced into joining pirate crews.

THE ILLYRIANS AND DALMATIANS

While pirate galleys of the Aeolian League hunted the waters off the western coast of Greece, a little further to the north pirates from Illyria and Dalmatia (now Albania and Croatia) raided the coasts of Greece and Italy, and plundered ships passing through the Adriatic Sea. These Illyrian and Dalmatian pirates were also known to have operated even further afield as, according to historical records, they were responsible for attacks as far as Sicily, Crete, and the coast of North Africa. Their activities reached a peak during the 3rd century BC, a time when Rome was emerging as a major political and economic power, and therefore Roman trading vessels were regularly sailing through these pirate-infested waters.

The main pirate bases in the region were the islands of Cephalonia, Corfu, and Santa Maria. When the Romans conquered Dalmatia and Illyria in the 2nd century BC the pirate threat was curbed, but not completely removed. As attacks continued the Romans resorted to sterner measures, and they launched a series of amphibious attacks on the pirate strongholds, wiping them out one after the other. However, small bands of pirates remained, and continued to operate from small hidden bases well into the mid-1st century BC, when Pompey eradicated the pirate threat once and for all.

Pompey, Caesar, and the Cilician Pirates

During the 2nd and early 1st centuries BC the most notorious pirate stronghold in the Mediterranean was Cilicia, on the southern-eastern coast of Asia Minor—now Turkey.

The Romans called the region Cilicia Trachea ("Rugged Cilicia"), as it was remote and inaccessible by land—making it the perfect pirate haven.

From this secure base the Cilician pirates ranged throughout the eastern Mediterranean, preying on merchant ships as far away as the coasts of Egypt and Greece. Then they encountered two implacable Romans—Caesar and Pompey—both of whom declared war on this last great pirate stronghold in an otherwise Roman sea.

THE CILICIAN HAVEN

Cilicia was a narrow strip of rocky coastline, with the Taurus Mountains behind it and the Mediterranean in front. This inhospitable coast was settled by a few struggling villages and fishing communities, with a host of hidden bays, natural harbors, and easily defensible rocky headlands in between. Cilicia also lay astride a major ancient sea route, linking Greece and Italy to Syria and Palestine. Pirates could sally out of secret harbors, attack passing ships, and be back in port within a matter of days.

When the Aetolian pirates were driven from Greek waters in the late 2nd century BC, many of them established themselves in Cilicia. The impetus behind their ejection from Greece was the expansion of Roman power into the region, a move that forced Asia Minor to divert its fleets to patrol the Aegean and prevent any further Roman expansion. This meant

Left: A young Julius Caesar depicted in 75 BC, standing, with his captors, Cilician pirates who held him for ransom. After his release, Caesar had them crucified.

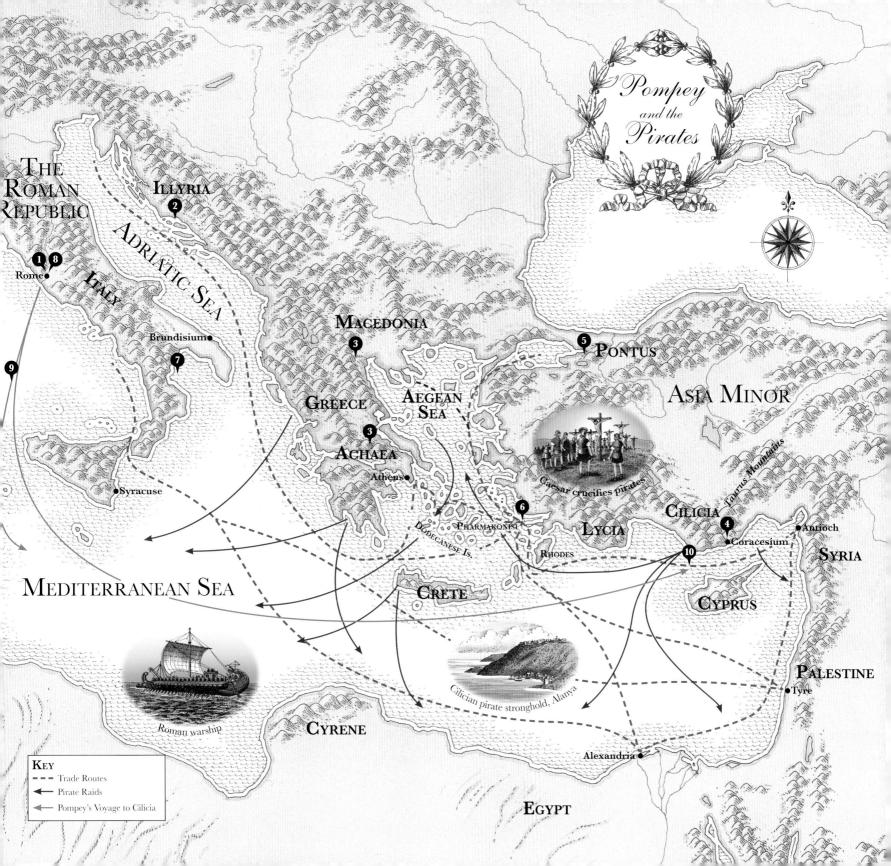

Pompey
and the
Pirates

THE
ROMAN
REPUBLIC

ILLYRIA

② ②

① ⑧
Rome•

ADRIATIC SEA

ITALY

Brundisium•

⑦

⑨

MACEDONIA

③

GREECE

AEGEAN
SEA

③

ACHAEA

Athens•

⑤
PONTUS

ASIA MINOR

Caesar crucifies pirates

Taurus Mountains

DODECANESE Is.

⑥

Pharmakonisi

CILICIA

④
•Coracesium

Antioch•

LYCIA

SYRIA

RHODES

⑩

Syracuse•

MEDITERRANEAN SEA

CYPRUS

CRETE

Roman warship

Cilician pirate stronghold, Alanya

PALESTINE

•Tyre

CYRENE

Alexandria•

EGYPT

KEY
- - - Trade Routes
→ Pirate Raids
→ Pompey's Voyage to Cilicia

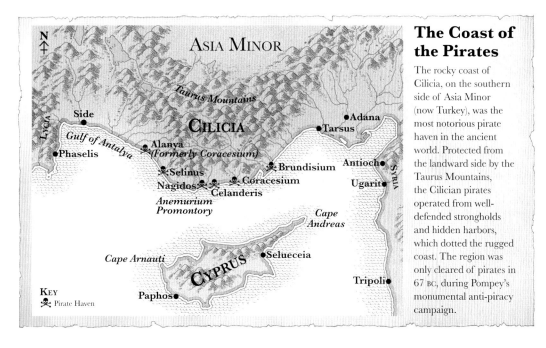

The Coast of the Pirates

The rocky coast of Cilicia, on the southern side of Asia Minor (now Turkey), was the most notorious pirate haven in the ancient world. Protected from the landward side by the Taurus Mountains, the Cilician pirates operated from well-defended strongholds and hidden harbors, which dotted the rugged coast. The region was only cleared of pirates in 67 BC, during Pompey's monumental anti-piracy campaign.

First, when the pirates demanded a ransom of twenty talents, Caesar burst out laughing. They did not know, he said, who it was that they had captured, and he volunteered to pay fifty. Then, when he had sent his followers to the various cities in order to raise the money and was left with one friend and two servants among these Cilicians, about the most bloodthirsty people in the world, he treated them so highhandedly that, whenever he wanted to sleep, he would send to them and tell them to stop talking.

For thirty-eight days, with the greatest unconcern, he joined in all their games and exercises, just as if he was their leader instead of their prisoner. He also wrote poems and speeches which he read aloud to them, and if they failed to admire his work, he would call them to their faces illiterate savages, and would often laughingly threaten to have them all executed. They were much taken with this and attributed his freedom of speech to a kind of simplicity in his character or boyish playfulness.

that no ships were available to patrol the waters of Cilicia, so the pirate bases were allowed to flourish. Soon, thousands of pirates were operating along the coast, their numbers swelled by refugees fleeing from the Romans. Worse, the new ruler of Asia Minor—King Mithridites of Pontus—actively supported the pirates, seeing them as a useful ally against the Romans. By the early 1st century BC the Cilician pirates had become a major power and were raiding coastal communities as far away as the Italian mainland. Captives were sold as slaves, and cargoes were sold on in the marketplaces of Asia Minor. By 75 BC, piracy in the eastern Mediterranean had become big business.

CAESAR AND THE PIRATES

According to the Roman historian Plutarch, a 26-year-old Julius Caesar was captured by Cilician pirates in 75 BC, while on his way to

Rhodes to study oratory. Realizing he was an important nobleman, the pirates held him for ransom on the island of Pharmakonisi, in the Dodecanese, just off the coast of Asia Minor. Plutarch described Caesar's encounter:

Pirate Galleys and Roman Warships

The Cilician pirates tended to operate in small, fast galleys, powered by pirate volunteers rather than by slaves. Their ships were really too light to be used as proper warships, but they rarely needed to fight a battle—most victims surrendered when the pirates overhauled them. Most merchant ships of the period were powered by sail, which meant that in most cases these pirate galleys were faster than their prey.

Earlier Roman warships had been slow, lumbering vessels. However, by Pompey's time, the Romans had begun to use biremes (galleys with two banks of oars), based on vessels used by the navy of Rhodes. They also used Roman-built Liburnians, which were purpose-built, fast privateering galleys.

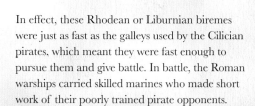

A votive model of a Roman bireme, dating from the mid-1st century BC.

In effect, these Rhodean or Liburnian biremes were just as fast as the galleys used by the Cilician pirates, which meant they were fast enough to pursue them and give battle. In battle, the Roman warships carried skilled marines who made short work of their poorly trained pirate opponents.

Left: An engraving based on a Roman bas-relief carving of the 1st century AD, showing the bireme galleys favored by pirates and pirate hunters alike.

When the ransom arrived, Caesar was set free. However, he returned soon afterwards with a naval squadron and captured the pirates, their base, and their ships. He took them to Pergamon in chains, and there he had them all crucified, as an example to others.

POMPEY AND THE PIRATES

During the 1st century BC the Romans made several half-hearted attempts to stamp out piracy in the Mediterranean, but none were particularly successful. The Roman attitude towards piracy hardened in AD70, when the Cilicians supported the slave revolt led by Spartacus. In 67 BC the Roman Senate voted to eradicate piracy in the Mediterranean, and chose Pompey to mastermind the campaign.

His plan was to launch a campaign on a monumental scale. He was granted sweeping military, financial, and economic powers, a force of 500 ships and 120,000 troops. This equaled about half of the annual total budget of the Roman Republic, so the Senate expected results. Pompey had already conducted small-scale campaigns against the Cilician pirates and he knew exactly what to do. His plan was simple— to start at one end of the Mediterranean, and drive the pirates eastward, toward the Cilician coast. He divided the Mediterranean into 13 districts and appointed a military commander to each of them. In a coordinated attack, each of these launched a simultaneous attack against the pirate bases in their area. First they blockaded known pirate bases, while warships scouted for pirate ships at sea or in unknown lairs. In each area, pirates were either pardoned or executed. Others were released in exchange for information.

For the next phase, Pompey started at the Pillars of Hercules (Gibraltar). He led the rest of his fleet east, driving any remaining pirates before him. Most of these fleeing ships were driven onto the blockading forces established by Pomey's deputies. These Roman warships looked into every port and bay as they advanced, making sure that no pirate ship was able to slip through Pompey's great net. Within 40 days the Mediterranean had been cleared of pirates—with one exception.

Pompey had deliberately left Cilicia untouched. He wanted the remaining pirates to flee there, seeking a safe haven. He then blockaded the Cilician coast, forming a tight cordon to trap them in their bases. If a few ships managed to slip through, Pompey had placed an outer ring of warships that waited just over the horizon. There was no escape.

Starting at the two ends of the Cilician coastline, he sent his marines ashore, exploring every bay, gully, and inlet. If a pirate ship was encountered it was besieged, and destroyed. In this manner the Cilicians were gradually driven back toward their main stronghold—a place called Coracesium at the end of a rocky peninsula—a place the pirates considered impregnable. But Pompey simply laid siege to it and in three months the pirates were starved into submission. Once again Pompey was lenient, executing the ringleaders but banishing their followers.

The operation had been a complete success. During the three-month campaign, the Romans had destroyed 120 pirate bases, killed or executed over 10,000 pirates, and destroyed over 500 of their ships. As a result, the Mediterranean was free of pirates for the first time in its history. It would remain so until the final collapse of the Roman world, some five centuries later.

Pompey the Great

In 67 BC, Gnaeus Pompeius Magnus—Pompey the Great (106–48 BC)—was Rome's most experienced general. He had defeated Spartacus, led successful campaigns in Italy, Sicily, Africa, and Spain, and had served as the Roman Consul—one of the two joint rulers of Republican Rome who were elected on an annual basis. He had even led minor campaigns against pirates. After his pirate campaign of 67 BC, he went on to lead Roman armies to victory in the east. Today, Pompey is best remembered as being the opponent of Caesar during the Roman Civil War. However, back in 67 BC this veteran general was simply the ideal man for the job.

597
POMPEIUS MAGNUS
d. 48 v. Kr.

Medieval Sea Rovers

After the collapse of the Western Roman Empire in AD 476, Europe and the western Mediterranean were plunged into a grim period of disorder, crime and brutality that lasted for around five centuries, popularly known as the "Dark Ages."

Above: A Byzantine illustration depicting an 11th-century sea battle between two Byzantine warships. The Byzantine navy maintained regular anti-piracy patrols in the eastern Mediterranean from the 5th century AD until the beginning of the 13th century, the sea being vital to the existence of Byzantium.

The Dark Ages was a lawless time, when trade collapsed, towns and cities crumbled, and weeds spread over the Roman roads. In most parts of Europe there was no effective government, which left communities vulnerable to attack by sea raiders.

In the eastern Mediterranean things were a little different. The Eastern Roman Empire survived the fall of the Western Empire, and Constantinople—now Istanbul—became the new center of the civilized world. But the Eastern Romans—the Byzantines—were unable to protect the coastal communities and merchant ships beyond their borders, and as a result pirate communities sprang up. When Byzantine fortunes started to wane, the Byzantine emperors called on these pirates to help defend them from attack by the new and growing threat posted by Islam.

The situation in northern Europe was much worse. The collapse of the Western Roman Empire meant that there was little or no central authority. In the ports of Europe—most notably in Britain—the locals struggled to form some kind of government. Ultimately, however, their efforts proved fruitless, as Britain was subjected to a series of invasions by barbarian tribes. The most notable of these were the Angles and the Saxons who invaded Britain from Denmark and Germany. They eventually conquered much of southern Britain, which became known as "Land of the Angles"—or England. Other raiders included the Irish from the west and the Picts and Scots from the north. Across western Europe the barbarians who brought down the Western Roman Empire carved out their territory—the Franks in Gaul (now France), the Vandals in Spain, and the Goths in Italy. All treated the sea as an avenue for attack, and ships and communities as a source of plunder.

Then, in the late 8th century, a new type of sea raider appeared—one that was more ferocious than any the long-suffering people of Britain and Europe had ever seen before. They came from the lands across the sea to the north, and so became known as the Northmen—or Norsemen. Today we know them as the Vikings.

The Fury of the Norsemen

For more than a century, the appearance of Norse longboats rowing inshore to Britain and mainland Europe heralded an orgy of death, destruction, and looting.

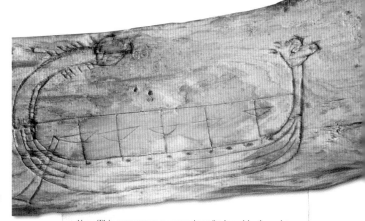

The origins of the word "Viking" are vague, but it is often argued that it comes from the Swedish word *vika*, meaning a "turn" or "shift," or the Norse *vikja*, which meant a shift of oarsmen. In other words, it probably means a Norse rower—one of the men who crewed the Norse longships.

THE COMING OF THE VIKINGS

The Anglo-Saxon monk Alcuin claimed that the Vikings first appeared off the coast of Britain on the morning of June 8, AD 793. They appeared unexpectedly from the North Sea, and raided the island monastery of Lindisfarne, just off the northeast coast of England. The monks were slaughtered, and the monastery looted and burned to the ground. Alcuin and his fellow monks saw the attack as an outrage—"an attack on the body and soul of Christian England." Worse was to come.

The year before, King Offa of Mercia, central England, had been warned that the Norsemen might come, so he

Left: A medieval Scandinavian *stele* (marker stone) depicting Norse scenes, one of which shows the setting sail of a Viking longboat.

The Viking Raider

Norsemen, or Vikings, were not really pirates in the truest sense of the word. They were sea raiders—just like the Sea Peoples of the ancient Mediterranean, or the buccaneers of the 17th-century Caribbean. For them, their ships were a means of transport—a vital tool which allowed them to sail or row from their bases on the coast of Norway, and then to launch attacks against coastal settlements in Britain or the mainland of Europe. Their ships were shallow drafted, allowing the Vikings to crew up rivers and attack targets far inland. They relied on their ships for speed, mobility, and surprise. When they reached their objective, the Vikings would land, overcome any resistance, and then loot the settlement, monastery, or township. They would then return to their longboats, laden with plunder.

Right: The 9th-century Oseberg Ship, found inside a Norwegian burial mound.

strengthened his defenses. However, it was too little, too late. Two years later, and a year after the attack on Lindisfarne, the Vikings returned and roamed the length of England's North Sea coast. In the years that followed, other raiders plundered the Scottish monastery of Iona, and the Welsh churches of Carmarthen, Llancarfan, and St. David. By AD 798 the Vikings weren't even returning to Norway—they built permanent settlements on Orkney and Shetland instead, where they spent the winter before they began raiding again in the spring. It was little wonder, then, that these early medieval monks saw the fury of the Norsemen as a precursor of the end of the world.

Below: This carved figurehead from the 9th-century Oseberg Ship is a particularly fine surviving example of the dragon heads that were used to decorate the bows of Viking longships. They were designed to intimidate.

Right: This 13th-century illustration shows that longships were in use for several centuries.

DANEGELD

By the early 9th century the Vikings had changed tactics. Having plundered the mainland of Britain, some turned their attention to Ireland, where the raids would continue for a decade. As one Irish monk put it:

The sea spewed forth floods of foreigners into Erin, so that no haven, no landing place, no stronghold, no fort, and no castle might be found, but it was submerged by waves of Vikings and pirates.

In England the Norsemen began offering communities their protection—in return for a hefty fee. This payment became known as *Danegeld*—"Dane's Money." This lasted until the 830s, by which time the Viking raiders began to establish their own settlements in the lands they had conquered, the most notable of which was Jorvik—now York.

VIKINGS IN FRANCE

Meanwhile, other sea raiders turned their attention to the mainland of Europe. Viking longships rowed far up the great river networks of the Rhine, the Seine, and the Loire, looting as they went. In AD 840 they sacked Rouen, and five years later they were at the gates of Paris. The city was only spared when its inhabitants paid the raiders off with a Danegeld of 7,000 pounds of silver. The Norsemen then established a permanent settlement at the mouth of the Seine and soon they claimed the surrounding land for themselves. This eventually became Normandy—"Land of the Norsemen."

THE FURY SPENT

These Viking raids lasted a little more than 50 years, and ended when there was nothing left to plunder. By the start of the 10th century the business of colonization had begun. By that time the raiders had become part of the emerging nations of Europe—Denmark, Norway, Scotland, England, and France. While the Viking age would continue for another century, the days of the sea raiders were over. Were the Vikings pirates? Well, as most of their attacks took place on land, they were technically sea raiders. However, to most Europeans of the time, the words Viking, sea raider, and pirate were one and the same.

Pirates of Medieval Britain

By the 11th century, western Europe was emerging from the Dark Ages. But as traders ventured back on to the high seas, so too did the pirates.

The new system of feudalism, whereby feudal overlords protected their lands in return for rent in money or produce, brought with it prosperity and a flourishing sea trade. However, not all traders stayed on the right side of the law. Some overlords turned a blind eye to piracy in return for a share of the profits.

ANGLO-FRENCH RIVALRY

This made it difficult for kings to maintain a royal fleet that could keep the sea lanes open, and so piracy flourished. Pirates also took advantage of the near-constant rivalry between England and France. Pirates and noblemen alike were often able to play the rival royal powers off against each other and in the process develop their own pirate havens, with little or no interference from either monarch. By the late 12th century most of the Channel Islands were seen as pirate havens. In theory they were ruled

This depiction of the Battle of Sluys (1340), which marked the start of the Hundred Years War, shows the brutal way in which medieval sea battles were fought. After an initial exchange of arrows and other missiles, both sides came alongside each other to fight it out hand to hand.

by the Norman kings of England, but in practice they were independent. Although attempts were made to suppress piracy in the Channel Islands during the 12th century, these activities continued.

EUSTACE THE MONK

The most notorious of these pirates was Eustace the Monk, also known as "The Black Monk." Tradition has it that he was the youngest son of a nobleman from Boulogne.

He joined a Benedictine monastery, but—it was said—he also dabbled in sorcery. The monk then served the Count of Boulogne as an administrator, but in 1204 he quarreled with his overlord. He is then said to have fled to Jersey in the Channel Islands where he joined the pirates.

Eustace rapidly became a pirate leader, and was responsible for attacks on both English and French ships as far afield as the Dover Straits. In 1205, King John of England hired Eustace and his men to attack the French.

Voyages of Eustace the Monk
c.1170–1217

Medieval cog

Eustace's beheading

Raid on Folkestone

SCOTLAND

Edinburgh

Berwick

Newcastle

IRISH SEA

Dublin

ENGLAND

NORTH SEA

LOW COUNTRIES

Amsterdam

Harwich

11 London

13 **14**

Sandwich

Dover

Folkestone

8

10

Southampton

Plymouth

Falmouth

ENGLISH CHANNEL

Cherbourg

GUERNSEY **5**

CHANNEL ISLANDS

JERSEY

Morlaix

Brest

BRITTANY

NORMANDY

Harfleur

Dieppe

Rouen

FRANCE

Paris **9**

Antwerp

Dunkirk

Calas

6

1

2

3

Boulogne

4 **7**

Dover Straits

12

FLANDERS

KEY
- - - Trade Routes

The Voyages of Eustace the Monk, c.1170–1217

1 **1170** Eustace is born in Boulogne, the son of a minor nobleman.

2 **c.1185** Eustace joins the Abbey of Samer, outside Boulogne, and trains to become a monk.

3 **1202** Eustace, now a monk, begins work as a cleric, in the court of the Count Ranault of Boulogne.

4 **1204** Eustace "the Monk" is accused of undisclosed crimes, and forced to flee. He becomes an outlaw.

5 **1205** Eustace the Monk establishes himself in the Channel Islands, which are already known as a pirate haven. He joins a pirate group, and rapidly becomes their leader. In one source, it is claimed he captured the islands using 30 galleys, lent to him by the English king.

6 **1206** After receiving payment from King John of England, Eustace and his followers raid Calais and the surrounding area. It is rumored he even raided up the River Seine, towards Rouen.

7 **1206** Eustace carries out an even larger pirate raid on Boulogne, forcing King Philip of France to pay Eustace protection money.

8 **1212** Eustace the Monk and his men raid Folkestone, earning the enmity of the English king.

9 **1214** Eustace the Monk forms an alliance with King Philip's son, Prince Louis of France.

10 **1215** Civil War brakes out in England, between the supporters of King John and rebel nobles. Prince Louis uses Eustace to transport arms and supplies to the rebels.

11 **October 1216** Death of King John. He is succeeded by his young son, Henry III.

12 **May 1217** Eustace is hired to transport the French army from Calais to Dover. Prince Louis besieges Dover.

13 **July 1217** Naval Battle off Dover. Eustace's fleet surprised and attacked by an English fleet, commanded by Hugh de Burgh. The pirates are defeated, and retreat to Sandwich.

14 **1217** Battle off Sandwich, fought on 24th August. Eustace's pirate fleet are attacked and defeated off Sandwich. Eustace is captured, and then executed.

The pirates attacked small French ports from Calais to Brest, forcing King Philip II of France to pay the pirates another fee to stop raiding his coast. Eustace was even paid to raid the English coast, and in 1212 he led a particularly devastating raid on Folkestone. He was now earning a fee from both countries.

Eustace then turned from piracy to protection—offering to protect shipping in return for a share of the cargo. However, the attack on Folkestone angered King John, who put together a fleet and attacked the Channel Islands. The pirate bases on Jersey and Guernsey were captured and destroyed, leaving Eustace without a safe refuge. He retaliated by allying himself with English rebels.

DOWNFALL OF THE PIRATE MONK

In early 1217, King Philip's son, Louis, hired Eustace to transport an even larger French force over to England. The pirate fleet anchored off Dover, when they were surprised by a smaller but better-equipped English war fleet. The English fired a volley of crossbow bolts and then threw quicklime in the faces of the pirates as they drew alongside. In the battle that followed the pirates were overwhelmed.

The Crooked Governor

Early medieval pirate chief Savary de Mauléon was the governor of La Rochelle on the Bay of Biscay, a port he held in the name of King John of England. Under his guidance the pirates preyed on French shipping—until de Mauléon switched sides and formed an alliance with the French king. For much of the early 13th century, La Rochelle was a pirate haven, a thorn in the side of English and French merchants alike.

Eustace fled with a handful of his ships, but a few weeks later he was surprised and cornered by the English fleet off the coast of Sandwich, south east England. He was captured and dragged before the English admiral, Hugh de Burgh. Technically, the pirates were privateers in French pay, but such niceties didn't suit de Burgh. He offered the pirate chief a choice—beheading at the center or the side of the ship. The chronicler Matthew Paris, who described the event, never said which option the monk chose. One way or another, Eustace the Monk and his fellow pirates were all put to the sword.

Below: The beheading of the pirate Eustace the Monk in 1217 shown in a medieval illustration accompanying the *Chronicles of Matthew Paris*.

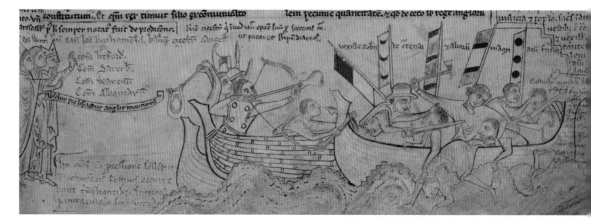

The Lords of the Mediterranean

As Byzantine rule faltered under attacks from Muslim warlords and Christian crusaders, the waters of the Aegean and Adriatic seas once again became the haunt of pirates.

After the collapse of the Western Roman Empire, the sea lanes of the Eastern Mediterranean were patrolled by the Byzantine navy. Unfortunately, when Byzantine power waned in the face of attacks by both Muslims and fellow Christians, the once great Empire lacked the resources to hunt down the growing number of pirates.

Below: A 14th-century warlike cog, fitted out with fighting "castles" at bow and stern.

THE COLLAPSE OF BYZANTIUM

The Byzantine Empire was effectively founded in AD 330 when the Roman Emperor Constantine "the Great" established himself in Byzantium, which he renamed Constantinople. The city became a major trading port, and Byzantine warships kept its sea lanes open, even after the collapse of the Western Roman Empire. By the 12th century things started to unravel, however. The growing power of Islam placed the Byzantines at the forefront of a new battleground, and after a major defeat in 1071 they appealed to the West for help. This appeared in the form of the Crusaders, who were as much interested in worldly wealth and power as in driving back the borders of Islam.

At the same time, the Venetians and the Normans of southern Italy began encroaching on Byzantine territory in the Adriatic, seizing islands and ports, and generally taking advantage of Byzantium's lack of naval muscle. Despite a temporary revival of Byzantine influence in the mid-12th century the decline continued, and in 1204 the Venetians and their crusading allies even captured and mercilessly sacked the great city of Constantinople during the Fourth Crusade. Western noblemen carved out small feudal fiefdoms in Greece and the Aegean basin, and faced with a barren landscape, many turned to piracy in order to make a living. This collapse of Byzantine authority meant that after 1204 the Adriatic and the Aegean had become breeding grounds for pirates.

The Pirate Islands of the Adriatic, 12th century

The eastern coast of the Adriatic Sea was a notorious pirate haven during the 13th century—the lair of Margaritone of Brindisi. His main bases were on the islands of Cephalonia and Zante.

THE PIRATE LORDS OF GREECE

Western (Latin) overlords now ruled much of Greece, and ports like Corinth and Athens became marketplaces for stolen goods and slaves. Many of these rulers saw piracy as a useful source of income, as they lacked the resources to develop legitimate maritime trade. Even Muslim rulers took advantage of this power vacuum—in northwestern Anatolia (now Turkey) the Turkish Karasi and Saruhan peoples developed a reputation for piracy, raiding the Aegean islands in search of slaves. Many of these islands became pirate havens in their own right, particularly Lesbos, Chios, and Samos. The ancient piratical island of Crete became a home for pirates once more, and soon only the ports and islands owned by the Venetians, Genoese, or Knights of Rhodes remained open to honest traders.

The Pirate Rock

The medieval pirates of the Aegean preferred to establish themselves in well-defended harbors, where they would be relatively safe from attack. The most impressive of these pirate havens was Monemvasia, on the southeastern corner of the Peloponnese. This harbor—known as the "Rock"—was an impregnable fortress built on the top of a rocky peninsula, joined to the Greek mainland by a narrow causeway. The "Rock" became a thriving pirate haven during the 13th century. It was situated on the easternmost "finger" of the Peloponnese, but the middle finger, the Mani Peninsula, had been a notorious refuge for pirates since ancient times. The locals—the Maniots—lacked any form of income apart from fishing, and so small-time piracy helped them to survive. Monemvasia remained a pirate stronghold until the 15th century, when it passed into the hands of the Venetians.

Above: A crusading ship of the 14th century, typical of the small single-masted merchant sailing vessels that plied the European waters during the Middle Ages. The ship is "carvel-built" (built with the hull planks lying flush or edge to edge rather than overlapping), which suggests it was constructed in the Mediterranean.

MARGARITONE OF BRINDISI

Pirates were also active in the Adriatic Sea. During the late 12th century Zante, Corfu, Cephalonia, and the picturesque islands of the Dalmatian coast all developed into safe havens for pirates. The most successful leader of these pirates was Margaritone of Brindisi (c.1149–97), an Italian knight who joined the Dalmatian pirates and soon rose to command their fleets.

Most of Brindisi's men were Italians—mainly renegade Venetian or Genoese sailors. In 1185 he became the self-proclaimed first count of Cephalonia and Zante when he captured the islands, and later Count of Malta. He was then hired by the Sicilians as a naval commander, and eventually became their Grand Admiral.

Brindisi was eventually captured during an attempt to relieve the siege of Naples by imperialist troops, and he ended his days in a German dungeon. His island bases remained thriving centers of piracy until the late 14th century, when they were annexed by the Venetians. By that time the center of piratical activity had moved again—this time to the Barbary coast of North Africa.

Störtebeker and the Baltic Pirates

Lucrative cargoes carried between German Baltic ports in the Hanseatic League attracted the attention of pirates—the most notorious of whom was Klaus Störtebeker.

After the passing of the Vikings, the waters of northern Europe were used more for trade than for raiding, and a great mercantile empire— the Hanseatic League—soon emerged. It was to transform the small harbors of the North Sea and the Baltic coast into bustling international ports.

THE HANSA

In 1241 merchants from the German Baltic port of Lübeck formed a trading alliance with the nearby city port of Hamburg. In the process they created the Hanseatic League, also known as the Hansa, a mercantile confederation that soon expanded to include several other major German ports, including Bremen, Stettin, Danzig, and Rostock. Other ports in the Baltic basin and the North Sea coast soon followed, and by 1300 the Hansa had become a major power in the region, with 19 ports united under its trading banner.

Rival trading organizations were squeezed out of business as the Hansa began to monopolize trade. The League became so powerful that neighboring states and cities felt threatened by the Hansa's economic power. The Danes consistently opposed the Hansa, as did smaller trading alliances such as the Cinque Ports of southern England. The greatest threat to the Hansa, however, came from pirates.

Left: A cog, as depicted on a 14th-century German seal. These round-hulled vessels became the standard ship types of northern Europe.

The Sea Cow's last fight

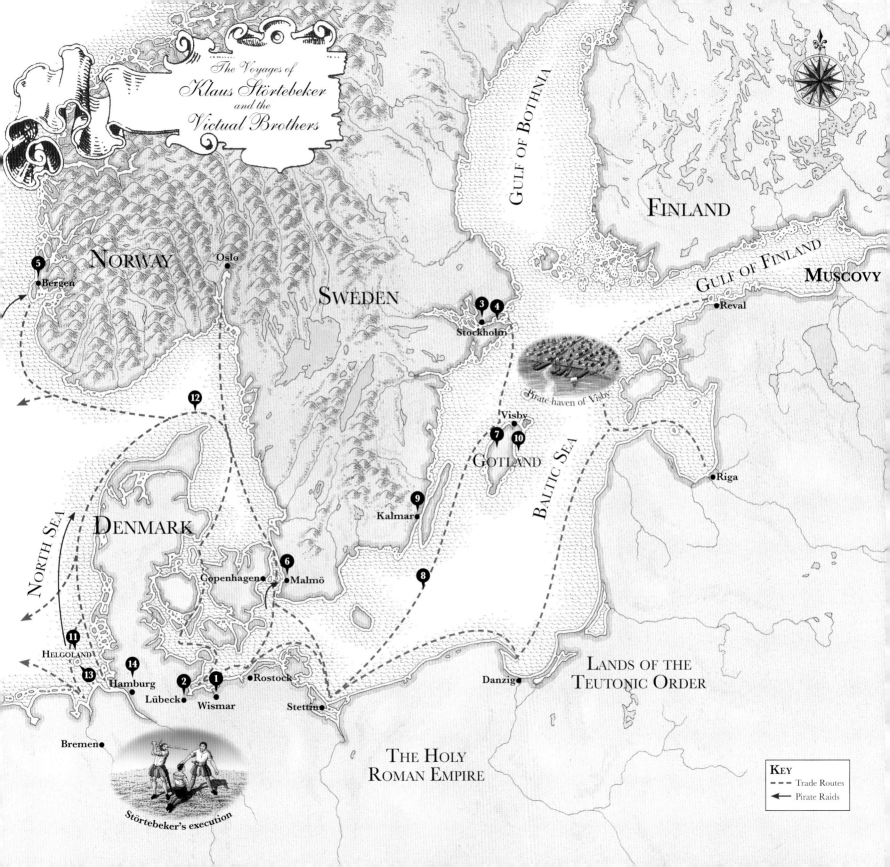

The Voyages of
Klaus Störtebeker
and the
Victual Brothers

NORWAY

SWEDEN

FINLAND

GULF OF BOTHNIA

GULF OF FINLAND

MUSCOVY

Bergen

Oslo

Stockholm

Reval

Pirate haven of Visby

Visby

GOTLAND

BALTIC SEA

Riga

Kalmar

DENMARK

NORTH SEA

Copenhagen

Malmö

Helgoland

Hamburg

Lübeck

Wismar

Rostock

Stettin

Danzig

LANDS OF THE
TEUTONIC ORDER

Bremen

THE HOLY
ROMAN EMPIRE

Störtebeker's execution

KEY

- - - Trade Routes

← Pirate Raids

THE VICTUAL BROTHERS

In the Baltic, a group of German pirates formed a confederation known as the Vitalienbrüder (Victual Brothers), which operated from the Hansa port of Lübeck and preyed on Danish ships. The name derived from one of their exploits when, in 1392, they broke the Danish blockade of Stockholm and brought supplies (in Latin, *victualia*) into the besieged port. However, the following year the Victual Brothers raided the Hansa port of Bergen in Norway, then attacked Malmö in southern Sweden. These actions led to the Hansa closing their ports to the pirates, who in turn retaliated in 1394 by seizing the Baltic island of Gotland.

During all this the pirates continued to attack Danish ships and to sell their stolen plunder in the Gotland harbor of Visby. The attacks became so bad that the Danes were even forced to hire warships supplied by the Cinque Ports to guard their Baltic convoys. At this time Denmark had become the dominant political power in the region, but Queen Margaret lacked the military and naval muscle to deal with the pirate threat. She solved the problem by ceding Gotland to the Teutonic Knights, a chivalric order based in Poland who possessed the troops and the ships needed to reconquer the island. In 1398, the Teutonic Knights attacked and captured the island, and the surviving pirates scattered. The Danes were then able to deal with most of the survivors, who had fled to Finland. By the end of the year only one group of pirates remained. However, these consisted of the toughest and most ruthless of them all—a pirate brotherhood that went by the name of the Likedeelers.

THE LIKEDEELERS OF HELGOLAND

The survivors of the Victual Brothers called themselves the Likedeelers, an egalitarian name meaning they shared all their possessions and plunder. Around 1399, they founded a new base on the banks of the River Schlei, at the estuary of the River Ems on the modern German–Dutch border. They also seized the North Sea island of Helgoland, which they turned into a pirate stronghold. From these bases they began preying on Danish and Hanseatic ships, smuggling their plunder ashore to sell in non-Hanseatic ports.

Above: This bronze statue of Klaus Störtebeker was erected in Hamburg in 1982, where today the pirate is seen as a kind of German Robin Hood.

KLAUS STÖRTEBEKER

The most famous of the Likedeelers was Klaus "Störtebeker," a name which equates very roughly to "emptying the mug in one gulp"! It seems his real name was Nikolas Klaus Störtebeker, who was reputedly born in Wismar around 1360. He joined the Victual Brothers and was one of those driven from Gotland in 1398. By 1400 he had become the leader of the Likedeelers of Helgoland.

Stortebeker began attacking Danish and Hanseatic ships, although it seems his men attacked any passing merchantman, regardless of nationality. German legend has it that his

The Haven of Helgoland

A small island about 45 miles (72km) from the German coast, Helgoland is a rocky outcrop less than a square mile in size. In the early 15th century the island was occupied by a small fishing settlement near its southwestern corner, which the Likedeelers claimed as their own pirate haven. The island was easily defensible, the settlement being surrounded by tall sandstone cliffs and wind-blown sand dunes. In 1400 it was owned by the Danes, which made the place an especially suitable sanctuary for the Likedeelers. Just as importantly, the island also lay close to the sea lanes linking Hamburg to Denmark and the Baltic ports.

flagship was called the *Seetiger* ("Sea Tiger"), and he was assisted by three captains—Gödeke Michels, Hennig Wichmann, and "Magister" Wigbold. By the summer of 1401 his attacks were crippling the economy of Hamburg as ships began to avoid the waters around Gotland and the mouth of the Elbe.

The Hamburgers called on the help of the rest of the Hanseatic League and, later that summer, a Hansa fleet appeared off Helgoland, forcing Störtebeker to sail out and meet it. The Hanseatic ships were commanded by Simon of Utrecht, a veteran sea captain whose flagship was a fighting cog called *Die Bunte Kuh* ("The Colorful Cow"). The running battle which followed lasted for three days, but eventually the pirates were defeated and the *Seetiger* was captured.

Another German legend tells how one of the pirates—a Helgolander—was paid by the Hansa to disable the rudder of the *Seetiger*, allowing Simon of Utrecht to overhaul his opponent. Störtebeker and the surviving Likedeelers were captured, and taken to Hamburg to answer for their crimes.

THE EXECUTION OF STÖRTEBEKER

Inevitably, Störtebeker and 71 Likedeelers were sentenced to death, despite the pirate chief's attempt to bribe the city magistrates. He is said to have offered them a gold chain long enough to encircle the port. In October 1401, the pirates were escorted to the executioner's block. Legend tells how Störtebeker supposedly struck a deal

Above: The execution of Störtebeker and his crew in Hamburg in 1401.

Right: A 16th-century medal, allegedly depicting Klaus Störtebeker.

whereby he should be first to face the axe, and if his headless body could walk down the line, past all the prisoners, then pardons would be granted to them all. The story goes that he managed to pass 11 of his shipmates before he fell—tripped up by the executioner. The heads of Störtebeker and his fellow pirates were stuck on to spikes, which lined the Hamburg waterfront. Today he is seen as a hero and his exploits have become the stuff of German legend.

The Barbary Pirates

Before the pirates came, the North African coast belonged to the nomadic Berbers—people the Greeks called *barbaroi*, or barbarians. Then came the Arabs, sweeping westward along Africa and into Spain, taking the faith of Islam with them.

By the late 15th century, the long coastline from Morocco to Libya was known as the Barbary Coast. From the late 15th century onward, the region became the base of a series of pirate communities. For the next two centuries or more these pirates operated in the western Mediterranean, turning it into one of the most dangerous seas on earth.

The Barbary pirates were highly organized and although they technically owed their allegiance to the Ottoman Turks, they were effectively a loose confederation of independent city-states—each port ruled by a bey, or overlord. The economy of the Barbary Coast was based on piracy and slavery. While pirate galleys ranged the Mediterranean in search of prey, the Barbary pirates also raided coastal communities in the northern Mediterranean. Their aim was to capture slaves, who could be sold for a profit in the slave markets of North Africa.

As well as being pirates, these corsairs (see page 41) also served as naval auxiliaries to the Turkish Sultan in Constantinople. For much of the 16th century they were at the forefront

Above: This 17th-century painting by Cornelis Vroom, a Dutch painter and draftsman, depicts the sinking of a pirate galley, while Spanish galleons engage the Barbary corsairs.

of a religious war between Christians and Muslims, fought on the sea and the coastline of the Mediterranean, from Greece to the Straits of Gibraltar. This meant the Barbary pirates faced the naval and military might of Spain, Venice, France, and several smaller states, including the zealous Knights of Malta.

For the most part, the Muslim corsairs not only managed to hold their own against their religious foes, but they managed to take the fight to their enemies, raiding and sacking Christian ports and helping the Turks to wage a relentless naval campaign for mastery of the Mediterranean.

The Rise of the Muslim Corsairs

In the 14th century a new breed of pirates arose—corsairs who combined their piratical activities with service to Allah and the Turkish Sultan.

For more than a century, the appearance of longboats rowing inshore along the Aegean coastline heralded an orgy of death, destruction, and looting.

The collapse of Byzantine power in 1204 created a power vacuum in the eastern Mediterranean. This encouraged the spread of piracy, a scourge which the new naval powers of Venice and Genoa were unable to prevent. Greek waters became a haven for pirates for more than a century, until a new power emerged that would impose order over the troubled waters of the Aegean. The rise of the Ottoman Turks created a new phenomenon—the combination of Islamic naval power allied to a whole new breed of Muslim pirates.

THE GREEK PIRATES

The 13th century was a time of trouble in Greece, and piracy thrived in the waters of the Aegean and Adriatic. According to the Italian historian Torsello, the majority of these pirates were Italians, mostly from Venice and Genoa. Many were opportunists and adventurers, eager to use piracy as a tool to gain power and territory. A typical Greek pirate of this period was Giovanni del lo Cavo, who in 1278 became the Byzantine governor of Rhodes as he was the only man powerful enough to hold the island in the name of the Byzantine Emperor. Others operated on a much smaller scale, many being simply local Greek fishermen who indulged in a little piracy on the side.

THE KNIGHTS AND THE LION

In 1308, the pirates of Rhodes were evicted when the island was captured by a crusading order, the Knights of St. John, or Knights of Malta as they were also known. They

Above: A Barbary corsair takes a young woman captive. Painting by Delacroix depicting Selim & Zuleika, featured in Byron's poem "The Bride of Abydos."

established a small fleet of galleys on the island, and the Rhodean navy began operating against pirates in the busy waters between Cyprus and Crete. Although their main aim was to keep the sea lanes open for crusaders bound for the Holy Land, they also made the waters safe for local merchant ships.

Another bulwark of naval power was Venice, which spent much of the 13th century expanding its control over the pirate islands of the Adriatic. It also carved out colonies on Crete, on the southern tip of the Peloponnese, and in several islands in the central Aegean. Their flag—the Lion of St. Mark—flew over Crete from 1206, and the port of Candia was turned into a major naval base, where Venetian war galleys could patrol the sea lanes. They even operated alongside the Rhodean and Byzantine fleets, to deal with troublesome nests of pirates in the northern Aegean. This meant that by the 14th century, piracy in the Aegean and Adriatic was on the wane.

Above: British sailors capture a black flag from Greek pirates in this imaginative 19th-century illustration.

The Pirate Galley

During the time of the Barbary pirates, the most common type of warship in the Mediterranean was the galley. These resembled the galleys used by the ancient Romans, but they now carried a battery of heavy guns, mounted in their bow. This made them formidable weapons of war, particularly as many war galleys were also crammed with soldiers, ready to capture the enemy using musket, sword, and shield.

Above: Barbary corsair galleys were light, fast, heavily manned, and armed with a small battery of guns in their bow.

A typical war galley could carry 20 to 30 oars per side, powered by three or four rowers apiece. On Christian galleys, these men were usually slaves, chained to their benches. A galley was fast, nimble, and in light winds it danced around a sailing vessel, keeping out of the angle of fire while pounding the foe with guns. Galleys were also fitted with at least one mast, allowing for sail-power as well as oars. They were ideal for overpowering merchant ships or fleeing pursuers.

THE COMING OF THE TURKS

Around 1300 the crumbling Byzantine Empire had lost control of most of Anatolia—now Turkey. At first the region was occupied by a patchwork of Muslim states, but during the 14th century one of these, led by Bey Osman I (ruled 1299–1326), expanded to incorporate its neighbors. In the process this state gained control of most of Anatolia. Osman's people became known as the Ottoman Turks, derived from his name. By the mid-14th century the Turks had reached the northeastern shores of the Aegean, and gained control of ports on the Sea of Marmara, which faced the great city of Constantinople.

During the later 14th century the Turks expanded their borders southward, working their way along the Aegean coast of Anatolia until in 1396 they conquered Bodrum and the province around it, which overlooked the island of Rhodes. From the 1360s the Turkish-held Aegean ports were turned into naval bases, and Ottoman Turkish galleys cleared the surrounding area of pirates. In truth, they didn't exactly eradicate piracy—rather the Turks favored hiring these pirate communities as mercenaries, so turning them into privateers who flew the Muslim standard.

PIRATES TURNED PRIVATEERS

Rather than build a completely new fleet, the 14th-century Turks preferred to use mercenary fleets, recruited from the Greek pirate communities in the Aegean. Ottoman regional governors often used these naval mercenaries as privateers, who were given a free hand to attack Christian shipping.

European sailors use superior firepower to fight off an attack from Barbary pirates in the 16th century.

The Barbary Coast

A notorious nest of cut-throats for almost four centuries, the Barbary Coast of North Africa was the ultimate pirate haven—home to some of the most dangerous pirates in history.

The coast of North Africa had been in Muslim hands since the 8th century. It was divided into several small states, most of which centered around a port such as Algiers, Tunis, or Tripoli. By the 15th century, these ports had developed into some of the most notorious pirate havens in the world.

ENCOURAGING THE PIRATES

During the Arab conquests of the 7th and 8th centuries the Mediterranean coastline of Africa fell under Muslim control, as did most of Spain. While much of this coast was uninhabited, a number of reasonably prosperous ports dotted the coast, each of which had a fertile hinterland that produced the food it needed. By the late 14th century,

Pirate Tactics

Barbary pirates usually tried to capture their prey without firing at them. After all, cannon fire could damage the cargo or the ship. These pirate galleys usually had the advantage of numbers over their opponents. Unlike the war galleys of the Spanish, the Venetians, or the Knights of St. John, Barbary galleys weren't powered by slaves, but by free men—all well-armed pirates. This meant that the pirates preferred to board an enemy and capture it in hand-to-hand combat. Unlike the galleys of antiquity, they never tried to ram an opponent, but fought using either sword or cannon.

when the Ottoman Turks were establishing a foothold in the Aegean, the Christian Spanish were engaged in the *reconquista*, the struggle to evict the Moors from Spain. The greater the Spanish success in evicting the Moors, the larger the number of refugees seeking sanctuary in the ports of the Barbary Coast; as the Moors in Spain grew weaker, the Barbary States grew stronger.

Pirates had operated along the North African coast since the collapse of the Western Roman Empire, but it was only in the 15th century that they seriously threatened trade. By this stage the *reconquista* had almost driven the Moors from Spain, and trade between Spanish, Italian, and French ports was on the increase. The ports of the Barbary Coast were now ideally placed to prey on these passing Christian traders. Until then, the Barbary ports had no real source of income. They lay on the edge of the Sahara Desert, and so any riches had to come from the sea. The growth of Christian maritime trade therefore came as a godsend to the beys of Algiers, Tripoli, and Tunis, and by the end of the 15th century they were actively encouraging pirates to use their ports. In return for

Above: The port of Oran on the Barbary Coast, from a 16th-century print. The port was captured by the Spanish in 1509.

commissioning these pirates as state-sponsored privateers, the rulers received a percentage of the profits. Privateering soon became a very profitable business, and the Barbary ports became bustling marketplaces for both slaves and plunder.

LOYAL TO THE SULTAN

In theory, those beys that ruled the Barbary States owed their allegiance to the Ottoman Turkish Sultan, who from 1453 was based in Constantinople (now Istanbul), which he had

Beys and Beyliks

The title of Bey is a Turkish word, roughly equivalent to "chief." It was traditionally a term for Turkish tribal leaders, but by the 15th century it meant "lord"—the equivalent to a duke in feudal Europe. The territory they ruled was called a Beylik, which meant a province or governorate, similar to a feudal duchy. This meant that the Bey of Algiers, the Bey of Tunis, or the Bey of Tripoli ruled the city itself, as well as the hinterland that formed part of the Beylik. A bey who was appointed directly by the Turkish Sultan was often called a Pasha—the equivalent of a royal governor, ruling on behalf of the Sultan.

The *rais* (captain) of each Barbary galley owned his own ship, and had complete control over the vessel and crew. This included the freedom to hunt for prey wherever he wanted. He was assisted by a scribe, appointed by the *Taife Raisi* to make sure everything was aboveboard. He also made sure that the captain followed the privateering rules approved by the bey. This meant only attacking non-Muslim shipping. Also, depending on the political situation at the time, ships from certain Christian countries might be off-limits too.

Above: The port of Tripoli, from a 16th-century chart. The city was the largest pirate haven on the Barbary Coast.

captured from the Byzantines. The reality was that the Sultan usually allowed the beys to rule themselves, and only demanded their help in time of war. Therefore the Barbary States are best seen as a series of independent city-states, whose freedom was guaranteed by serving as naval auxiliaries to the Turkish Sultan. The Barbary pirates took part in several naval campaigns alongside the Turks, but operated mostly on their own.

THE COUNCIL OF CAPTAINS

By the early 16th century many of the beys were elected from among the pirate captains. A ruling council of captains called the *Taife Raisi* supervised the privateering fleet, but it remained answerable to the bey, and ultimately to the Ottoman Sultan. The council dealt with disputes among the crews, supervised the selling of slaves and plunder, and made sure the bey received his share of the profits. Usually he received 10 percent of the spoils. Everyone benefited—apart from the Christians who filled the slave markets.

THE SPANISH THREAT

In 1492, the Spanish finally managed to drive the Moors out of Spain. While Moorish refugees helped swell the numbers of the Barbary fleets, this also meant that the Spanish were now a serious threat to the Barbary States, who were now on the front line in the war between Christian and Muslim. The Spanish soon began launching attacks on the western end of the Barbary Coast, seeking a foothold in North Africa, and trying to use it to push the pirates eastward. When two Greek-born pirate captains, the Barbarossa Brothers (see page 46), began attacking Spanish shipping and coastal settlements, the Spanish retaliated by launching full-scale expeditions against the Barbary States.

Pirate, Privateer, or Corsair?

Technically, the Barbary pirates weren't really pirates at all, but privateers. These men were granted privateering licenses by the various beys, who in turn owed their authority to the Turkish Sultan. Therefore, the Barbary pirates operated as privateers, in Ottoman Turkish service. The problem was that most of the western maritime powers in the region—France, Spain, Venice, Genoa, and the Knights of Malta—refused to recognize the authority

Seventeenth-century sketch by Van de Velde the Younger, depicting a fight between pirates and Dutch sailors.

of the beys. They saw these Muslim galley crews as pirates, or corsairs. "Corsair" is a French term meaning privateer, but by the 16th century the term was also used to describe pirates. After all, if the Christian powers of the Mediterranean didn't recognize the authority of the beys, then the men who served in their galleys were pirates.

Right: Christian slaves disembarking on the Algiers waterfront, from a 16th-century engraving. The port housed a bustling slave market.

The Galiot

An even more nimble version of the galley was the galiot—a popular type of vessel on the Barbary Coast. These sleek craft were smaller and faster than regular galleys, and were fitted with six to twelve oars per side, crewed by just two men apiece. Another variant was the Lanterna—a big, powerful flagship galley, with 30 or 40 oars each side. These monsters were the battleships of their day, and while they weren't ideally suited to the needs of the Barbary pirates, they were sometimes used as the flagships of pirate fleets.

Between 1510 and 1525 the Spanish captured several Barbary ports, including Oran, Algiers, and Tunis. For a time it looked like the Barbary pirates would be wiped out, but help arrived from the Ottoman Turks—ships, men, and money—and in 1529 the Turks were able to launch a counter-attack that managed to recapture most of the lost cities. It was a brutal war where prisoners were usually killed, and civilians of the wrong

The Redemptionist Fathers were dedicated to buying freedom for Christian slaves held by Barbary pirates.

religion were put to the sword. By the late 16th century this war had reached a stalemate and both sides eventually wearied of the fight. An undeclared truce led to a tenuous peace, which lasted until the first decades of the 19th century.

AN OTTOMAN BACKWATER

When Uluch Ali, Bey of Algiers, died in 1587 he was the last in a long line of piratical rulers in the Barbary States. From that point on the Turkish Sultan took a direct interest in who ran the states, and most of the subsequent beys were appointed directly by him. In other words, they were men he could rely on. As a result, because the Ottoman Turks and the Spanish had made peace with each other almost 15 years earlier, the Spanish were forced to recognize the Barbary States as Ottoman Turkish territory.

Of course, the Barbary pirates still attacked Christian ships—they just avoided Spanish ones. This period of direct rule by

the Ottoman Turks lasted six decades—until 1659. Then a series of revolts in the Barbary States led to freedom from Turkish rule, and the re-establishment of independence. From then until the early 19th century the beys ruled, and their pirate fleets helped to guarantee their autonomy. While the Barbary States survived, by the 17th century they were no longer considered to be a serious threat in the western Mediterranean.

Below: HMS *Aurora* guarding a convoy attacked by Barbary pirates, 1812, by Thomas Buttersworth.

The Barbarossa Brothers

Two red-haired brothers from Greece ruled the Mediterranean and became the most feared Barbary pirates of the 16th century.

The first successful Barbary pirate leaders were Aruj and Hizir—known as the "Barbarossa Brothers." Already accomplished pirates when they arrived on the Barbary Coast in 1505, they soon established a reputation as the fiercest pirates in the western Mediterranean.

BEWARE THE GREEKS

Aruj and his younger brother Hizir were both born on the Aegean island of Lesbos during the 1470s. Tradition has it that their father was Yakup Aga, a retired Ottoman soldier who married an island girl. At the time, Lesbos was owned by the Turks, and was a known pirate haven. It was also a bustling, cosmopolitan port where Muslim and Greek merchants mixed freely.

Another legend has it that Aruj and an older brother were serving aboard a local trading ship when they were captured by the Knights of St. John. His older brother was killed and Aruj Aga spent a year in Rhodes before his family could raise the money to pay his ransom. On his release, Aruj boarded a visiting Egyptian ship and sailed to Alexandria. There the local Egyptian ruler Qansuh al-Ghawri lent him the funds

The Barbarossa Brothers—who became the most notorious and ferocious of the Barbary pirates.

to fit out a privateering galley, and soon his younger brother joined him. Together they spent a decade preying on ships trading with Rhodes as a way of seeking revenge for the death of their eldest brother.

THE PIRATES OF DJERBA

The brothers soon became highly regarded as skilled pirate captains. In 1504 the Ottomans made peace with the Knights of St. John, and

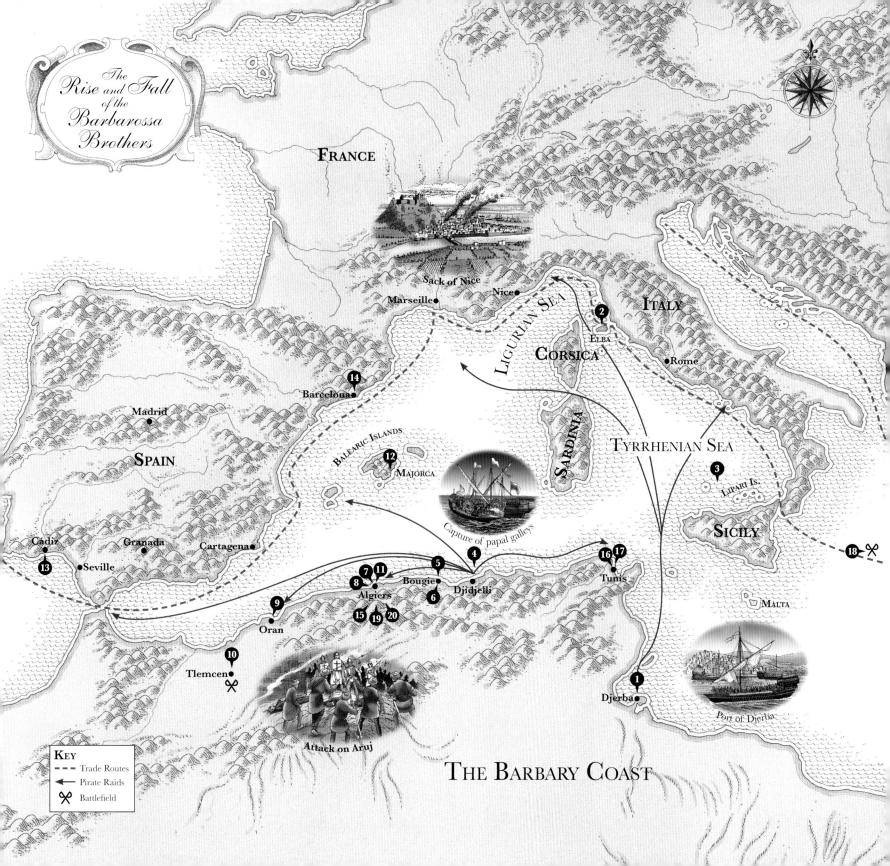

The Rise and Fall of the Barbarossa Brothers

FRANCE

Sack of Nice

Nice

Marseille

LIGURIAN SEA

ITALY

Elba

2

CORSICA

Rome

Barcelona

14

SARDINIA

TYRRHENIAN SEA

SPAIN

Madrid

BALEARIC ISLANDS

MAJORCA

12

Capture of papal galleys

3

LIPARI IS.

SICILY

Cadiz

Granada

Cartagena

18

Seville

13

9

7 11

8

Bougie

5

4

16 17

Tunis

Oran

Algiers

6

Djidjelli

15 19 20

MALTA

10

Tlemcen

1

Djerba

Attack on Aruj

Port of Djerba

THE BARBARY COAST

KEY
- - - Trade Routes
← Pirate Raids
✗ Battlefield

Above: Dutch ships engage a heavily armed flotilla of Barbary pirates in oared galleys, in a 17th-century oil on canvas by Flemish painter Sebastian D. Castro.

Red-Bearded Brothers

In 1507, the Spanish historian Diego Haedo wrote of one of the brothers:

*T*he wonder and astonishment that this notable exploit caused in Tunis, and even in Christendom, is not to be expressed, nor how celebrated the name of Aruj Rais was to become from that very moment. He was held and accounted by all the world as a most valiant and enterprising commander. And by reason his beard was extremely red, or he was generally called Barbarossa, which in Italian means "Red Beard."

In a Mediterranean world of black-haired people, the two red-bearded Barbarossa Brothers would have been instantly recognizable.

so the brothers moved their privateering operation westward to the Barbary Coast. In 1505 the Bey of Tunis granted them the use of the small island port of Djerba, 200 miles (322km) away to the south of his Beylik. The two brothers commanded a galley each, and soon the pair were ranging far to the north, preying on Christian shipping in the Tyrrhenian and Ligurian seas. They had some spectacular successes. In 1506, Aruj captured two galleys belonging to Pope Julius II off the island of Elba, while his brother Hizir captured the

Right: A large and prestigious Florentine galley is surrounded and attacked by a substantial squadron of smaller Barbary galleys.

Sardinian warship *Cavalleria* in the Lipari Islands to the north of Sicily. These successes meant that other pirates flocked to join them, and soon the brothers found themselves in command of a pirate fleet.

SCOURGE OF THE SPANIARDS

In 1511, they fell out with the Bey of Tunis because he demanded a greater share of their profits. The brothers moved their fleet to a new base, this time in the small port of Djidjelli, near Algiers. With the Spanish-held ports of Bougie and Oran on either side of them, there was no shortage of enemy ships to attack. In 1512 the brothers launched an attack on Bougie but were driven off, and Aruj lost an arm in the fighting. Seeking revenge, he attacked the port again in 1514, but once again they were repulsed. The brothers were becoming impatient with the Bey of Algiers, who took his share of their plunder but did nothing to help them fight his enemies.

THE DEATH OF ARUJ BARBAROSSA

In 1516, Aruj seized his chance. Using a popular revolt against the Bey as a distraction, he entered the city at the head of his men, killed the Bey in his palace, and claimed the title for himself. He now had the men and resources he needed to renew his offensive against the Spanish. In early 1518 he defeated a Spanish attempt to capture Algiers. Later that summer the Spanish gathered an army at Oran, led by the Emperor Charles V. Aruj struck first, but his pirates were intercepted, and besieged in the town of Tlemcen. After three weeks the Spanish assaulted the walls, and the pirate leader was killed, together with the rest of his men.

KHAIR-ED-DIN

Hizir Barbarossa now took command of Algiers. He was soon known as Khair-ed-Din ("Gift of God"), as he successfully rallied the pirates to the defense of his Beylik, with a little help from the Turkish Sultan. In 1519, he managed to repulse the Spanish attack on Algiers, forcing the Spanish to abandon the campaign. Algiers was secure, and Khair-ed-Din—now named Pasha (see Beys and Beyliks, page 44) by the Sultan—took the war to the enemy. He raided the Spanish-held Balearic Islands and even burned shipping off the great Spanish harbor of Cádiz.

With the Spanish at bay, the pirate leader then answered the summons of the Sultan, and led his men to join in a Turkish attack

Left: A contemporary depiction of younger brother, Hizir Barbarossa (Khair-ed-Din), one of the most successful of the Barbary pirates.

against Rhodes. The island fell in 1523 and Khair-ed-Din and his men had their pick of the spoils. During the decade that followed, his Algerian galleys launched repeated raids on Spanish coastal towns. In 1531 he attacked Tunis, which had been captured by the Spanish but was now defended by the Knights of St. John. The Barbary pirates were defeated. It was Hizir's first real setback since coming to power.

He had more success campaigning against a new Holy League, an alliance of Venice and the Papacy. In 1538, his joint Turkish and Barbary fleet defeated the League's fleet at Prevesa, on the Adriatic coast of Greece. Two years later he repulsed a third and final Spanish assault on Algiers. By the time of his death in 1545, Hizir Barbarossa had turned Algiers into a fortress, a secure base from which his successors could continue the fight against the enemies of Islam.

Murat Rais

Embracing piracy when he was just a boy, Murat Rais went on to become the scourge of the Spanish. He was a maverick pirate who earned a reputation for skill and daring.

A worthy successor to the Barbarossa Brothers was Murat Rais, who rose to prominence in the late 16th century. An audacious and wily corsair, he was once regarded as the most dangerous pirate in the Mediterranean, but he ended his days as a respected admiral in the service of the Turkish Sultan.

Below: A French merchantman, pictured being attacked by Barbary pirates. Sailing vessels were particularly vulnerable to galleys in calm weather.

A Rising Star

Born in Albania around 1534, Murat Rais was a teenager when he was captured by Barbary pirates. He converted to Islam and joined the crew, and by the 1560s he had command of his own pirate galiot. He developed a reputation for daring—and for impetuosity, a trait that did little to endear him to his superiors, including the Barbary pirate leaders Turgut Rais and Uluj Ali.

The Beys of the Barbary Coast, 16th Century

Turgut Rais

1 **1520** The Barbary corsair Turgut Rais joins the fleet of Khair-ed-Din, based in Algiers, and serves under his command.

2 **1538** He is made an admiral in the Ottoman Turkish fleet, and serves under Khair-ed-Din at the Battle of Preveza. They win a spectacular victory over their Christian opponents.

3 **1539** In his first independent command, he campaigns in the northern part of the Adriatic Sea, his galleys ranging as far north as Venice.

4 **1540** Establishes an operational base at Djerba, and uses it to launch a raid on Malta.

5 **1540** Leads raids throughout Corsica and Sardinia.

6 **1541** Captured by the Genoese and spends the next three years as a galley slave.

7 **1544** Khair-ed-Din threatens to attack Genoa, to secure the release of Turgut Rais.

8 **1550** Turgut Rais forced to yield Djerba to the Christians.

9 **1551** Recaptures Tripoli from the Knights of St. John.

Battle with Knights of Malta

10 **1565** Killed during the Siege of Malta.

Murat Rais

A **1565** Murat Rais becomes the commander of a Barbary galiot.

B **1568** Earns the disfavor of his superior Uluj Ali, so promotion is slow.

C **1574** Given command of the Algerian fleet.

D **1574** Captures the Spanish Viceroy of Sicily off the southern tip of Sardinia—an achievement which secures his reputation.

E **1584** Becomes the Beylerbey of Algiers—the *de facto* commander of the Barbary corsairs.

F **1586** Leaves the Mediterranean, to lead a raid against the Canary Islands.

G **1594** As commander of the Ottoman fleet, he leads a major raid on the coast of southern Italy.

H **1595** Defeats a powerful Christian naval force off the southern coast of Sicily.

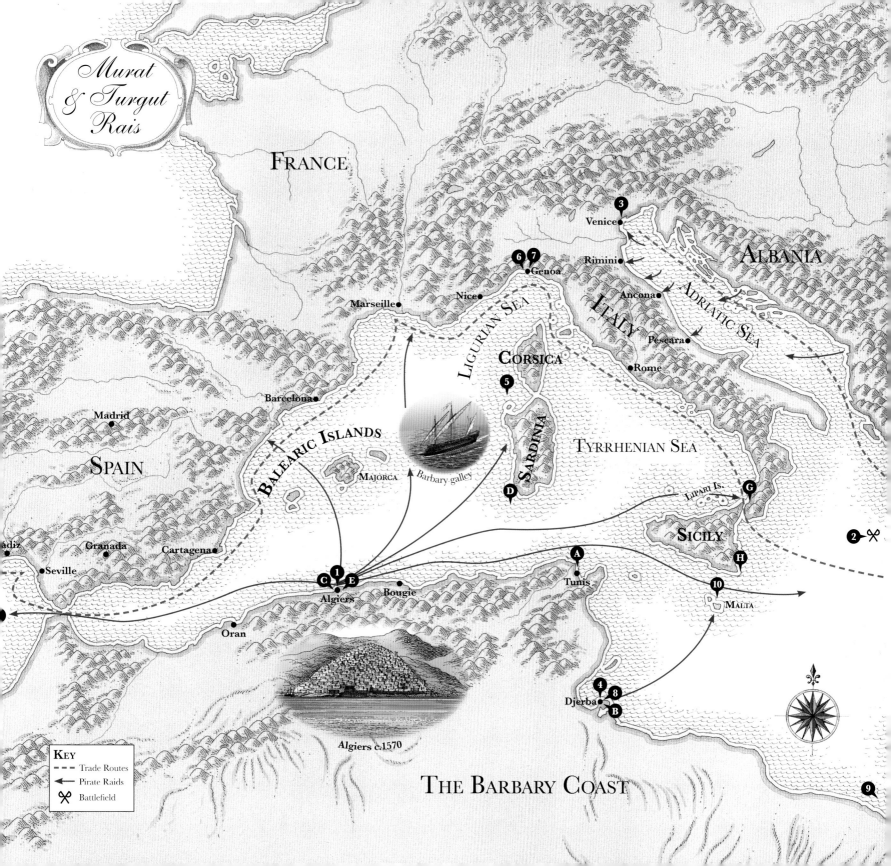

Murat & Turgut Rais

FRANCE

ALBANIA

Venice ●③

Rimini

ANCONA

Pescara

Rome

ITALY

ADRIATIC SEA

⑥ ⑦

Genoa

Nice

Marseille

LIGURIAN SEA

CORSICA

⑤

TYRRHENIAN SEA

Barcelona

BALEARIC ISLANDS

SARDINIA

Ⓓ

Lipari Is.

Ⓖ

SICILY

②✂

Madrid

SPAIN

MAJORCA

Barbary galley

Ⓗ

Ⓐ

Granada

Cartagena

Tunis

Ⓒ ①Ⓔ

Algiers

Bougie

Seville

Oran

④

⑧

Djerba

Ⓑ

⑩

Malta

Algiers c.1570

⑨

THE BARBARY COAST

KEY
- - - Trade Routes
→ Pirate Raids
✂ Battlefield

Turgut Rais (1485–1565)

Unlike many Barbary captains, Turgut Rais never regarded himself as a pirate, or even a privateer. His origins are obscure, but sources suggest he was brought up near Bodrum in Asia Minor (now Turkey) as the son of a Turkish farmer. He began his career in the Ottoman Turkish army, and it was only in 1517 that he went to sea, reputedly after acquiring a part-share in an Egyptian galiot. He soon mastered the nautical skills he required; for more than two decades he pursued a career as a Barbary corsair, serving under Khair-ed-Din, the younger of the Barbarossa Brothers, and leading raids throughout the western Mediterranean.

In 1538 both Turgut Rais and Khair-ed-Din were called on to serve the Turkish Sultan, and

Left: Turgut Rais, as portrayed in a dramatic 18th-century engraving. Many Europeans viewed the Barbary pirates as romantic figures, but they were hard-bitten, merciless fighters.

while Khair-ed-Din commanded the fleet, Turgut Rais took charge of the Muslim reserves. As a reward for his performance, he was given the Governorship of Djerba. Then, in 1540, he was surprised at anchor, and captured by a Spanish squadron. Turgut Rais was forced to serve as a galley slave for three years and then imprisoned in Genoa until Khair-ed-Din negotiated his release. Freeing him proved a costly mistake, as Turgut Rais spent the rest of his career seeking revenge, refusing to negotiate with his Christian opponents.

After the death of Khair-ed-Din, he rose to command the Turkish fleet, and later became the Beylerbey ("leader of leaders") of Algiers, and then the Pasha of Tripoli. However, his great love was waging war against the Christians, and therefore it is appropriate that he died in action, besieging the Christian stronghold of Malta.

CAPTAIN OF THE SEA

In 1584 Murat Rais became the Bey of Algiers, and the Sultan commissioned him as "Captain of the Sea." He won fame when he captured a Spanish galley with the Spanish Viceroy of Sicily aboard. Murat Rais proved a real thorn in the side of the Spanish, and spent a decade raiding their coast, sinking their merchant ships, and filling the marketplace of Algiers with Spanish slaves. In 1586, he attacked Lanzarote in the Canary Islands and held the inhabitants for ransom.

ADMIRAL OF THE TURKISH FLEET

Eight years later he was appointed Admiral of the Turkish fleet, and promptly led the Ottoman fleet to victory over the Spanish

Right: English warship in action with Barbary corsairs, c.1680, in a painting by Van de Velde the Younger.

off the coast of Sicily. Having successfully turned his back on piracy, he spent the remainder of his days living in the eastern

Mediterranean, in the service of the Sultan. Murat Rais reputedly was over 100 years old when he died in 1609.

The Last of the Barbary Pirates

The son of an Italian fisherman, Uluj Ali became one of the last great corsairs of the Barbary Coast, a man of legendary skill and courage.

One of the last great pirate leaders of the Barbary Coast, Uluj Ali combined his activities as a pirate chief with service to the Turkish Sultan. In the process, he not only preserved the independence of the Barbary States, but he also helped save the Turkish empire from collapse in the wake of a catastrophic naval defeat.

Below: A 16th-century depiction of the Barbary port of Algiers, a natural harbor that was home to a sizeable fleet of pirate galleys. The port was also well defended by walls and fortifications.

FROM SLAVE TO PIRATE

Born to a fisherman in southern Italy, Uluj Ali was captured by Barbary pirates when he was in his teens. He became a slave but won his freedom when he converted to Islam. He duly became a Barbary pirate, dropping his Italian name, Giovanni Dionigi.

During the 1550s he rose to prominence under the corsair leader Turgut Rais, and by 1560 had gained command of his own pirate galiot. He fought at the battle of Djerba (1560), when his skill and bravery were noted by Piyale Pasha, the Turkish admiral. His performance was also noted during the Siege of Malta (1565).

SUPREME LORD OF THE PIRATES

Uluj Ali was rewarded by being made Pasha of Tripoli, and in the years that followed he developed the city into one of the most active pirate havens on the Barbary Coast. In 1568 a grateful Sultan rewarded him with the prestigious post of Beylerbey of Algiers. A Beylerbey was a Supreme Bey, holding authority over the other beys and pashas.

Above: Not all Barbary vessels were galleys—apart from its triangular "lateen" sails, this 17th-century North African merchantmen is little different from the European trading vessels that sailed the waters of the Mediterranean.

The following year he launched a full-scale attack on Tunis, and against the odds he succeeded in capturing the port from the Spanish who had occupied it since 1535. From there he waged a naval war with the Knights of St. John based on Malta, and in 1570 he even captured a powerful Maltese squadron, an achievement which was lauded throughout the Mediterranean.

SAVIOR OF THE MUSLIM WORLD

The following year Uluj Ali was ordered east to join the main Turkish fleet, and he was present when it was comprehensively defeated at the Battle of Lepanto (1571).

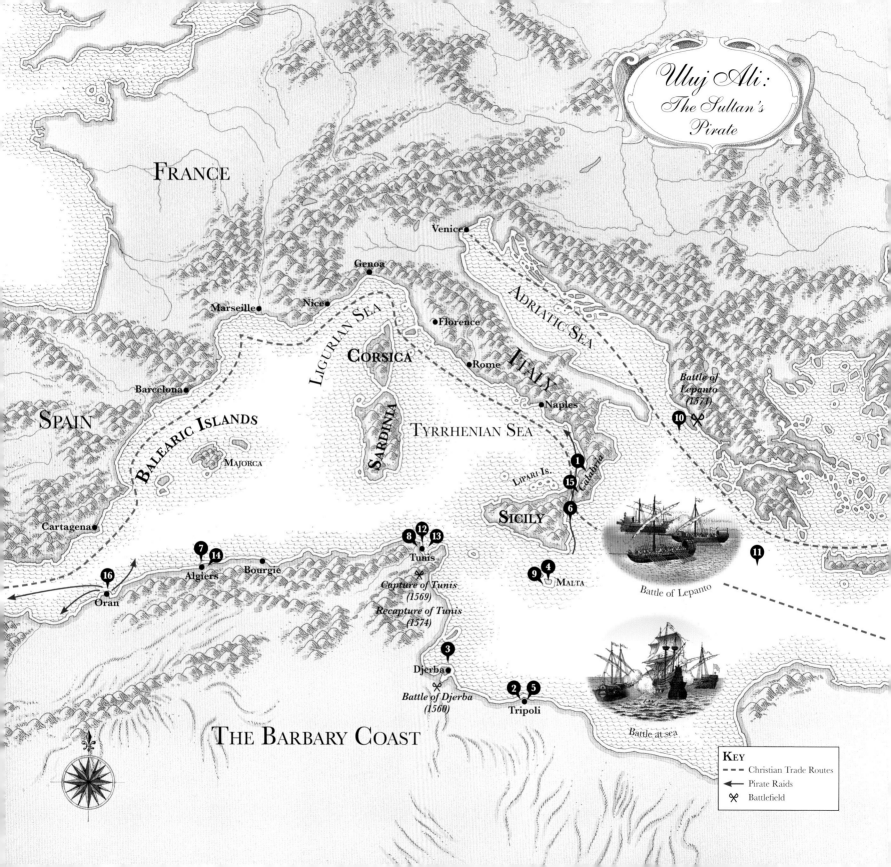

Uluj Ali: The Sultan's Pirate

FRANCE

SPAIN

Venice

Genoa

Marseille

Nice

Florence

Rome

LIGURIAN SEA

CORSICA

ADRIATIC SEA

ITALY

Barcelona

BALEARIC ISLANDS

Majorca

SARDINIA

TYRRHENIAN SEA

Naples

Battle of
Lepanto
(1571)

10

Cartagena

16

Oran

7 **14**

Algiers

Bourgie

8 **12**

13

Tunis

Capture of Tunis
(1569)

Recapture of Tunis
(1574)

LIPARI IS.

1

15

Calabria

6

SICILY

9 **4**

Malta

11

Battle of Lepanto

3

Djerba

Battle of Djerba
(1560)

2 **5**

Tripoli

Battle at sea

THE BARBARY COAST

KEY
- - - Christian Trade Routes
→ Pirate Raids
✂ Battlefield

Uluj Ali: The Sultan's Pirate, 1536–1587

1 **1536** Born Giovanni Dionigi on the coast of Calabria, southern Italy. His father was a fisherman.

2 By the late 1550s he is known as Uluj Ali, a Barbary Corsair, who commands a galiot in the fleet of Turgut Rais, based in Tripoli.

3 **1560** Distinguishes himself during the naval battle off Djerba.

4 **1565** Participates in the Siege of Malta.

5 **1566** Succeeds Turgut Rais as the Bey of Tripoli.

6 **1567–68** Tripolitanian galleys raid the coasts of Sicily and southern Italy, causing widespread destruction.

7 **1568** Uluj Ali named as the Beylerbey of Algiers, thereby gaining control over all the Barbary Corsairs.

8 **1569** Leads the Barbary Corsairs of Algiers in an assault on Tunis, which liberates the city from the Spaniards.

9 **1570** Defeats and captures a squadron of Maltese galleys, crewed by the Knights of St. John. His reward is a commission as admiral in the Ottoman Turkish fleet.

10 **1571** The Battle of Lepanto—this climactic naval engagement ends in disaster for the Turks, and halts Turkish expansion into the western Mediterranean. Uluj Ali commands the Turkish rearguard with distinction.

11 **1572** Commands the Turkish fleet, rebuilding it after the Lepanto disaster and securing Turkish control over the waters of southern Greece and the Aegean Sea.

12 **1573** Don Juan of Austria captures Tunis in the name of Spain.

13 **1574** Uluj Ali recaptures Tunis from the Spaniards, and from that point on the city is placed under Ottoman Turkish rule.

14 **1574** He then strengthens the Muslim defenses of Algiers and Morocco.

15 **1576** Leads a major raid on Calabria, in southern Italy.

16 **Late 1570s** Raids Oran, and other Spanish enclaves along the North African coast.

The Battle of Lepanto (1571) as depicted here was the battle that decided the fate of the whole region. The victory of the Christians over the Turks ended Ottoman expansion into the western Mediterranean.

His tactical skill almost saved the day and the following year he became the Admiral in Chief of the Turkish fleet. While he rebuilt the shattered fleet, he also prevented the Christians from taking advantage of their victory. The corsair had almost single-handedly preserved the Ottoman Empire.

Oran and their other footholds on the coast. From then until his death in 1587, Beylerbey Uluj Ali strengthened the defenses of his ports, and used them to launch piratical and naval raids throughout the Mediterranean. To the end, he considered himself a pirate first, and an Ottoman admiral second.

THE HERO OF TUNIS

However, while he was distracted the Spanish managed to recapture Tunis. Then, in the summer of 1574, Uluj Ali led the Turkish fleet into the western Mediterranean, where he blockaded Tunis, then recaptured the city in a masterly combined amphibious and land assault. He went on to consolidate his control over the whole of the Barbary Coast, ejecting the Spanish from

By the time the British bombarded Algiers in 1816, the Barbary pirates were no longer considered a serious threat to trade.

The Spanish Main

In 1492, not only were the Moors driven from Spain and the country finally united under the banner of the "Catholic Monarchs" Ferdinand and Isabella, but Christopher Columbus discovered the New World and claimed it for Spain.

Spain's policy of colonization and conquest led to her controlling the Caribbean basin, as well as most of Central and South America. Under the 1494 Treaty of Tordesillas, all this territory, apart from Brazil, belonged to them. This overseas empire was a source of glory and riches.

After conquest came exploitation, and soon a regular convoy of ships was transporting New World wealth to Spain. When French privateers intercepted one of the first of these shipments, the rest of Europe discovered just how lucrative the New World had become.

By the mid-16th century, the first European "interlopers" appeared in the Caribbean—waters which were generally called the Spanish Main by these French, Dutch, and English newcomers. The first Spanish settlements were attacked, prompting the Spanish crown to divert resources to the protection of her colonies. Her main ports were fortified and garrisoned, warships patrolled the Caribbean, and Spanish treasure shipments were transported in well-protected convoys. For a century, these defenses were adequate, and the Spanish overseas empire continued to flourish.

This all changed during the 17th century, as other European settlers established their own colonies. By the mid-17th century, these newcomers had started to launch regular attacks on Spanish settlements and shipping, which would lead to the sacking and destruction of several important Spanish settlements, and the disruption of Spain's vital annual treasure convoys.

While the Spanish weathered this storm and retained their possessions in the Americas for another 150 years, by the 1690s the Spanish Main was no longer an exclusively Spanish preserve. It had become a hunting ground for pirates, buccaneers, and privateers of all nationalities.

Below: A Spanish fleet arrives in a Caribbean port, as depicted in a 17th-century painting by Andries van Eertvelt.

Spain's Overseas Empire

Within three decades of Columbus planting the flag of Spain on a beach in the Bahamas, the Spanish had carved out a vast empire.

Spain's overseas empire stretched from Florida down to the mountains of southern Peru. Conquistadors battled with the jungles of Central America or the lofty heights of the Andes, as well as with the peoples who lived there. Their reward was a share in the great riches of the Americas—gold, silver, and precious stones—all available for the taking.

THE TREATY OF TORDESILLAS

The first voyage of Christopher Columbus in 1492 established that there was land for the taking on the far side of the Atlantic Ocean. While he thought the islands he discovered were in Asia, the Spanish crown still wanted to establish control of these new lands—this New World. Therefore, in 1492, representatives of Spain and Portugal sat down to discuss the partition of the undiscovered world between them. The agreement—the Treaty of Tordesillas—was ratified by Pope Alexander VI in June 1494. It effectively divided the undiscovered world into two parts. The dividing "line" was set along a line of longitude—at 38° west— which ran down the Atlantic Ocean, passing within 100 miles (161km) of the Azores.

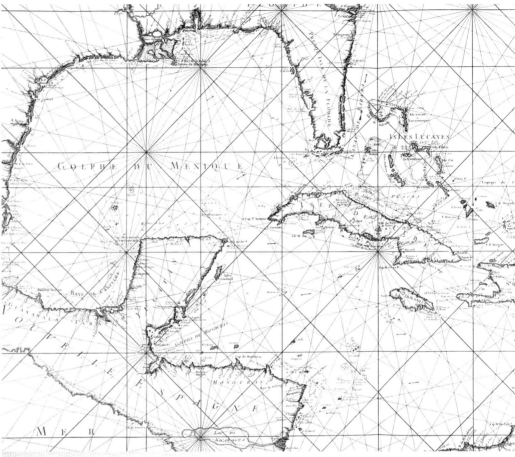

This 18th-century French chart depicts the area known as the Spanish Main. Originally referring solely to the Caribbean coast of South America, by the mid-16th century it encompassed the entire Caribbean basin.

The Portuguese now controlled all undiscovered lands to the east of this line. This included the coast of Africa and more importantly the lands which lay to the east, including what is now India and Indonesia. After the discovery of Brazil, the two nations met again, and the line was moved further westward—to 46° 37' west. The Spanish now controlled everywhere to the west

Interlopers

The Spanish viewed any other European who crossed the "line" into their territories as "interlopers." For them, the word referred to any non-Spaniards who appeared in the Spanish Main during the 16th and early 17th centuries. They were seen as intruders, and regardless of whether they came to trade or to raid, they were viewed as enemies.

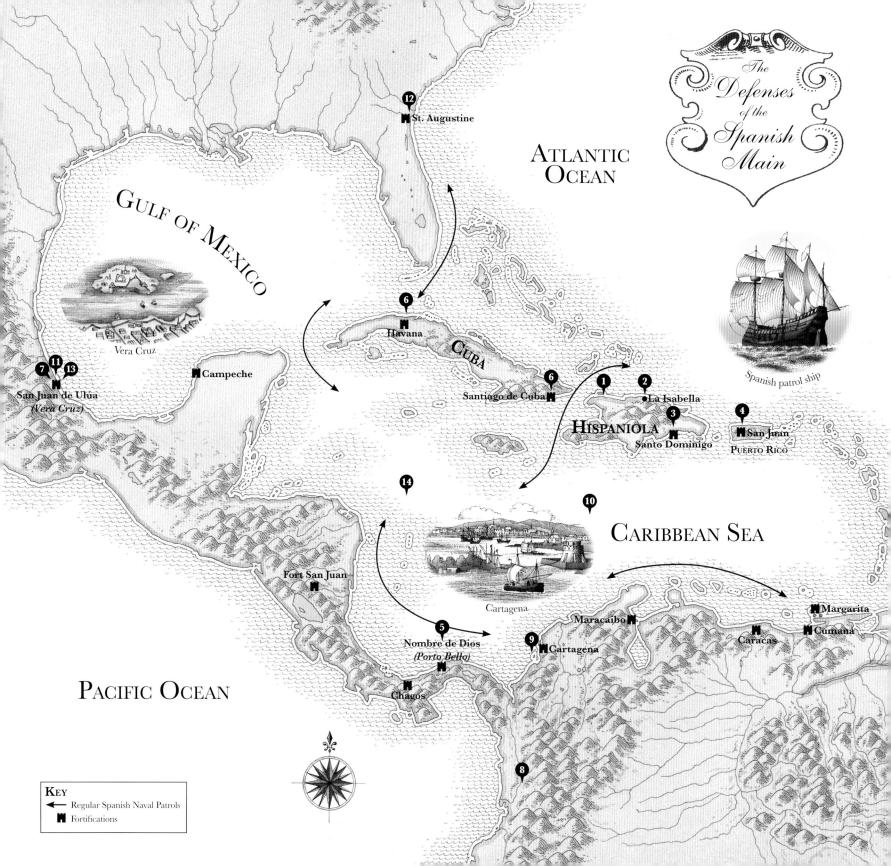

The Defenses of the Spanish Main

ATLANTIC OCEAN

GULF OF MEXICO

Vera Cruz

⑫ St. Augustine

Spanish patrol ship

⑥
Havana

CUBA

⑦ ⑪ ⑬
San Juan de Ulúa
(Vera Cruz)

Campeche

⑥
Santiago de Cuba

① ②
La Isabella

③
Santo Dominigo

HISPANIOLA

④ San Juan
PUERTO RICO

⑭

⑩

CARIBBEAN SEA

Fort San Juan

Cartagena

⑤
Nombre de Dios
(Porto Bello)

⑨
Cartagena

Maracaibo

Caracas

Margarita

Cumaná

Chagos

PACIFIC OCEAN

⑧

KEY

→ Regular Spanish Naval Patrols

Fortifications

How the Spanish Main was Defended, 1492–1564

1 **1492** Christopher Columbus discovers the Americas, and establishes the fortified settlement of La Navivad on the northern coast of Hispaniola.

2 **1494** The settlement of La Isabella is founded in Hispaniola. It is abandoned four years later. The same year the Treaty of Tordesillas establishes that all territory to the west of Brazil belongs to Spain.

3 **1498** The town of Santo Domingo is founded, on the southern coast of Hispaniola. Four years later work begins on its fortification.

4 **1508** Juan Ponce de León establishes a settlement at San Juan, in Puerto Rico. It too is fully fortified by 1521.

5 **1510** A fortified colony is established at Nombre de Dios, on the Isthmus of Panama. Ten years later the regional capital is moved to Panama, on the Pacific coast.

6 **1511** The settlement of Cuba is begun, and within two years a fortified settlement is established at Havana and Santiago de Cuba.

Havana

7 **1519** The conquistador Hernán Cortés invades Mexico, and establishes the fortified town of Vera Cruz. Within two years, all of Mexico is under Spanish control.

8 **1526** The conquistador Francisco Pizarro leads a small army south from Panama, to invade the Incan Empire in Peru. Within nine years the whole region is under Spanish control.

9 **1533** A strongly fortified settlement is established at Cartagena.

10 **1535** The first French "interlopers" cross the "line" and attack Spanish shipping in the New World.

11 **1558** The port of Vera Cruz is fortified.

12 **1565** A fortified colony is established at St. Augustine in Florida.

13 **1568** English interlopers are defeated at San Juan de Ulúa, the newly constructed fortress protecting Vera Cruz.

14 **1564** The Spanish crown orders the improvement of its New World defenses, and a major fortress-building program is instituted.

Above: The Spanish repulse an attack by Dutch interlopers in an early 17th-century painting by Adam Willaerts.

of the line—which included the entire Caribbean basin, the whole of Central America, and most of South America.

THE FIRST SETTLEMENTS

The first Spanish settlements in the Americas were tiny, defended by little more than a wooden stockade. The first Spanish colony was sited on the northern coast of Hispaniola, but this was soon abandoned, and in 1498 a more suitable site was chosen on the southern coast. This became the town of Santo Domingo, and in 1502 work began on a castle to defend the settlement from both Indians and European interlopers.

During the next few decades other small Spanish settlements appeared in Puerto Rico, Cuba, the Isthmus of Panama, and the Caribbean coast of South America. Then in 1519 the conquistador Hernán Cortés landed on the coast of Mexico, where he founded the settlement of Vera Cruz. Within two years he had defeated the Aztec Empire, and established a fortified Spanish settlement in the Aztec capital—now Mexico City. In 1523, he shipped his Aztec plunder back

Beyond the Line

The Spanish were very protective about their new-found overseas Empire. As they saw it, no other Europeans were allowed across the "line," and they threatened to evict any interlopers by force if they had to. Of course, the French, English, and Dutch didn't agree, and by the mid-16th century they began venturing into these Spanish waters. The Spanish reacted vigorously, and whenever they could they used force to expel the interlopers. For the Spanish, there would be "no peace beyond the line."

Founded in 1498, Santo Domingo in Hispaniola is the oldest Spanish city in the Americas.

Right: A publication from 1581 depicting the Potosi silver mine.

to Spain. Unfortunately his ships were captured by French privateers off the southern tip of Portugal. As a result, Spain's European rivals learned just how lucrative Spain's overseas empire had become—and of course they wanted some of those riches for themselves.

Meanwhile, conquistadors led by Francisco Pizarro conquered the Incan Empire in South America. Pizarro soon discovered that this land—Peru—was rich in silver. He even discovered a mountain at Potosí that was almost literally a mountain of silver, and by 1530 the first shipments of Peruvian silver had begun to be sent back to Spain. This coincided with the first arrival of interlopers in the Spanish Main, eager for their share of this fabulous wealth. During the next decade, as the annual shipments to Spain from the New World became increasingly substantial, the numbers of interlopers grew, until small fleets of French corsairs were prowling the waters of the Caribbean, attacking Spanish

settlements and capturing Spanish ships on the high seas. From the 1570s they were joined by illegal traders from England and Holland, which meant that the Spanish crown had to divert resources to defend her New World possessions, or risk losing them altogether.

DEFENDING AN EMPIRE

As a result of these attacks by interlopers, the Spanish began fortifying their ports. The raids by Francis Drake in the 1580s on Cartagena, Santo Domingo, and St. Augustine highlighted the vulnerability of the ports, including those where gold, silver, and other treasures were picked up by the annual treasure fleets.

In 1588, King Philip II of Spain approved a grandiose plan to improve the fortifications of his major harbors in the Americas, and work began almost immediately. The success of this scheme was demonstrated by the failure of Drake's last expedition in 1595, when his English interlopers were repulsed at San Juan in Puerto Rico and also on the Isthmus of Panama.

However, the treasure ports were still vulnerable. A combination of lethargy, corruption, and disease had reduced the effectiveness of Spain's garrisons, and so when a new wave of interlopers arrived in the early 17th century, the Spanish were unable to drive off these incomers. Having established firm bases "beyond the line," these French, Dutch, and English colonies would be used as springboards for attacks on Spanish cities, towns, and settlements throughout the Spanish Main. The Spanish remained on the defensive throughout the 17th century and were ill-prepared to cope with the likes of Henry Morgan, François L'Olonnais, and the other buccaneering captains of the age. For these men, the Spanish Main was little more than a collection of rich towns, just waiting to be plundered.

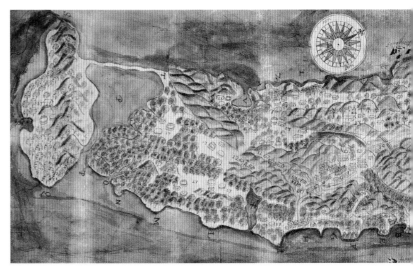

Above: The fortified island of Margarita lay off the Venezuelan coast.

The Treasure Fleets

Having found gold and silver aplenty in the New World, the Spanish had to ship this bounty to Spain. To do this, they set up a complex, highly organized, and lucrative convoy system.

Above: The embarkation of veteran Spanish troops on to a *flota* of galleons, a scene that would have been commonplace on the Spanish Main. By Andries van Eertvelt.

During the first few decades of Spanish exploration and colonization in the New World, ships made the transatlantic crossing on their own. However, in 1523, three richly laden ships were captured by pirates as they returned home to Spain. If the king wanted to guarantee an annual windfall from the Americas, he needed to protect his treasure ships.

SETTING UP THE FLOTAS

Only a portion of this New World treasure actually belonged to the crown. The looting of the Americas was run as a business, conducted by individuals and companies. The king taxed this production of wealth by charging the owners a *quinta* (fifth)—a 20 percent tax on all goods shipped across the Atlantic. He also levied a tax to pay for

the building of galleons that were designed to protect the treasure ships.

In 1526, four years after the pirate attack, the king decreed that transatlantic shipping should travel in convoys, to reduce the risk of attack by pirates. That was the birth of the annual treasure *flotas* (fleets of vessels), a virtually foolproof way of transporting gold, silver, emeralds, spices, and other valuable cargo from one side of the Atlantic to the

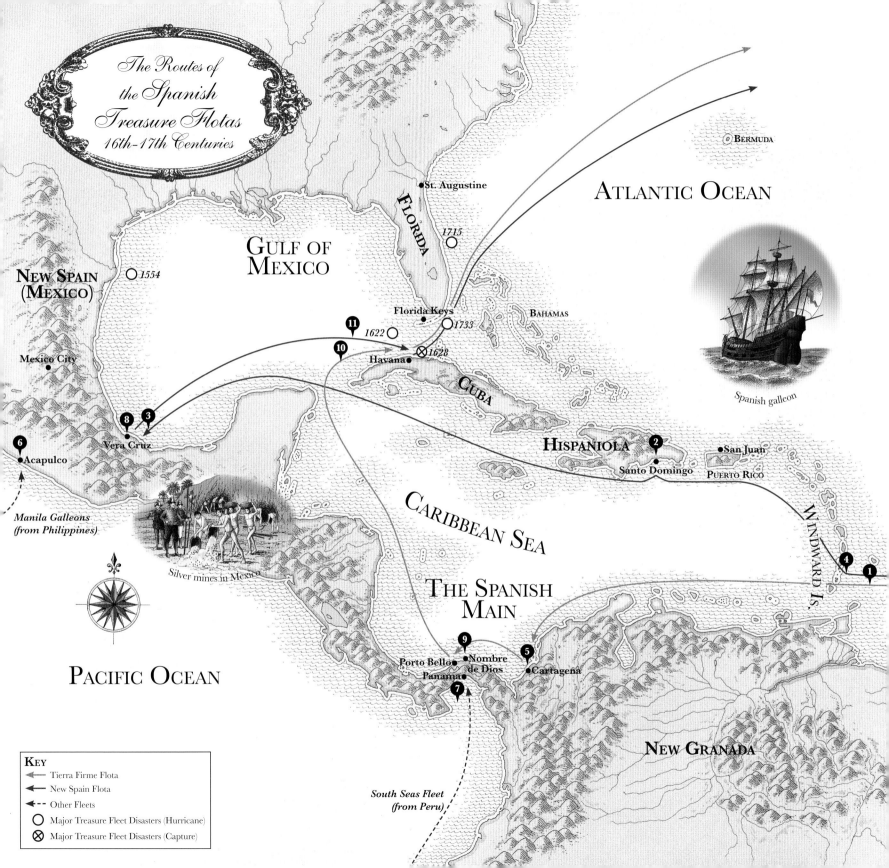

The Routes of
the Spanish
Treasure Flotas
16th–17th Centuries

ATLANTIC OCEAN

BERMUDA

St. Augustine

FLORIDA

1715

GULF OF
MEXICO

NEW SPAIN
(MEXICO)

○ *1554*

Mexico City

Florida Keys

11

1622 ○

BAHAMAS

○ *1733*

10

⊗ *1628*

Havana

CUBA

Spanish galleon

Vera Cruz

8 **3**

HISPANIOLA

2

San Juan

6

Acapulco

Santo Domingo

PUERTO RICO

*Manila Galleons
(from Philippines)*

CARIBBEAN SEA

WINDWARD IS.

4

Silver mines in Mexico

THE SPANISH
MAIN

1

PACIFIC OCEAN

9

Porto Bello ● Nombre
de Dios
Panama

5

Cartagena

7

NEW GRANADA

*South Seas Fleet
(from Peru)*

KEY
→ Tierra Firme Flota
→ New Spain Flota
--→ Other Fleets
○ Major Treasure Fleet Disasters (Hurricane)
⊗ Major Treasure Fleet Disasters (Capture)

The Routes of the Spanish Treasure Fleets, 16th and 17th Centuries

1 The New Spain Flota (fleet) leaves **Seville**, as it does every April, and in July it makes landfall in the **Windward Islands**.

2 Part of the fleet puts into **Santo Domingo**, on the southern coast of Hispaniola.

3 The rest of the New Spain Flota heads directly to **Vera Cruz**, on the Caribbean coast of New Spain (now Mexico). It usually arrives in September, and remains in the port throughout the winter.

4 The Tierra Firme Flota leaves Seville in September, as always, and makes landfall in the **Windward Islands** in late November.

5 The fleet visits the small ports of the **Tierra Firme coast** (the Caribbean coast of South America), as far as **Cartagena**, where it spends the winter. During the winter, Colombian emeralds and Venezuelan gold are gathered, for shipment to Spain.

6 Around February, a Manila galleon arrives in **Acapulco**, on the Pacific coast of New Spain. It carries spices and porcelain from the Far East. These are then transported overland to Vera Cruz. Silver from Mexican mines is also sent there, for shipment to Spain.

7 In March the South Seas Fleet arrives in **Panama**, laden with silver from the Peruvian mines. This silver is then transported across the Isthmus of Panama to Nombre de Dios.

8 A small coastal *flota* transports logwood and spices from **Trujillo** to Vera Cruz.

9 Around April, the Tierra Firme arrives in **Nombre de Dios**, where it takes on board its consignment of Peruvian silver. It then sails directly to Havana.

Quayside of Nombre de Dios

10 In May the New Spain fleet also sails to **Havana**.

11 The two fleets rendezvous in **Havana** in June, and usually sail back to Spain together the following month, before the onset of the hurricane season.

---

other. The *flota* system would remain in operation for the best part of two centuries, making it the longest-running shipping operation in history. From 1555, these annual convoys were each escorted by a minimum of four royal warships.

THE TWO FLOTAS

This highly organized convoy system involved two annual sailings from the port of Seville in southern Spain, each bound for the New World. The first was called the New Spain Flota—New Spain being the Spanish name for what is now Mexico. It sailed from Seville in April each year, followed four months later by the Tierra Firme Flota. Tierra Firme was the term given to the Caribbean coast of South America—the coastline that interlopers called the "Spanish Main." Both convoys began the voyage by sailing southwest to the Canaries, where the ships took on water and supplies. They then sailed into the Atlantic Ocean, making landfall in the southern part of the West Indies about eight weeks later.

THE NEW SPAIN FLEET

The New Spain fleet then sailed westward to Vera Cruz, where it collected silver produced in the rich mines of Mexico. Another treasure route crossed the Pacific Ocean, from the Philippines to Acapulco on the western coast of New Spain. This was the route charted by the Manila galleons, which transported spices from the Orient and porcelain from China. These goods were then transported across Mexico to Vera Cruz on the Caribbean coast, ready for shipment by the New Spain Flota.

Above: King Philip II of Spain (ruled 1556–98) relied on silver from the Americas to pay for his military endeavors in Europe.

The fleet spent the winter in Vera Cruz, then sailed on to Havana in Cuba in the following spring, laden with silver, spices, and porcelain, as well as other cargo, including indigo dye produced in Central America.

THE TIERRA FIRME FLEET

Similarly, the Tierra Firme Flota wintered in Cartagena after its transatlantic crossing. There the ships were loaded with gold from the mines of Colombia and emeralds from Venezuela. In the early spring the treasure ships made the short crossing to the town of Nombre de Dios on the coast of Panama, where the annual cargo of Peruvian silver

Cartagena's Strength

The port of Cartagena comprised a small inner harbor and large outer roads. The entrance to the outer roads was guarded by a fort at the end of a sandspit, while two more forts covered the approaches to the inner harbor. The city itself was encircled by walls and bastions, making it one of the most strongly held cities in the Spanish Main.

was waiting to be loaded. This silver had been mined in Potosí and other Peruvian mines, then transported to the Pacific coast, where it was shipped north to Panama. From there the silver was carried by mule trains across the Isthmus of Panama to Nombre de Dios.

In the late 16th century the Caribbean terminus for this silver was moved a little further up the coast to Porto Bello, as this second port was easier to defend than Nombre de Dios. After loading the silver, the Tierra Firme Flota made its way to Havana, where in most years it joined the New Spain fleet, which had not yet sailed. Sometimes the two fleets made their own way home, but in times of war or danger they sailed home together, even though that might mean a slight delay. The fleets sailed home using the same route—north through the Florida Straits and the Old Bahama Channel, then eastward across the Atlantic to the Azores. There the treasure *flotas* would take on stores and water again, before completing the final leg of their journey to Seville, which they reached around October or November.

PAYROLL AND PREDATORS

This huge undertaking followed a strict timetable, and the whole enterprise formed the largest maritime trading system in the world. It was usually too powerful to attack, as the treasure ships themselves were well-armed as well as being escorted by warships. Only on one occasion—in 1628—were the annual *flotas* attacked and captured by an enemy fleet. In that particular case the attackers were the Dutch, who drove the fleet ashore at Matanzas Bay to the east of Havana, then looted the ships, and took the plunder home to Amsterdam.

The Spanish crown came to rely on this annual fleet of silver, gold, and precious minerals. The revenue it produced was used by the Spanish crown to pay Spanish troops, and to fund Spain's political and military endeavors in Europe. If for some reason the fleet didn't arrive, the country was plunged into financial turmoil. Therefore the *flotas* were extremely important to Spain, and a great deal of effort was made to keep the treasure ships and their precious cargoes out of the hands of any interlopers, pirates, privateers, or buccaneers who might try their luck against the richest and best-protected fleet in the world.

The Hurricane Season

A far more significant danger to ships was posed by hurricanes. The annual hurricane season in the Caribbean started around June, and continued until October. The plan was that the *flotas* would sail from Havana before the hurricane season got underway, but this wasn't always possible because sometimes the departure of the fleets was delayed. On four occasions—in 1554, 1622, 1715, and 1733—the treasure *flotas* were caught in a hurricane and many of the ships were wrecked. The loss of the 1715 fleet on the eastern coast of Florida resulted in a frenzy of treasure hunting, which in turn played a significant part in the development of the Bahamas as a pirate haven.

Treasure hunter Mel Fisher (left) displaying some of the treasure recovered from the wreck of the Spanish galleon *Nuesta Señora de Atocha*.

The Spanish Galleon

Long associated with pirates and the Spanish Armada, the galleon has become an emblem of Spanish power during the 16th and 17th centuries.

When we think of Spanish galleons, we imagine one of the most romantic ship types in history—the grand vessels portrayed on film, just waiting to be captured by pirates. The real galleons, however, were completely different.

THE CREATION OF THE GALLEON

Unlike the slow, lumbering galleons of fiction, the real ships were nimble and designed for speed. Rather than floating status symbols, they were the workhorses of Spain's overseas

Above: Elegant and well-armed Spanish galleons such as this were the workhorses of the treasure fleets throughout the 16th and 17th centuries.

empire, designed to protect the shipments of Spanish treasure from the New World to Spain. The word "galleon" first appears in the early 16th century. The earliest galleons were powered by oars as well as sails, but by the 1540s the term referred to a type of small sailing warship in the service of the Spanish crown.

In 1536, the Spanish determined just how these ships should be built, and how they should be armed. Clearly they had become fast, powerful warships—ideally suited to the long, grueling voyage to the Spanish Main and back, and perfectly able to defend themselves against all but the most determined attack by pirates.

From the 1570s, the typical large galleon of the treasure fleets weighed around 500 tons and was armed with up to 24 heavy bronze guns; the crew included a company of veteran Spanish soldiers. In times of war, a typical treasure *flota* might include four or more of these ships, all of which were considered more than a match for any

French, Dutch, or English warship that tried to attack the fleet. The only time a Spanish treasure fleet was defeated in battle was in 1628, and while the battle exposed minor problems with Spanish ship design and gunnery, the main problem lay with the way the ships were commanded rather than the way they had been built. Therefore, for the best part of 150 years, from the mid-16th century onward, the galleon remained the mainstay of the Spanish treasure fleet, and the best guarantee the King of Spain had that his treasure would be safely delivered to his royal exchequer.

How Big Were They?

During the early 16th century, most galleons were quite small—weighing little more than 150 to 200 tons. However, by the 1550s galleons displacing 350 tons were built, carrying a larger armament than the earlier galleons. This was a reaction to the growing threat posed by French corsairs in the Spanish Main, and therefore the increased risk of an attack against the treasure *flotas*. By the 1570s, galleons with a displacement of 700 tons were commonplace, and during the Spanish Armada campaign of 1588 the Spanish fleet included a group of Portuguese galleons, most of which weighed more than 1,000 tons and were designed to fight in European waters.

The Sea Dogs

While the English regarded men like Drake and Hawkins as heroes—Elizabethan "sea dogs"—to the Spanish they were little more than pirates, who along with French and Dutch equivalents were plundering their New World riches.

In May 1523, off Cape Sagres on the southwest tip of Portugal, three small Spanish ships sighted land after a dull and uneventful transatlantic voyage. Their home port of Seville lay just three days away.

The ships expected to rendezvous with a squadron of warships, which would escort them home in safety. Instead the Spanish lookout saw five ships approaching them

from the wrong direction. The Spaniards altered course, but after a brief chase the mysterious ships overhauled them. Their pursuers turned out to be well-armed French privateers. Outgunned and outnumbered, the Spanish had little option but to surrender.

The French ships were commanded by Jean Fleury, an experienced pirate who now sailed as a privateer under the French flag. Even this hard-bitten corsair would have been amazed at the plunder he found inside the holds of the Spanish ships—chests filled with Aztec gold, sparkling jewelry, and religious statues; precious jewels, including an emerald the size of a man's fist; even a live jaguar in a cage. In all, the plunder was valued at more than 800,000 gold ducats—the equivalent of a staggering 234

Left: In this lively early 17th-century painting, an English and a Dutch warship attack a larger Spanish galleon.

million dollars today. It was probably the richest treasure haul in the history of piracy. When the privateers returned to their home port of Dieppe, the news of their success spread like wildfire. Now everyone in Europe knew that there was fabulous wealth to be had in the Americas. It was there for the taking for anyone willing to make the voyage, and risk the wrath of the Spanish.

During the next seven decades French and English pirates made regular incursions into Spanish territory, raiding Spanish settlements, intercepting treasure shipments, and generally causing havoc throughout the Spanish Main. Strangely enough, the Spanish could have avoided much of this if they had pursued a more inclusive policy toward these illegal traders. When John Hawkins, the first English "interloper," appeared in the Spanish Main, he came to trade rather than to plunder. However, after being attacked by the Spanish in 1568, Hawkins and his men vowed to seek revenge by attacking their poorly defended overseas empire.

One of Hawkins' followers was Elizabethan "sea dog" Francis Drake, who did exactly that, returning to the Caribbean to harry the Spanish and to plunder their treasure.

The First Interlopers

Naturally, after Jean Fleury's capture of the Spanish treasure ships and the discovery of untold riches, a host of French privateers took to the seas in search of another windfall.

A Huguenot squadron are depicted attacking Spanish ships off the coast of Cuba in this mid-16th century engraving. The attacks by these corsairs caused widespread disruption to Spanish trade, and the loss of income threatened the very survival of some of Spain's overseas colonies.

French Corsairs

To the French, the word *corsair* meant the same as "privateer." The word came from the French *la course*—a nautical cruise. To confuse things, the French also used the word when speaking about the Barbary pirates of the Mediterranean. In general, though, a corsair should be seen as a French privateer, although he could also be a pirate. As the Spanish showed when they executed Fleury, to those who fell victim to these corsairs they were nothing more than pirates.

While most French privateers operated in European waters, an intrepid few ventured beyond the line drawn up by the Treaty of Torsedillas. The French plunder of Spanish treasure ships would continue for the next 40 years.

THE FIRST CORSAIRS

Within a year of Jean Fleury's success, French corsairs were cruising off the Azores hoping to intercept more Spanish ships. The Spanish, meanwhile, started operating in convoys, which meant the corsairs were unable to achieve anything. In 1527 Jean Fleury was captured by the Spanish, after a six-hour long sea battle, and he was duly executed as a pirate. This didn't deter his fellow corsairs, who by that time had ventured as far afield as the coast of Brazil.

In 1533 another Spanish ship was captured in the Azores after it became separated from its convoy during a storm. During the next 15 years the Spanish lost another 23 ships during the transatlantic crossing, although not all of these were laden with treasure. Still, by this time French corsairs were regularly operating "beyond the line," and they had become a major nuisance to the Spanish. In 1537 alone, nine Spanish ships were captured, producing a haul of more than 30,000 ducats. While this wasn't anything like the plunder captured by Jean Fleury, it still represented about half of Spain's annual income from the New World.

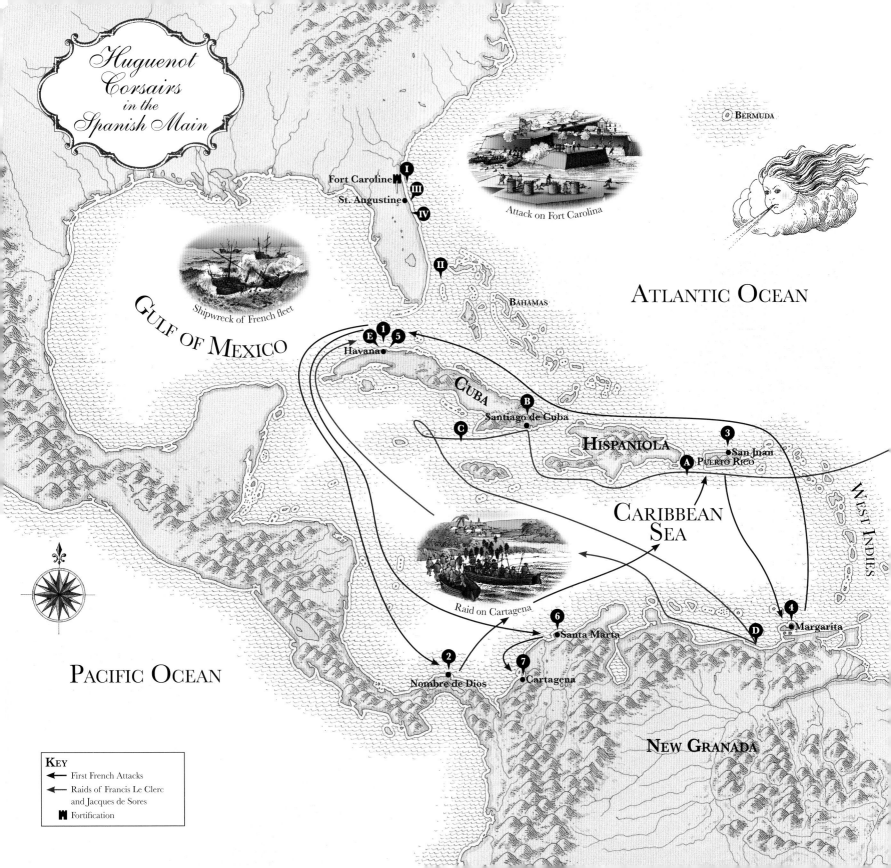

Huguenot Corsairs in the Spanish Main

BERMUDA

ATLANTIC OCEAN

Fort Caroline **I**
III
St. Augustine **IV**

Attack on Fort Carolina

II

BAHAMAS

GULF OF MEXICO

Shipwreck of French fleet

E **1** **5**
Havana

CUBA

B
Santiago de Cuba

C

HISPANIOLA

3
San Juan
A PUERTO RICO

CARIBBEAN SEA

WEST INDIES

4
D Margarita

PACIFIC OCEAN

Raid on Cartagena

6
Santa Marta

2
Nombre de Dios

7
Cartagena

NEW GRANADA

KEY

← First French Attacks

← Raids of Francis Le Clerc
and Jacques de Sores

⚑ Fortification

Raids of the Huguenot Corsairs in the 1500s

The First French Attacks on the Spanish Main

1 **1536** French "interlopers" attack Havana and sack the settlement.

2 **1537** Nombre de Dios sacked by the French.

3 **1540** San Juan in Puerto Rico attacked and plundered.

4 **1541** The pearl farms of Margarita ransacked by Huguenot corsairs.

5 **1542** Havana attacked and pillaged for a second time.

6 **1544** Santa Marta ransacked by the French and burned to the ground.

7 **1544** The city of Cartagena falls to French raiders—it is their largest prize yet in the Spanish Main.

The Raids of François Le Clerc and Jacques de Sores

A **Late 1553** François Le Clerc makes landfall in the West Indies, and raids settlements on the coast of Puerto Rico and Hispaniola.

B **Early 1554** The Huguenot raiders descend on Santiago de Cuba and sack the city.

C **Summer 1554** Le Clerc returns to France, but his deputy Jacques de Sores remains in the Caribbean.

D **Late 1554** Jacques de Sores raids settlements on the Tierra Firme coast.

E **July 1554** The French descend on Havana, and capture the port after a brief siege. It is plundered for the third time in two decades, and then burned.

Jean Ribault and the Huguenots of Fort Caroline

I **1564** The French establish a settlement at Fort Caroline, on the coast of Florida.

II **1565** A Spanish force led by Pedro Menéndez is sent north from Havana to deal with interlopers.

III **September 1565** After landing at St. Augustine Menéndez marches north and attacks Fort Caroline. The fort is destroyed, and its defenders massacred.

IV **October 1565** Ribault's fleet is overtaken by a hurricane and the French are shipwrecked on the Florida coast. The Spanish round up the survivors and massacre them.

Above: In 1555, the Huguenot corsair de Sores attacked and plundered Havana, the Spanish capital of Cuba.

THE HUGUENOT RAIDS

In 1536, a group of French Huguenot corsairs attacked Havana, which lacked any adequate defenses, and the city was plundered. Just five years later the city was captured again, by which time there couldn't have been much left for the corsairs to take. These attacks in the very heart of the Spanish Main represented a new departure for the French—for the first time they were attacking Spanish settlements rather than just Spanish shipping. By 1537, these raids had spread to the Tierra Firme (the Caribbean coastline of South America), to Honduras,

Religion and Piracy

The Huguenots were French Protestants who regarded the Catholic Spanish as their religious enemies. Many of the French corsairs who operated in the Spanish Main during this period were Huguenots; these French Protestant reformers had found a receptive audience in the ports of the French Atlantic seaboard. From 1534 the Huguenots had been persecuted in France, forcing many of these Protestant seamen to quit their native country in order to pursue their own private war against the Spanish. In so doing they lost any claim to being privateers. If caught, they were liable to be executed as both heretics and pirates.

Above: The assault on Cartagena in 1544 took the Spanish unawares.

and to the lucrative pearl-farming station on the island of Margarita. In 1540, the French even raided the prosperous town of San Juan on Puerto Rico, while other smaller settlements were repeatedly attacked and plundered. In 1544, Cartagena was sacked, disrupting the annual treasure shipments in the process.

JACQUES DE SORES

One of these French Huguenot corsairs was François Le Clerc, known as Jambe de Bois ("Peg Leg"). In 1553, he arrived in the Caribbean with ten ships and worked his way westward, plundering Spanish coastal settlements on Puerto Rico and Hispaniola as he went. The following year he sacked Santiago de Cuba, then returned home via the Canary Islands, where he sacked Las Palmas. One of his captains—

Jacques de Sores—elected to remain in the Caribbean, and with three ships he cruised the Tierre Firme coast before heading north. In July 1555, he attacked Havana, laying siege to the city for two days before capturing it. When he did, he plundered then burned the city to the ground. To add insult to injury, he even desecrated the city's churches before putting the torch to them.

Peace between France and Spain in 1559 ended further raids—at least for the time being—and a religious civil war back in France meant that most corsairs were too busy in home waters to consider attacking settlements on the far side of the Atlantic.

However, in 1564, the French returned—with a vengeance. The only difference was, this time the Spanish were ready for them.

JEAN RIBALT AND FORT CAROLINE

In 1564, a group of Huguenots founded the settlement of Fort Caroline on the banks of the St. Johns River in northeastern Florida. Fearing this would become a haven for interlopers, the Spanish ordered Pedro Menéndez de Avilés to sail north from Havana and destroy the fledgling colony. The Spanish landed at St. Augustine and marched north. In September 1565 Menéndez attacked the fort and captured it with ease. He discovered that Jean Ribault, a French Huguenot leader, had already sailed, leaving behind a small garrison. The Spanish massacred them and marched south.

Ribault had hoped to attack the Spanish ships off St. Augustine, but his own fleet was hit by a hurricane and dashed against the Florida coast. The survivors were captured by Menéndez, and those who refused to convert to Catholicism were executed. The Spanish had successfully dealt with a serious threat to their overseas empire. However, more interlopers would follow, and these newcomers would pose a far greater threat.

Left: In 1564, Spaniards led by Pedro Menéndez stormed the Huguenot stronghold of Fort Caroline in northern Florida.

John Hawkins

The accession of Queen Elizabeth I to the throne of England meant that the Spanish Main was considered a legitimate target for interlopers. Admiral Sir John Hawkins was one of the first.

Above: The Elizabethan "sea dog" Sir John Hawkins (1532–95) made his fortune as a slave-trading interloper on the Spanish Main.

Until 1558, Spain and England were often allies, united by a common distrust of France. However, the accession of Queen Elizabeth I was to change all that. Whether to trade or to plunder, the wealth of the Spanish empire became fair game.

CROSSING THE LINE

According to the Spanish, the first English interloper to appear on the Spanish Main did so in 1527. However, such ventures "beyond the line" were rare, discouraged by an English crown who sought Spanish support in a long-running feud with France. The accession of Queen Elizabeth I in 1558 marked a change in this policy. As a Protestant, Elizabeth saw the Spanish king as a rival and a threat, and the Spanish Main was no longer considered off limits to English traders and adventurers. So began a "cold war" between the two powers, which would last almost 25 years, before finally erupting into full-scale war.

A Devon sea captain, John Hawkins was destined to be one of the first of these Elizabethan interlopers. However, he first ventured across the line in peace, planning to trade with the Spaniards rather than to attack them. In 1562 he collected a cargo of slaves on the west African coast, then crossed the Atlantic to make landfall in the West Indies the following spring. His three small ships were laden with over 300 African slaves. Avoiding the strongly garrisoned town of Santo Domingo, Hawkins landed further down the coast of Hispaniola and sold his human cargo to local plantation owners. He returned to England as a wealthy man.

In 1564 he made a second voyage, this time with several ships, including the royal warship *Jesus of Lubeck*, which had been leased to him by the queen. Once again he collected a cargo of slaves, but this time he headed south, to the Tierra Firme. Fearing reprisals from their own government, the Spanish settlers of

Queen Elizabeth I of England (ruled 1558–1603) was a major investor in the New World slave-trading ventures of Admiral Hawkins.

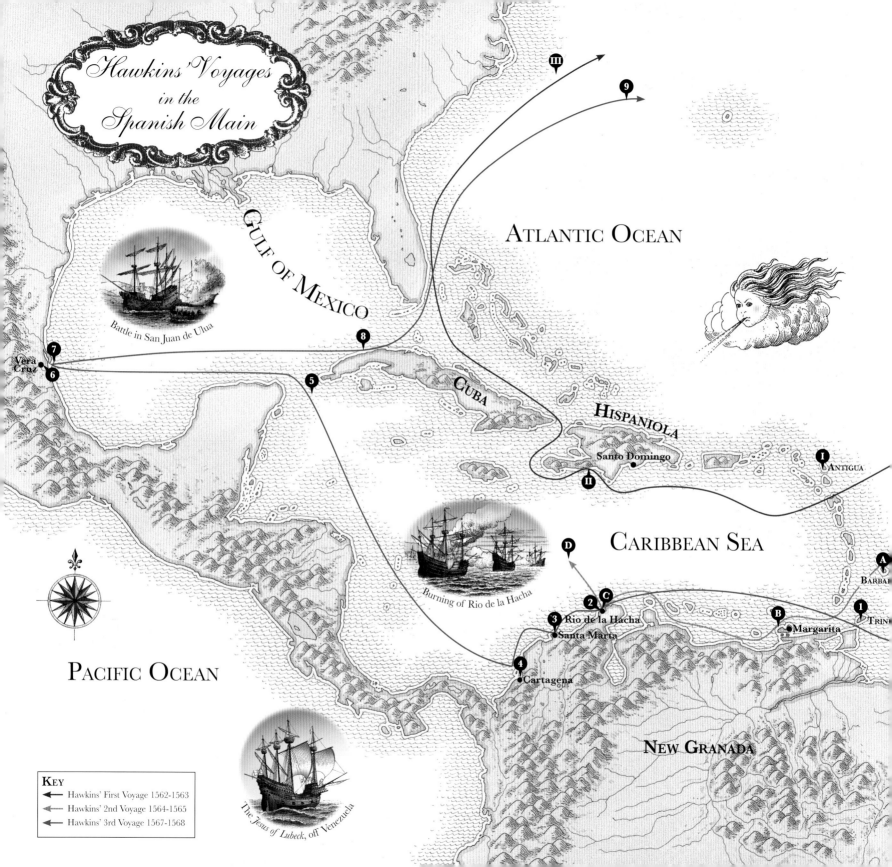

Hawkins' Voyages
in the
Spanish Main

ATLANTIC OCEAN

III

9

GULF OF MEXICO

Battle in San Juan de Ulua

Vera Cruz
7
6

8

5

CUBA

HISPANIOLA

Santo Domingo

II

CARIBBEAN SEA

D

Burning of Rio de la Hacha

2 C

3 Rio de la Hacha
Santa Marta

4 Cartagena

PACIFIC OCEAN

I
ANTIGUA

A
BARBA

B
Margarita

1
TRIN

NEW GRANADA

The Jesus of Lubeck, off Venezuela

KEY
Hawkins' First Voyage 1562-1563
Hawkins' 2nd Voyage 1564-1565
Hawkins' 3rd Voyage 1567-1568

John Hawkins in the Spanish Main, 1563–68

Hawkins' First Voyage, 1562–63

I **Spring 1563** Hawkins makes landfall near Antigua, then continues on to the west.

II Avoiding Santo Domingo, he lands further down the coast of Hispaniola and sells his cargo of slaves to local plantation owners.

III Hawkins returns to England via the Bahamas Channel.

Hawkins' Second Voyage, 1564–65

A **Spring 1565** Hawkins makes landfall near Barbados, and this time he sails south, toward the Tierra Firme coast.

B He tries unsuccessfully to sell his slaves on the island of Margarita.

C He manages to do so at Rio de la Hacha, after threatening to bombard the town.

D He returns to England.

Hawkins' Third Voyage, 1567–68

1 **Spring 1568** Hawkins makes landfall off Trinidad and sails west.

2 **June** He tries unsuccessfully to sell his cargo of slaves at Rio de la Hacha.

3 **July** He manages to sell half his cargo in Santa Marta, after threatening to bombard the town.

4 **August** Hawkins is fired upon as he approaches Cartagena, so he avoids the city.

5 **September** His squadron encounters a hurricane off the western tip of Cuba and is badly battered.

6 Hawkins puts into Vera Cruz for repairs. To safeguard his squadron he captures the fortress of San Juan de Ulúa. Two days later, the annual Spanish treasure *flota* arrives, but the two sides agree a truce.

7 **September 23** The Spaniards launch a surprise attack, and Hawkins' men on the island fortress are overrun. The Spanish then attack the English ships. After a brutal struggle, Hawkins manages to escape in the *Minion*, accompanied by Francis Drake in the tiny *Judith*.

8 **October** More than a hundred starving crewmen beg to be put ashore rather than die of starvation. Most are eventually killed or captured.

9 Hawkins and Drake return to England with the survivors.

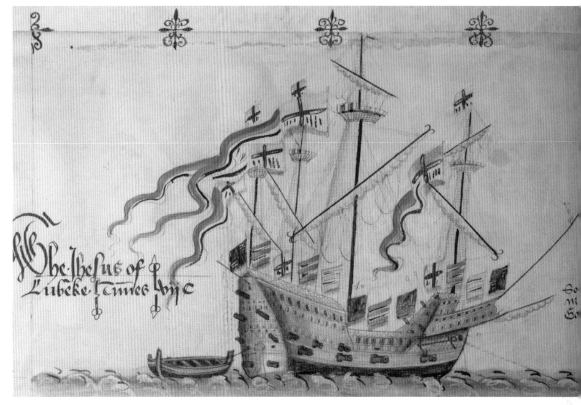

Above: The warship *Jesus of Lubeck* was lent to Hawkins by the Queen, for use on his 1567 voyage to the Spanish Main. Unfortunately, she was captured by the Spanish at San Juan de Ulúa the following year.

Margarita refused to trade with the interloper. He finally managed to sell his cargo of slaves in Rio de la Hacha after threatening to turn his guns on the town. This seems to have been a pre-arranged gesture, concocted between Hawkins and the local mayor as a means of saving face, and avoiding retribution from the Spanish authorities. In late 1565, Hawkins returned to Plymouth, and once again his expedition had been highly profitable.

HAWKINS' THIRD VOYAGE

Inevitably, Hawkins decided to make another voyage. Once again he leased the *Jesus of Lubeck*, which sailed from Plymouth in October 1567 accompanied by four smaller ships. This time everything went wrong. First, when Hawkins arrived on the west African coast, he found the coastal tribes unwilling to trade with him. He then led a slaving raid on an inland tribe, only to be repulsed with the loss of eight men. Finally, he found two tribes who were at war with each other. He backed one faction over the other and used his muskets to assure victory. His reward was a cargo of 500 African prisoners.

In June 1568, Hawkins appeared off Rio de la Hacha again, but this time he found the garrison had been changed and the Spanish fired on his ships. He managed to sell about half his slaves in the nearby port of Santa Marta, but again he had to resort to threatening to bombard the town in order to force the settlers to trade with him. Following this, the garrison of Cartagena drove him back out to sea, so Hawkins headed north. It was now September. Somewhere off the western tip of Cuba his fleet was overtaken by a hurricane, and the aged *Jesus of Lubeck* almost foundered. Hawkins was forced to put into a port for repairs—the nearest being Vera Cruz on the Mexican coast.

SAN JUAN DE ULÚA

The town was defended by an island fort, San Juan de Ulúa, which he captured by guile, pretending his ships were Spanish and in need of repair. So far he had been lucky, but

two days later this spell of fortune ran out. The annual treasure *flota* arrived, trapping the English in the harbor. The commander of the Spanish treasure fleet, Admiral Luján, declared a truce, but he and the newly arrived Governor of New Spain had no intention of honoring it. Instead they laid plans to launch a surprise attack.

At dawn on September 23, the Spanish launched an assault and captured the fortress of San Juan de Ulúa. They then turned the guns on the English ships. Meanwhile, the galleons in the *flota* joined in the firing, catching the English in a deadly crossfire. Hawkins had no option but to try to escape. *The Jesus of Lubeck* was in no condition to sail, so she was abandoned, along with two other small ships. Hawkins made his escape

Above: The quayside at San Juan de Ulúa, where Hawkins fought his disastrous battle in 1568.

in the *Minion*—another royal ship—followed by the tiny *Judith*, which was commanded by his kinsman, Francis Drake.

A DANGEROUS FOE

Barely 300 men managed to escape the debacle, and the ships lacked enough provisions to make it home. More than 100 sailors asked to be put ashore, hoping to take their chances with the Spaniards and Indians rather than face starvation. Of the remainder, less than two dozen were still alive when the ships finally reached Plymouth. Hawkins and Drake were among the survivors. Both captains vowed to make the Spanish pay for their treachery, but it was Drake rather than Hawkins who would eventually return to the Caribbean, seeking revenge. The incident had awoken a burning hatred of the Spanish in Drake—and he was determined to avenge his old shipmates.

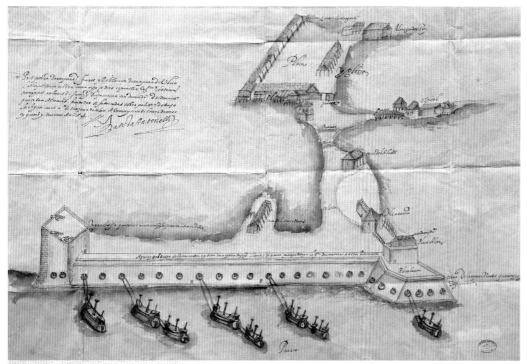

This late 16th-century illustration shows the Spanish fortress of San Juan de Ulúa, which sat on a small island, guarding the harbor and treasure *flota* anchorage of Vera Cruz, in New Spain (now Mexico).

Drake's Raid

In 1570, Francis Drake returned to the Spanish Main and embarked on his own private war against the Spanish. He was a formidable enemy.

Over the next ten years Francis Drake would earn such a fearsome reputation that the Spanish referred to him by using a variant of his name. They called this English "sea dog" *El Draque*, which meant "The Dragon."

RETURN TO THE SPANISH MAIN

In 1570—just over a year after Francis Drake returned from San Juan de Ulúa— Queen Elizabeth granted the 30-year-old sea captain a "letter of reprisal." This was an official peacetime version of a privateering license called a "letter of marque," which allowed those who felt they had a grievance against a foreign government to seek redress by attacking that country's possessions. This meant that Drake could wrest from the Spanish reimbursement for the losses he had suffered on the Mexican coast. That year he led a small force of two ships into Spanish territory, but there is no record of where he went or what he achieved. Presumably, this first expedition was a reconnaissance. After all, Drake planned to return.

In the spring of 1571, he returned to the Spanish Main in the tiny 25-ton *Swan*. He cruised off the isthmus of Panama, but lacked the strength to attack Nombre de Dios or any of the smaller Spanish ports in the area. He joined forces with a group of Huguenot corsairs instead, who he encountered in the mouth of the River Chagres. Together the privateers captured passing Spanish ships, and plundered river traffic. By the time Drake returned to Plymouth he had amassed plunder valued at over 40,000 ducats (approximately $10.5 million in today's money). Drake found himself one of the richest men in Devon, and was well on his way to becoming a national hero.

THE ATTACK ON NOMBRE DE DIOS

In 1572, Drake launched another raid on the Spanish Main. He sailed from Plymouth with two small ships—the *Swan* and the *Pasco*— and 73 men. By July he was off the isthmus of Panama, where he moored his ships in a hidden anchorage he called Port Pheasant— probably Puerto Escoces—where more than a century later the Scots would make their own doomed bid at establishing a New World colony. There he was joined by Captain Raunce, an English privateer who commanded another small vessel.

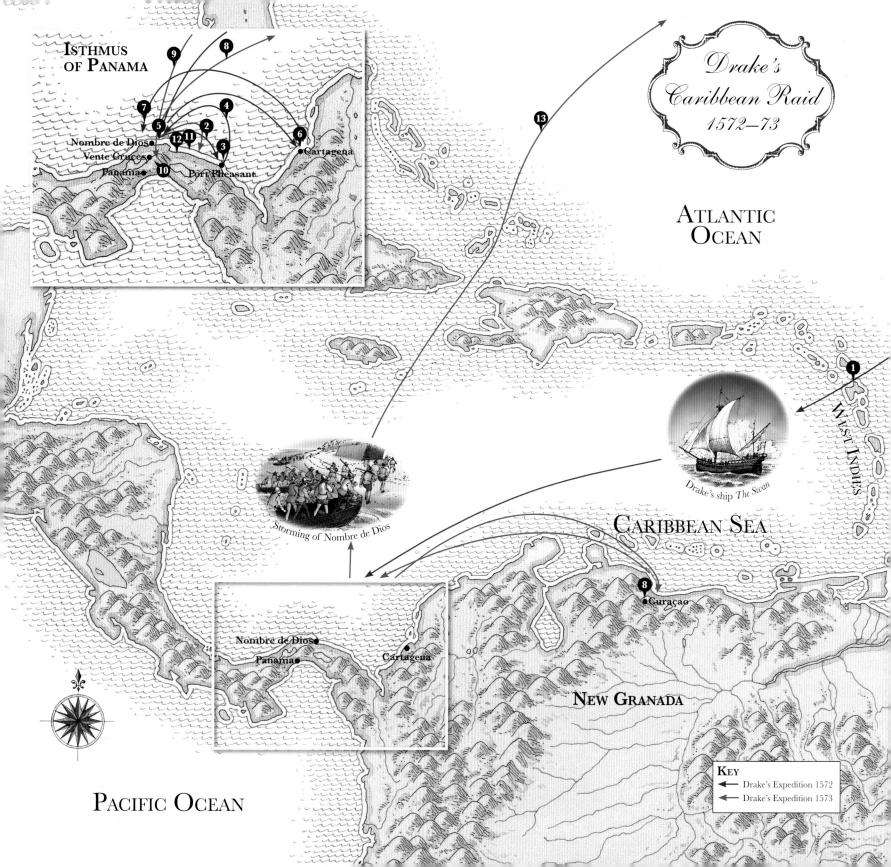

ISTHMUS OF PANAMA

⑨ ⑧

⑦ ④
⑤ ②
Nombre de Dios ⑫⑪
Vente Cruces ③
Panamá ⑩ Port Pheasant
⑥ Cartagena

Drake's
Caribbean Raid
1572–73

⑬

ATLANTIC
OCEAN

①

WEST INDIES

Drake's ship The Swan

Storming of Nombre de Dios

CARIBBEAN SEA

⑧
Curaçao

Nombre de Dios
Panamá Cartagena

NEW GRANADA

PACIFIC OCEAN

KEY
← Drake's Expedition 1572
← Drake's Expedition 1573

Francis Drake's Caribbean Raid of 1572–73

1572

1 **Spring 1572** Francis Drake makes landfall in the West Indies in two ships (*Pasco* and *Swan*) and heads toward the Isthmus of Panama.

2 **July** Arrives off Nombre de Dios and sails east.

3 **August** Establishes a base at Port Pheasant. There he is joined by another English ship, commanded by a Captain Raunce.

4 **July 26** Leaving Raunce to guard the ships, Drake approaches Nombre de Dios in longboats and lands just outside the town.

5 **July 28** Attacks the port at dawn and reaches its central marketplace. There he is wounded. His men lose heart and retreat back to their ships, taking their commander with them.

6 **Autumn 1572** After recovering, Drake sails west toward Cartagena. Raunce sails home.

7 **Autumn 1572** Having captured a few small prizes, Drake abandons the *Pasco*, and sailed back to the Isthmus of Panama in the *Swan*. However, the Spanish learn of his presence, and shipping remains in port.

1573

8 **January 1573** Drake returns to the Tierra Firme coast and sails eastward as far as Curaçao in an unsuccessful search for prizes.

9 He then decides to return to the Isthmus of Panama, hoping to attack the Spanish silver shipment from Panama to Nombre de Dios.

10 Drake sets up an ambush at Vente Cruces, 18 miles west of Panama. The Spanish detect his force and the attack fails. Drake and his men return to their ships.

11 **April 1573** Drake makes another raid on the silver train, this time landing 20 miles (32km) east of the treasure port of Nombre de Dios, and setting up another ambush close to the port. This time the attack is a success.

Ambush of a silver train

12 Unable to evade his pursuers, Drake decides to bury the silver, hoping to recover it later. However, the Spanish retrieve it first.

13 **June 1573** Drake returns to England.

Leaving Raunce in charge of the ships, he led his men up the coast in longboats and landed a few miles west of Nombre de Dios. He planned to launch a surprise attack on the city, a port of call for the Tierra Firme treasure fleet which came every year to pick up gold and silver, but a passing fisherman had seen the longboats and raised the alarm. The local militia were ready, and although Drake managed to capture the town, he knew the Spanish would return. On top of this, Drake and several of his men were badly wounded. When Drake fainted from loss of blood, his men retreated back to their ships. His first raid had been an ignominious failure.

THE SILVER TRAIN ATTACKS

Raunce abandoned Drake, leaving him with too few men to man his two ships. The *Swan* was abandoned, and Drake cruised offshore wondering what to do next. Then in January 1573, he learned that the annual silver shipment was about to be transported from Panama to Nombre de Dios by mule train. Drake decided to attack it. After hiding his ship he used local guides to lead him to the Camino Real (Royal Road), which linked the two ports. He decided to ambush the silver train outside the village of Vente Cruces, some 18 miles (29km) from Panama.

Drake only had 18 sailors with him, one of whom had been drinking heavily. Drake was spotted by the Spanish before his trap could be sprung, and the guards covered the pack mules until they could be spirited away to safety. His second attack had been another failure. Determined to retrieve something, Drake then joined forces with the French corsair Guillaume Le Testu. Together they decided to attack the silver train again, on its next attempt to reach Nombre de Dios.

Elizabethan Naval Guns

During the age of the Elizabethan "sea dogs," most naval guns were muzzle-loading pieces, cast in bronze. A few smaller breech-loading guns (the size of modern machine-guns) were also used as anti-personnel weapons, and toward the end of the period the first reliable cast-iron guns began to appear.

However, the big advantage the English enjoyed over the Spanish was in the ability to fire far more often. This was largely because the English used maneuverable four-wheeled carriages like the one shown here, while the Spanish still relied on more cumbersome two-wheeled ones, which were far less easy to operate on board a ship.

This bronze "demi-culverin" gun was recovered from the *Mary Rose*, which sank in 1545, but it is typical of the guns carried by later Elizabethan warships.

This time the mule train was taken by surprise, and the English and French sailors succeeded in driving off the guards. The only casualty was Captain Le Testu, who had to be left behind when the rest of the attackers retreated into the jungle, carrying over 15 tons of silver and a few hundred pounds of gold between them. When the Spanish returned, the French captain was executed on the spot. Unable to carry the silver back to the ships, Drake decided to bury it and come back for it later. Unfortunately, the Spanish captured one of his local guides, who was tortured until he revealed the hiding place. All Drake now had to show for his efforts was a few small chests of gold.

Even after dividing the plunder with the French, Drake still returned to Plymouth in August 1573 with a treasure haul valued at approximately 25,000 ducats or 50,000 pieces-of-eight—the equivalent of $6.6 million today. His backers were delighted with the success of their protégé, and Drake immediately began planning an even more ambitious expedition.

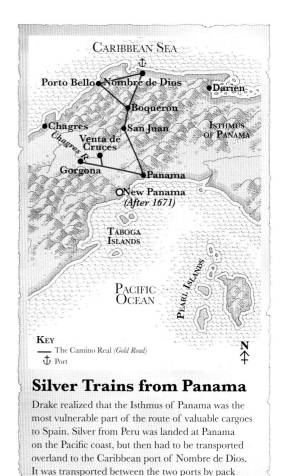

KEY
— The Camino Real *(Gold Road)*
⚓ Port

N ↑

Silver Trains from Panama

Drake realized that the Isthmus of Panama was the most vulnerable part of the route of valuable cargoes to Spain. Silver from Peru was landed at Panama on the Pacific coast, but then had to be transported overland to the Caribbean port of Nombre de Dios. It was transported between the two ports by pack mule, in a series of convoys known as "silver trains."

Sir Martin Frobisher (c.1535–94)

Like Drake and Hawkins, Frobisher is always seen as an archetypal Elizabethan "sea dog." However, unlike the others he was more of an explorer than a privateer. He made three unsuccessful voyages in search of a Northwest passage—a fabled route around the northern tip of North America, connecting the Atlantic and Pacific oceans.

One of the ablest seamen of his time, in 1585 he sailed as Drake's deputy during his raid on the Spanish Main, and served as an English vice-admiral during the Spanish Armada campaign of 1588, during which he was knighted. Frobisher went on to lead a naval expedition that raided the Spanish coast, and in 1594 he led a naval force to the relief of Brest, which was being besieged by the Spanish. He was badly wounded in a naval skirmish there and taken back to his native Plymouth, where he died of his wounds.

Left: Sir Martin Frobisher, as depicted in a full-length portrait by Cornelius Ketel.
Frobisher served as Drake's deputy during the raid on the Spanish Main in 1585–86.

Drake's Raid into the Pacific

Between 1577 and 1580 Drake led another expedition into Spanish waters—one whose scope was considerably more ambitious than his last venture, and which led to a knighthood.

Drake's next expedition resulted in his capture of a fabulous treasure, and in Drake becoming the first Englishman to circumnavigate the globe. It may well also have set England on the road to war with Spain.

Drake's Secret Voyage

In December 1577, Drake sailed from Plymouth with five small ships, two of which weighed less than 30 tons each. By the following April he was off the coast of Brazil. He headed south, down the Atlantic coast of South America. On the way he overcame a mutiny by executing one of his captains, abandoned a leaking ship, and renamed his flagship the *Golden Hind*. It took two weeks to pass around Cape Horn and all went well until they entered the Pacific. Then a major storm blew up, the ships were scattered, and one of them foundered with all hands. Another two failed to find Drake again and returned home. However, the *Golden Hind* survived the storm and eventually made it safely to calmer waters.

Drake headed north, plundering the town of Valparaiso in Chile as he went. After waiting to see if any other English ships had made it

Right: Francis Drake in the *Golden Hind* is shown here attacking the Spanish Manila galleon *Nuestra Señora de la Concepción* in 1579. Its capture yielded a fabulous haul of treasure.

Above and right: This replica of the *Golden Hind*, launched in 1973, retraced the route of Drake's voyage of circumnavigation.

that far, he continued on up the coast toward Peru. Next he raided Arica, the port which served the silver mines of Potosí, and then he sacked Callao. While he managed to take silver, most of the produce of the Peruvian mines had already been shipped north. But Drake captured Spanish charts of the Pacific coast and he used them to plot his next move.

A RICH HAUL

Drake learned that the annual silver shipment had just sailed in a 120-ton galleon called *Nuestra Señora de la Concepción* (known to sailors by the more colorful name of *Cacafuego* or "Shitfire"). Drake set off in pursuit. He picked up the trail from local fishermen, and on March 1, 1579, sighted his prize. He slowed down to appear more like a slow merchantman, but as dusk approached picked up speed and overhauled his prey. The Spanish were taken completely by surprise. Even more significantly, they never expected an interloper to reach the Pacific and so the treasure galleon was completely unarmed.

Drake and his men began taking stock of their plunder. In all the *Cacafuego* contained coin chests filled with silver, gold bars, and over 26 tons of silver ingots. The total haul was estimated at 400,000 pieces-of-eight—the equivalent of $53 million today. At the time it represented about half of England's annual income—a staggering sum and one of the richest pirate hauls in history. Now Drake had to get home with his plunder.

He decided not to return the way he had come but to return the long way, by completing a voyage of circumnavigation. Avoiding the well-protected ports of Panama and Acapulco, he headed north as far as what is now California. Exactly where he landed is still a mystery, but it might well have been in Drake's Bay—not far from where San Francisco's Golden Gate Bridge stands today. He named the land there New Albion. After a month in California, he set sail toward the west, heading for the Spice Islands of the East Indies. Until then these islands were the preserve of the Portuguese, who kept their location secret. Now Drake had learned the secret, and he added a cargo of spices to his already laden ship.

Finally, in September 1580, the *Golden Hind* sailed back into Plymouth. Drake was now a hero, and one of the richest men in Europe. Once again, his investors were overjoyed. His largest backer was the Queen herself, who honored Drake by visiting his ship as she lay at anchor in Deptford on the River Thames. She celebrated the occasion by knighting Francis Drake on the quarterdeck of his own ship. The Spanish were furious, but their protests were ignored by Elizabeth. Significantly, she called Drake "my pirate," which infuriated the Spanish even more. War between England and Spain was beginning to look impossible to avoid.

Ducats and Doubloons

In 16th-century Europe, the standard gold coin in circulation was the "ducat," which weighed about a tenth of an ounce (2.8 grams). The Spanish version of the ducat was the "escudo," although they also minted a double-sized two-escudo coin, called the "dublon." This piece became the doubloon of pirate fact and fiction.

The smallest silver coin used by the Spanish was the "real," which contained an eighth of an ounce of silver. Before the market was swamped by a huge influx of Peruvian silver, 11 silver reales were considered the equivalent of 1 gold escudo. However, from the 1560s, the rate was set at 16 reales to the "escudo." By that time, the most common silver coin in circulation was the one-ounce eight-real coin, known as the "peso" or dollar. To interlopers, this peso of eight reales became a "piece-of-eight."

A silver "piece-of-eight" in 1580 was worth the equivalent of $130 today, while the value dropped to the equivalent of $87 by 1675.

Drake's Great Expedition

By 1585 it was clear that a war between England and Spain was inevitable, and so Queen Elizabeth ordered Drake to launch a full-scale raid on the Spanish Main.

Drake's raid was designed to disrupt Spain's income from the New World, as well as to divert attention away from England's preparations for war.

THE 1585 EXPEDITION

In late 1584, Queen Elizabeth's spymaster Sir Francis Walsingham began planning a large scale raid on the Spanish Main, and Drake was the obvious candidate to lead such an expedition. During the summer of 1585, he gathered an impressive fleet of 21 ships, including two royal warships, one of which—the *Elizabeth Bonaventure*—became Drake's flagship. His fleet was crewed by 1,000 sailors and 800 soldiers, the latter commanded by Walsingham's son-in-law, Captain Carleille.

In mid-September 1585, when word reached Plymouth that the Queen was having second thoughts, Drake hurriedly put to sea before the expedition could be recalled. His first objective was the port of Vigo in north-western Spain, which he captured. He then sailed on to the Canary Islands, where he hoped to intercept the returning treasure fleet. Although Drake missed the *flota*, he landed Carleille's troops and stormed the island's capital of Santiago (now called Praia). Finding nothing to plunder, Drake burned the town, and sailed on toward the west.

SANTO DOMINGO

He landed just before Christmas, after a voyage marred by disease. After taking on water and stores the expedition continued on to Santo Domingo, the capital of Hispaniola. This time he landed Carleille and his men some 20 miles (32km) from the city. On New Year's morning they attacked it from the landward side at the same time as his ships bombarded it from the sea. Drake was soon master of the city. He held it for ransom, threatening to demolish the principal buildings unless the inhabitants paid him 25,000 ducats. It worked. Drake then sailed toward the south.

BATTLE FOR CARTAGENA

Drake's next target was Cartagena, a city the Spanish thought was impregnable. They had already been warned that Drake was in the area, so the governor had had time to reinforce the garrison, which now consisted of 10,000 troops—over ten times that of Drake. Undeterred, he arrived off Cartagena on February 9, and under cover of darkness landed his troops on the tip of La Caletta—a coastal spit which protected the

Above: Drake's surprise attack on Santo Domingo, the capital of Hispaniola, on New Year's Day 1586, yielded a hefty 25,000-ducat ransom. Illustration by Howard Pyle (1853–1911).

entrance to the harbor. The forts guarding the entrance were captured, allowing Drake to sail his ships into the anchorage.

As dawn broke the Spanish found their harbor in English hands, while Carleille's men were now on the western end of the spit, on the edge of the city. The English soldiers launched a charge, and the defenders were bundled back into the streets of the port. Governor Fernandez tried to hold the English in the market square, but Carleille's men were better armed and the Spanish soon broke and fled. Against all the odds, Drake had captured the second largest city on the Spanish Main, and at the cost of just 30 casualties. Some 250,000 pieces-of-eight were plundered in the city, while Drake raised another 100,000 by holding the town to ransom. By the time the English sailed away on April 12, Drake had gleaned plunder worth another 100,000 pieces-of-eight in the form of guns, slaves, and even church bells.

St. Augustine

Before he returned home with his plunder, Drake decided to launch one more raid. He wanted to attack Havana, but after probing its defenses he decided the port was just

Above: Drake's greatest success during the Caribbean voyage was his capture of Cartagena, in February 1586.

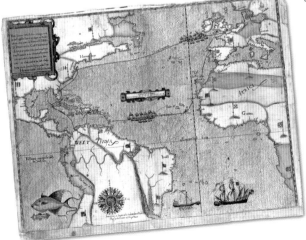

Above: This chart, produced in 1588, traces the route of Drake's Caribbean voyage of 1585–86.

too well defended. Instead he targeted St. Augustine, on the northeastern coast of Florida. The oldest settlement on the mainland of North America, St. Augustine was a small, sleepy town, which lacked adequate defenses.

Late on May 27, 1586, Carleille's troops were landed at the mouth of the Matanzas River, and marched through the sand dunes until they reached the town, which lay a mile inland, on the far bank of the river. Carleille's artillery pounded St. Augustine's small wooden fort into submission and Drake's men made camp, ready to sack the town the following morning. A nocturnal attack by

Indians and Spaniards was repulsed, and at dawn Drake entered the town, only to discover that it had been abandoned during the night. The only treasure to be had was a strongbox, containing the garrison's wages.

The expedition returned home in late July, where Drake discovered that the long-expected war with Spain had finally broken out. The great expedition of 1585–86 was a strategic success, but the large number of participants and backers meant that it was not as financially successful as many had hoped. Still, as England prepared to face the might of the Spanish Armada, few would have realized that this had been Drake's last successful expedition to the Spanish Main.

Drake's Last Voyage

In 1595, Francis Drake and John Hawkins joined forces for one last great expedition to the Spanish Main. They were under secret orders.

England's war with Spain had been dragging on for ten years. Elizabeth's advisors hoped to force the Spanish to the negotiating table by causing mayhem in the New World.

Two Old Sea Dogs

In August 1595, Drake and Hawkins sailed from Plymouth in a fleet of 27 ships, with orders to capture a port and turn it into an English settlement. The two veterans shared command of the expedition but they now rarely spoke to each other after Hawkins had publicly censured Drake for his behavior during the Spanish Armada campaign seven years earlier. As a result, the commanders couldn't agree on strategy.

Disaster off San Juan

The expedition arrived in the Canary Islands, but a major attack was called off due to bad weather. In mid-November, it arrived off the port of San Juan, Puerto Rico. By that time disease was rife aboard the English ships, and on November 20 Hawkins died of fever.

Word of Drake's approach had already reached San Juan, and the harbor entrance was blocked; batteries covered all the

Above: An Elizabethan warship, typical of the larger royal ships that formed the core of the 1595 expedition.

seaward approaches. Drake was driven back by Spanish fire. On November 23 he tried landing troops, but his men were driven back. After a second landing was repulsed, Drake bowed to the inevitable and sailed away.

The End of an Era

He made for the Tierra Firme, where he raided several small ports before heading west to the isthmus of Panama. Nombre de Dios had been abandoned in favor of nearby Porto Bello, so Drake used the now undefended harbor as a base and marched on Panama. He soon found his path blocked by well-entrenched Spanish troops. Unable to force his way through, he retreated to his ships, burning the port behind him.

By that time many of the crew were suffering from yellow fever, and Drake himself caught the disease. He died on December 27, 1595, and was buried at sea just off Porto Bello. The death of these two great sea dogs marked the end of an era. Within a few years Elizabeth would be dead, and England and Spain would conclude a peace treaty. The Spanish territories, however, would soon be plagued by a new wave of raiders.

The Buccaneers

By the mid-17th century the Spanish colonies had become a hunting ground for buccaneers. And as predators like Francois L'Olonnais and Henry Morgan became ever bolder, the power and wealth of the Spanish overseas empire began to wane.

During the first decades of the 17th century, it seemed to the Spanish that their empire in the New World was prospering. Peace with both England and Holland ensured that for the most part the Spanish colonists were left alone and not subject to attack.

However, this apparent peace was an illusion. Already other European interlopers had established themselves on the eastern edges of the Spanish Main, while the renewal of the Dutch War meant that Spain's tenuous but vital sea links with her overseas colonies were once again under threat.

The Dutch managed to pull off one of the most audacious privateering attacks in history, which highlighted the vulnerability of the Spanish in their territories beyond the line. Spanish steps to improve the situation were not always successful. One step in particular—the forcible resettlement of Spanish colonies on Hispaniola—sowed the seeds of disaster.

By the mid-17th century the Spanish Main had become a hunting ground, preyed on by thousands of buccaneers, who plundered Spanish settlements, attacked Spanish ships, and generally brought the whole creaking empire to the brink of apparent disaster.

The establishment of buccaneer bases in the Spanish Main itself meant that these predators had secure bases from

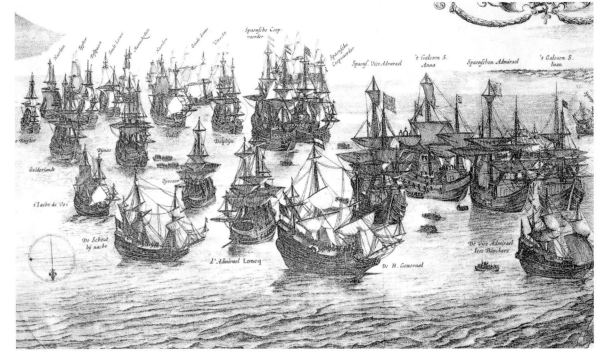

Left: In 1628, the capture of Spanish treasure flota off the coast of Cuba caused economic chaos in Spain, as the country was embroiled in a major war, and needed the money.

Right: Howard Pyle's spirited depiction of a mid-17th-century buccaneer captures the essence of these men—uncouth and ragged, dressed in captured finery and well-armed with musket, pistols, and sword.

which to launch their raids. Places like Port Royal and Tortuga became the archetypal "pirate dens," where plunder was sold and successful buccaneers squandered their loot on high living. However, what set these men apart from previous interlopers and raiders was their burning hatred of the Spanish. When they raided a Spanish town, they didn't just come to plunder its riches—they came to burn, kill, and destroy. Men such as François L'Olonnais became notorious, not only for their buccaneering exploits, but also for their cruelty.

Plundering the Spanish Main became big business. By the time of Henry Morgan and Jean du Casse, these raids were being carried out by large fleets and miniature armies, making it all but impossible for the Spanish to defend themselves. The more successful these raids were, the less money there was available to the Spanish to improve their defenses, or to send men and ships to defend their ports. As a result, the Spanish overseas empire was no longer a source of wealth. Instead it became a struggling backwater, while the real centers of power and wealth in the region moved elsewhere—first to ports like Port Royal in Jamaica and then to the burgeoning colonies of North America and the sugar islands of the West Indies.

This particular era of buccaneering, therefore, marked a watershed in the New World—a period that saw power slip from the hands of the Spanish and into the clutches of their European rivals.

The Coming of the Dutch

The Spanish and the Dutch had been at loggerheads since 1572, almost all the fighting at sea taking place in European waters. However, by the 1590s the Dutch were venturing further afield and within two decades, Dutch warships were prowling the waters of the Spanish Main.

Above: The Dutch attack on San Salvador on the Brazilian coast in May 1624, depicted by Andries van Eertvelt.

During the Dutch Revolt (1568–1648), the epic struggle against Spanish rule, the Dutch rebels relied heavily on privateers to protect their coastline and to harass Spanish shipping. However, by the time of the 12-year truce (1609–21), the Dutch had already ventured as far afield as the East Indies, the Philippines, and the coast of Chile in search of Spanish prey.

The Capture of Bahia

By the end of this wary truce, the Dutch were ready to contest Portuguese control of the East Indies and Spanish domination of the Caribbean. The first big raid came in March 1624, when a Dutch fleet captured the Portuguese port of Bahia (now San Salvador) in Brazil. Although the Spanish and Portuguese recaptured Bahia the following year, the Dutch had already moved on and

were cruising the waters of the Spanish Main. Bahia was recaptured by the Dutch in 1626, their fleet led by a former privateer turned admiral called Piet Heyn. In Holland, he was viewed as a Dutch naval hero in the mold of Francis Drake in England.

Matanzas Bay

In 1628, Piet Heyn returned to the Spanish Main with a fleet of 36 Dutch privateers. He loitered in the Florida Straits hoping to intercept the treasure fleets as they made their way to Havana, ready for their return voyage across the Atlantic. The Tierre Firme Flota was warned in time to avoid the Dutch, but the New Spain Flota had no warning. The Spanish were driven eastward into Matanzas Bay, ten miles past Havana, where their ships were trapped and captured.

The haul of plunder came to more than 11.5 million ducats. This was a blow that the Spanish could ill afford, and it plunged their economy into a downward spiral from which it never recovered. By contrast, by the time the Spanish and Dutch ended their war in 1648, Holland had become a thriving economic power. They also had permanent settlements in the Caribbean, and while these were primarily trading colonies they could also serve as bases in any future struggle with their old enemy.

The Buccaneers of Hispaniola

Spain was still trying to exclude other European nations from the Caribbean until well into the 17th century, and the Spanish fought hard to drive interlopers from their waters.

In the process of keeping them out, the Spanish unwittingly drove a group of landless settlers to take up arms against the Spanish crown. These became known as "buccaneers."

THE HUNTERS OF HISPANIOLA

Philip III of Spain (ruled 1598–1621) saw interlopers and illegal trade with his colonies as a serious problem. He responded by fortifying the ports of the Spanish Main, and by setting up naval patrols charged with hunting down smugglers. Similarly, he began launching expeditions to expel foreigners whenever they tried to establish their own settlements within the region. He was equally strict with his own people. When the Spanish settlers of Hispaniola refused to stop trading with interlopers, he ordered the abandonment of the north coast of the island. His colonists were moved closer to Santo Domingo, where they could be supervised by the island's governor.

As a result, many cattle farms were abandoned, and the animals roamed wild throughout the island. This move also created a political vacuum, and a haven for *renegados*—those who existed outside the law. Spanish colonists who elected to stay behind lived off the wild cattle, which also provided them with a source of income, as leather and meat could be sold to passing ships.

The Original Buccaneers

The *renegados* and hunters who roamed the hinterland of Hispaniola came to be known as *boucaniers*—a French word meaning "meat smokers." It came from an old Arawak word—*buccan*—which referred to a frame used to smoke fish or meat. By the 1640s these people were called "buccaneers." Whatever their origins—hunters, sailors, or adventurers—they all shared an abiding hatred of the Spanish, and were willing to fight their own private war against Spain, regardless of the political climate back in Europe.

Above: This small sloop is typical of the vessels used by buccaneers in the 17th century.

Above: An early 17th-century buccaneer of Hispaniola, clothed in home-made clothing, and accompanied by his hunting dog.

During the first decades of the 17th century, these early buccaneers lived off the land, evaded Spanish patrols, and traded with interlopers. These unwashed backwoodsmen were no seamen—that came later. However, their numbers were soon swelled by others—refugees from settlements like St. Kitts, which had been attacked and destroyed by the Spaniards. Like the hunters of Hispaniola, these newcomers wanted to make the Spanish pay for their actions. Inevitably, the two groups would join forces, and in the process they started a resistance movement that would all but destroy Spain's

Tortuga and the Brethren of the Coast

Off the northwest coast of Hispaniola lay the island of Tortuga, a watering place for passing mariners. It also became a refuge for buccaneers—and soon the first pirate den in the Americas.

Above: The fort on Tortuga island, built in the 1640s to provide a refuge if the island was attacked.

In the early 17th century, the small island was a haven for mariners, and a place where *boucaniers* sold hides and meat to passing ships. The island's name—Isla Tortuga (Turtle Island)—came from its shape.

THE SAFE HAVEN

Resembling a giant turtle when viewed from the sea, Tortuga had only one harbor on its south side; the rest of its coast was protected by cliffs or mountainous slopes. This made it easy to defend. The Spanish occasionally attacked the island—in 1631, 1635, and again in 1638—but the inhabitants simply hid on Hispaniola until they sailed away.

In theory, Tortuga was owned by the Spanish, but in practice it was ruled by an English trading company, at least until 1642 when it became a French settlement. According to the buccaneer historian Alexander Exquemelin, during the 1630s some of these buccaneers or mariners turned to piracy. Under French rule buccaneers were actively encouraged to use Tortuga as a pirate haven, and it developed a notorious reputation as a wild, lawless place.

THE FRENCH PIRATE COLONY

Despite—or more likely, because of—this the colony prospered. During the 1640s Governor Le Vasseur built a fort to defend the harbor, but he and his islanders offered little more than token allegiance to France, and welcomed buccaneers from throughout Europe. The Spanish recaptured the island in 1652, and garrisoned it for a year before withdrawing the troops back to Santo Domingo. When they left, Tortuga was occupied by the English, who used it as a base from which they could raid Hispaniola. It was recovered by French corsairs in 1659, and

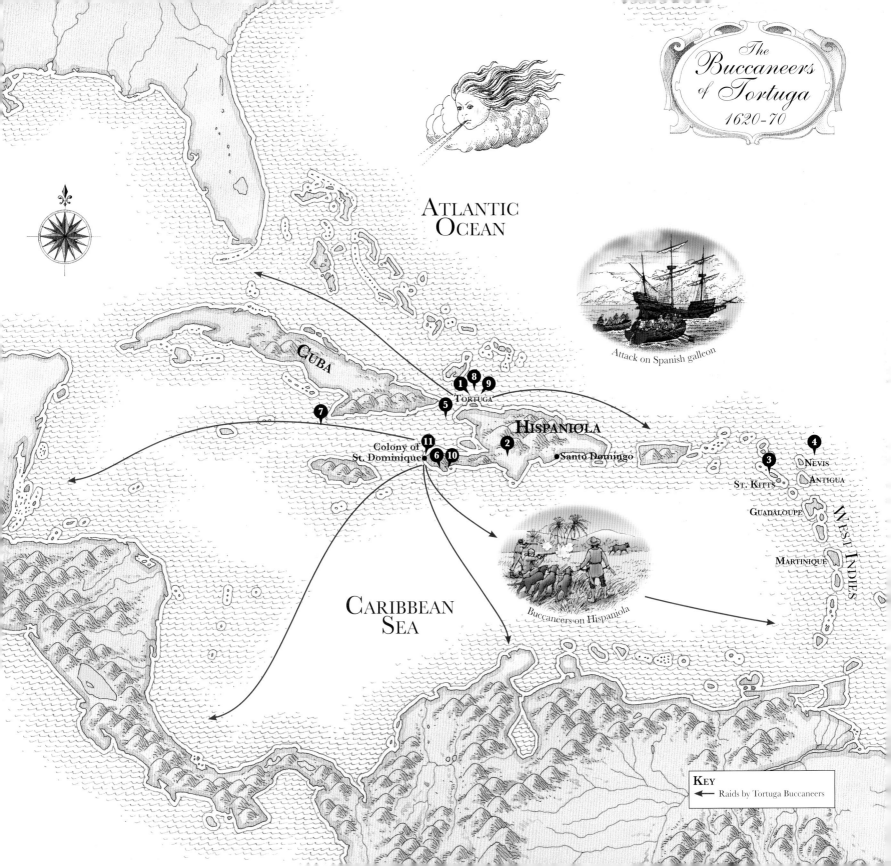

ATLANTIC
OCEAN

The
Buccaneers
of Tortuga
1620–70

Attack on Spanish galleon

CUBA

7

1 **8**
9
5 TORTUGA

HISPANIOLA

11
Colony of
St. Dominique **6** **10**
2
• Santo Domingo

4

3
NEVIS

ST. KITTS
ANTIGUA

GUADALOUPE

W
E
S
T
I
N
D
I
E
S

MARTINIQUE

Buccaneers on Hispaniola

CARIBBEAN
SEA

KEY
← Raids by Tortuga Buccaneers

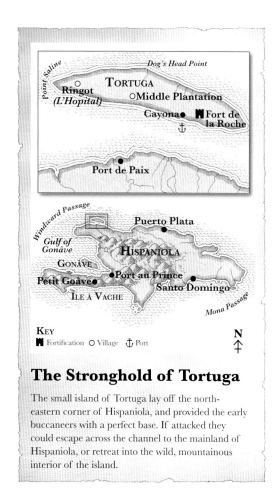

The Stronghold of Tortuga

The small island of Tortuga lay off the north-eastern corner of Hispaniola, and provided the early buccaneers with a perfect base. If attacked they could escape across the channel to the mainland of Hispaniola, or retreat into the wild, mountainous interior of the island.

the French governor relied on buccaneers to defend the island from the Spanish.

During the 1660s, Governor D'Ogeron encouraged the colonization of north-western Hispaniola, and these settlements eventually developed into the French colony of St. Dominique (now Haiti). This was the heyday of the French buccaneers. Plunder from as far afield as Panama and the coast of Venezuela was brought back to Tortuga and squandered in its bars and brothels. However, by the 1670s the buccaneers had moved on—preferring the larger and more prosperous new settlement of Petit Goâve on the south coast of St. Dominique. The

Right: Frontispiece of Alexandre Exquemelin's *The Buccaneers of America*, first published in Amsterdam in 1678.

island's swashbuckling history ceased in 1713, when the end of a long war with England and Spain meant that France had no more need of buccaneers, corsairs, or privateers. Legality proved the death knell for the island, which soon lapsed into obscurity.

EARLY BUCCANEER ATTACKS

During the 1640s, the Spanish authorities in Santo Domingo reported to Madrid that their ships were being attacked in the Windward Passage by pirates based on Tortuga. The Windward Passage lies between the western coast of Hispaniola and the eastern end of Cuba. Tortuga was located at the upper end of the passage, which was a popular route for for transatlantic vessels that had landed in the Bahamas and were bound for the Spanish Main.

In his book *The Buccaneers of America,* published in 1678, Alexandre Exquemelin revealed how these buccaneers operated. The pirates used small sailing or rowing boats and attacked at night. Their preferred tactic was to creep up astern of a Spanish ship and board it before a lookout could sound the alarm. While marksmen shot the helmsmen and officers, others jammed the ship's rudder to prevent escape. They then overpowered its crew. The buccaneers earned a reputation for cruelty, which worked in their favor as

the Spaniards hoped that submission meant their lives would be spared.

Exquemelin claimed that the first of these attacks was carried out by a Frenchman called Pierre Le Grand (Peter the Great). According to the biographer, the buccaneer hailed from Dieppe and arrived in Tortuga during the early 1640s. He began his career by cruising the waters off Tortuga in a small canoe. He and his handful of men captured a small Spanish trading ship, which they then used to hunt larger prey. After several months of fruitless searching he came across a treasure galleon. To encourage his men, he scuttled his own vessel as he pulled alongside his prey. The buccaneers had no escape—they had to capture the ship or die. According to Exquemelin, they succeeded, and Le Grand triumphantly sailed his prize into Tortuga harbor.

The Brethren of the Coast

According to the historian Exquemelin, the buccaneers of Hispaniola operated in groups of six to eight men, pooling resources and making decisions together. They also formed male pairings—a system known as *matelotage,* where the men supported each other. The early buccaneers developed their own laws (known as "the way of the coast"), and in time their society became collectively known as the "Brethren of the Coast." It wasn't a formal confederation—more a collection of individuals united by common laws and ideals. By the 1670s, this term was normally applied to English buccaneers, who operated from Port Royal in Jamaica.

François L'Olonnais

Known more for his cruelty than for his successes, François L'Olonnais was a pirate operating out of the safe haven of Tortuga who fought his own brutal war against the Spanish.

Even among the buccaneers, known for their brutality, François L'Olonnais was singled out as a man of exceptional cruelty. In his war against the Spanish no mercy was asked for—or indeed given.

Left: L'Olonnais earned a reputation as a most brutal buccaneer. Here he is shown ripping the heart from a Spanish captive, and smearing it in the face of another.

EARLY DAYS

François L'Olonnais was born Jean-David Nau, c.1635, in the small port of Les Sables d'Olonne on the French coast of the Bay of Biscay. As a child he was sent to the Caribbean as an indentured servant, but by the mid-1650s he was living with the buccaneers of Hispaniola. By the early 1660s, he had made his way to Tortuga, where he completed two or three cruises with the buccaneers, before being given his own small privateering vessel by the island's French governor. France and Spain were at war at the time, and Governor de la Place was adamant that Tortuga should reap the profits from privateering.

L'Olonnais' first voyages were highly successful, but—according to the biographer Exquemelin—he became notorious for his cruelty, to the extent that Spanish crews preferred to fight to the death rather than face excruciating torture and a lingering death. Around 1665, L'Olonnais was shipwrecked off the coast of Campeche, now part of Mexico. When a Spanish patrol massacred the survivors on the beach, the injured L'Olonnais hid among the bloody

L'Olonnais, shown here in a suitably menacing pose, with Maracaibo burning in the background.

corpses until the Spanish departed. He then talked a group of slaves into stealing a canoe and paddling him to Tortuga.

THE LAGOON OF MARACAIBO

Back in Tortuga, L'Olonnais managed to find another small vessel, and used it to capture a small warship ship off the Cuban coast. He massacred all the crew save one, who was sent to the Governor of Havana with a note in which L'Olonnais claimed responsibility and threatened no quarter to any other Spaniards he captured. After recruiting more men in Tortuga, he led a buccaneering expedition to the Gulf of Venezuela, and entered the Maracaibo

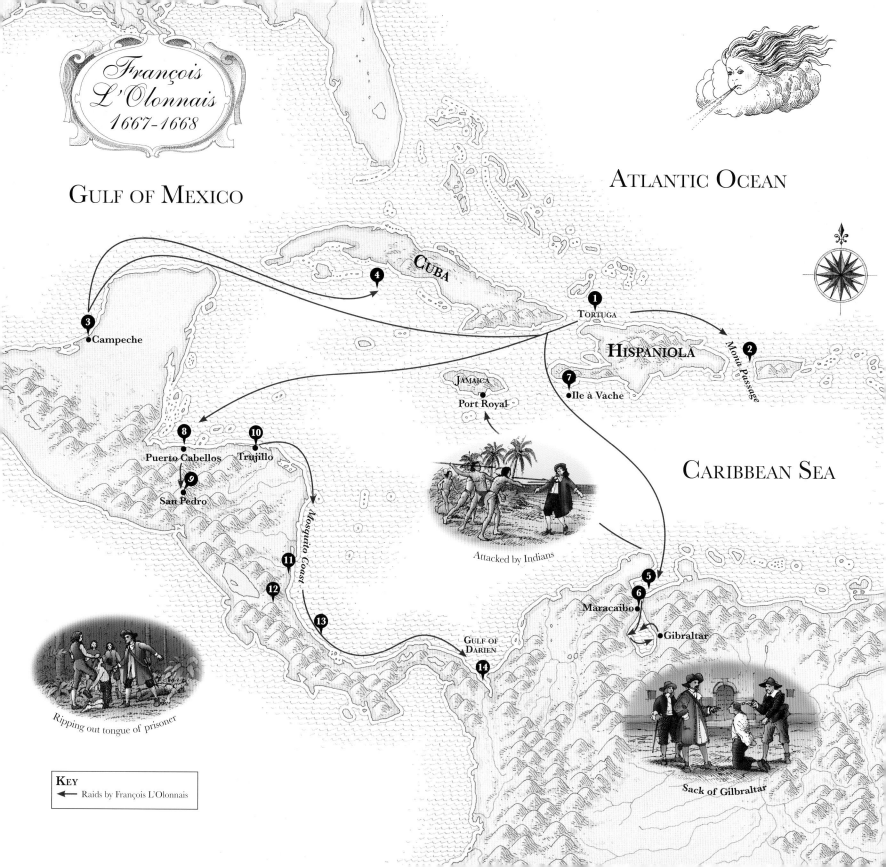

François L'Olonnais
1667-1668

GULF OF MEXICO

ATLANTIC OCEAN

CUBA

4

3
●Campeche

1
Tortuga

HISPANIOLA

Mona Passage

2

7
●Ile à Vache

JAMAICA
●Port Royal

CARIBBEAN SEA

8
Puerto Cabellos

10
Trujillo

9
San Pedro

Mosquito Coast

Attacked by Indians

11

12

13

Gulf of Darien

14

5

6

Maracaibo●

●Gibraltar

Ripping out tongue of prisoner

Sack of Gilbraltar

KEY
← Raids by François L'Olonnais

Voyages of the Despotic French Buccaneer François L'Olonnais, 1667–68

1 **Spring 1667** Governor d'Ogeron of Tortuga gives L'Olonnais a privateering "letter of marque."

2 The buccaneer captures his first prize in the Mona passage.

3 **Summer 1667** He is shipwrecked near Campeche, but evaded Spanish attempts to capture him.

4 Captures a Spanish patrol vessel off the southern coast of Cuba and sails his prize back to Tortuga.

5 **September 1667** Enters the Gulf of Maracaibo with eight ships, and storms the battery guarding its entrance.

6 He then sacks the port of Maracaibo, and crosses the gulf to sack Gibraltar. He returns to Maracaibo to round up any townspeople who had escaped his clutches. He rips out victims' tongues if they don't reveal where valuables are hidden. He then sails away with his plunder.

7 The French buccaneers divide their loot on the Île à Vache (Cow Island). L'Olonnais then visits Port Royal to sell goods, before returning to his base on Tortuga.

8 **1668** L'Olonnais sails to Honduras, where he captures Puerto Cabellos.

9 He marches inland to sack the regional capital of San Pedro. The town yields little in the way of plunder.

10 On his return to the coast he captures a Honduran galleon, off Trujillo. The raid proves a failure, so many of his men desert him, leaving him with just one ship and 400 men.

11 L'Olonnais heads south, down to the Mosquito Coast (now Nicaragua), but is shipwrecked off Punta Mono. The survivors establish a camp on the coast.

12 Leads a raiding expedition up the San Juan River, but is ambushed by the Spanish and forced to retreat back to his camp.

13 His men build a small boat and L'Olonnais sails it south to the Gulf of Darien.

14 On reaching the Gulf of Darien, he goes ashore in search of food, but is ambushed and killed by local villagers.

Lagoon. First he raided the town of Maracaibo, where many of the inhabitants had fled into the jungle with their valuables. After torturing and killing his captives, he crossed the lagoon to Gibraltar, where he spent a month ravaging the area. He then returned to Maracaibo under cover of darkness and captured the town and its inhabitants, which he held for ransom. By the time the buccaneers returned to Tortuga they had plundered more than 260,000 pieces-of-eight. As Exquemelin put it, "The tavern keepers got part of their money and the whores the rest."

A BLOODY END

The following year, L'Olonnais led six ships and 700 men to Central America. After raiding the ports on the coast, L'Olonnais led his men inland, torturing prisoners to reveal the presence of towns or Spanish troops. In one infamous incident, he supposedly ripped the heart out of a captive, gnawed at it, and smeared it into the faces of the other prisoners. However, the raid proved a failure as there was little to plunder.

Disappointed with their spoils, L'Olonnais' other captains abandoned him, leaving him in his own ship. The buccaneer cruised the Mosquito Coast of Nicaragua, but he ran his ship aground on a small island. After rowing to the mainland he headed south, but attacks from local Indians whittled away his party until finally L'Olonnais and a handful of starving survivors were ambushed and killed. Appropriately enough, one survivor reported that L'Olonnais—the most bloodthirsty of the buccaneers—was "hacked to pieces, and roasted limb by limb."

Gulf of Maracaibo, c.1665

The Gulf of Maracaibo (now called the Gulf of Venezuela) is an inlet of the Caribbean, some 150 miles (240km) long and 70 miles (113km) across at its widest point. However, during the 17th century its already narrow entrance was blocked by sandbanks and sand spits, allowing its one remaining channel to be guarded by a powerful gun battery.

Buccaneers threatening a captive to make him reveal the location of hidden plunder during L'Olonnais' Maracaibo raid.

Port Royal

Founded by the British in the 1650s, Port Royal on the southern coast of Jamaica was the ultimate pirate town, one that was to become known as "the richest and wickedest city on earth."

By the 1670s, Port Royal had become a large and busy town, practically overrun by buccaneers. From here, they raided the Spanish Main, and then squandered their plunder in the town's many bars and brothels.

OLIVER CROMWELL'S COLONY

In 1655, an English expedition sent by Oliver Cromwell captured Jamaica from the Spanish and set about fortifying the island's main harbor. By the 1660s this port had become known as Port Royal, a bustling town of around 3,000 inhabitants. And from the outset, the English relied on the buccaneers to defend Jamaica from attack.

The governor lured English buccaneers from Tortuga by offering them lucrative privateering contracts. More importantly, Port Royal had merchants willing to buy Spanish plunder. It also lay closer to the rich heart of the Spanish Main. By 1660, over a dozen buccaneering captains were operating out of Port Royal. The numbers of buccaneers kept on growing, and by 1670 it had become a largely buccaneer-run town, filled with bars, brothels, and gambling dens.

Above: For half a century, Port Royal was the most notorious buccaneer haven in the Caribbean. It had a sheltered deep-water harbor, and was well-protected by fortifications. Painting by Richard Paton.

The Voyages of Bartolomeo el Portugues and Roche Brasiliano, c.1662–70

Port Royal

1 **1655** An expedition sent from England by Oliver Cromwell captures Jamaica from the Spaniards. Spanish Town becomes the English colony's new capital.

2 **c.1662** The capital's harbor—Port Royal (originally known as Cagway)—develops into a thriving haven for buccaneers. It becomes one of the richest and wildest towns in the Americas.

3 **June 7, 1692** Port Royal is hit by an earthquake, which causes widespread devastation. A third of the port falls into the sea—a disaster from which Port Royal never recovers.

Bartolomeo el Portugues

4 **c.1662** Bartolomeo el Portugues captures a Spanish ship off the southern coast of Cuba, but is overtaken by a Spanish warship and captured after a brisk fight.

5 He is taken to Campeche but escapes shortly before his scheduled execution.

6 Reaches the coast near Cancún and finds a friendly ship which takes him back to Jamaica.

7 **c.1663** Returns to Campeche in a small boat, and captures a ship in the harbor.

8 Runs aground on Cuba's Isle of Pines, and is forced to return to Jamaica in a small boat. He reputedly ends his days begging on the streets of Port Royal.

Roche Brasiliano

A **c.1665** Roche Brasiliano (Rock the Brazilian) begins his career preying on Spanish shipping off the western end of Cuba.

B **c1666** Captures a Spanish ship off Vera Cruz, but is overtaken by a hurricane and shipwrecked near Campeche.

C He is captured, but escapes, and makes it back to Jamaica.

D **1669** Returns to Campeche, but his ship runs aground.

E Leads his men across the Yucatán Peninsula, fighting off Spanish patrols until he reaches the coast. He then steals two small boats and returns to Port Royal.

F **c.1670** Dies shortly after his return to Port Royal.

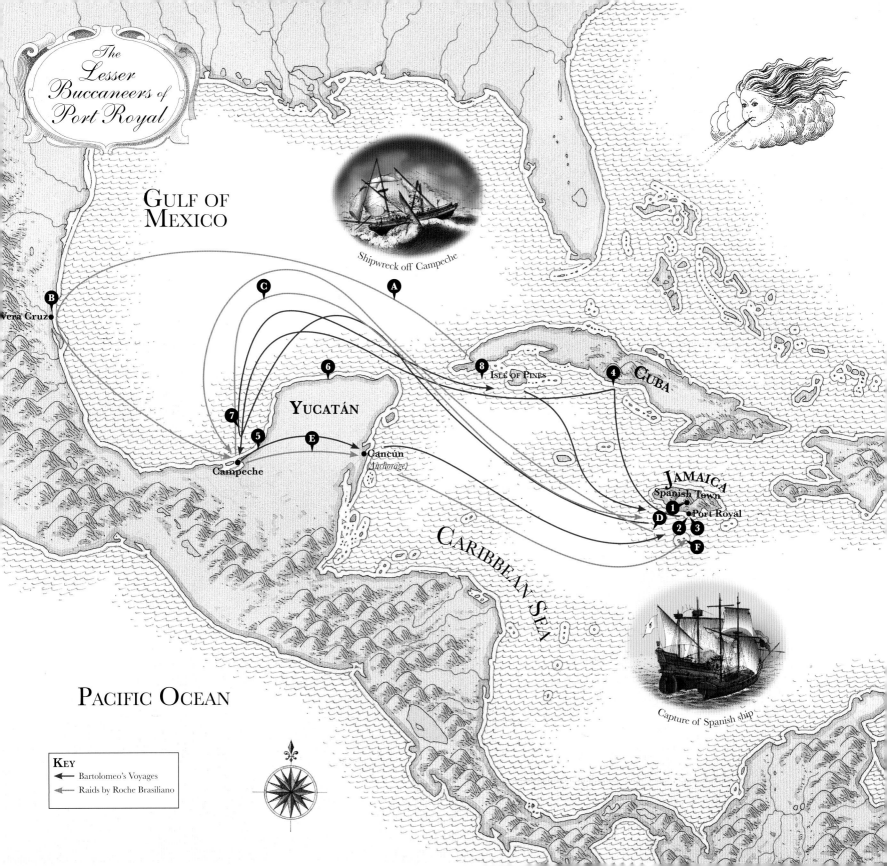

The
Lesser
Buccaneers of
Port Royal

GULF OF
MEXICO

Vera Cruz **B**

C

A

Shipwreck off Campeche

8 Isle of Pines

4 CUBA

6

YUCATÁN

7

5

E

Cancún
(Anchorage)

Campeche

JAMAICA
Spanish Town
D **1**
2 **3** Port Royal
F

CARIBBEAN SEA

PACIFIC OCEAN

Capture of Spanish ship

KEY
→ Bartolomeo's Voyages
→ Raids by Roche Brasiliano

THE GREAT EARTHQUAKE

At its height, during the 1660s and 1670s, Port Royal was the busiest port in the Americas. However, on the morning of June 7, 1692 an earthquake hit the town, followed by a succession of great tidal shock waves. The sand on which the town was built liquefied and dissolved, plunging whole streets into the harbor. By the time it ended, more than 2,000 people had died, and two-thirds of the town had disappeared. Port Royal never recovered and nearby Kingston became the island's main settlement. Many saw the destruction of Port Royal as God's punishment of a city of sin and wickedness.

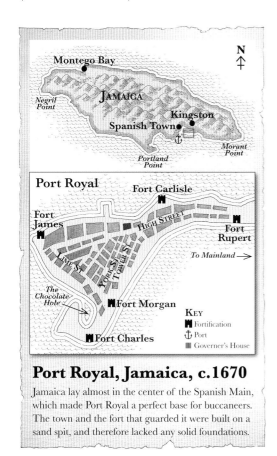

Port Royal, Jamaica, c.1670

Jamaica lay almost in the center of the Spanish Main, which made Port Royal a perfect base for buccaneers. The town and the fort that guarded it were built on a sand spit, and therefore lacked any solid foundations.

BARTOLOMEO EL PORTUGUES

Bartholomew "the Portuguese" was typical of the small-time buccaneers who operated from Port Royal during the 1660s. He began by capturing a Spanish merchantman during a battle that cost him half his crew. On his way home, he was captured by Spanish warships and imprisoned in Campeche. He escaped and made his way through the jungles to the Yucatán coast, where he found a ship which took him home. Bartholomew returned to Campeche and captured one of the warships, but the unlucky buccaneer ran it aground off the Cuban coast. Although he made it back to his home port, he was considered unlucky by his old shipmates and died "in the greatest wretchedness in the world."

ROCHE BRASILIANO

Another Port Royal celebrity was Rock "the Brazilian," who began his career with just a canoe. He captured a Spanish trading sloop but lost it during a storm off Campeche. He managed to escape from prison and returned to the port in 1669, with several fellow buccaneering captains. This time he ran aground and was forced to make his way with his men across country to a known buccaneer rendezvous.

On the coast he captured two ships, and returned to Port Royal in triumph. Nothing is known about him after that, although Exquemelin noted that in Port Royal, "He would roam the town like a madman. The first person he came across, he would chop off his arm or leg, and anyone daring to intervene, for he was like a maniac." It sounds unlikely that the buccaneer died peacefully!

Above: Brasiliano's buccaneers encounter a Spanish patrol during their escape from Campeche.

Roche Brasiliano, taken from Exquemelin's *The Buccaneers of America*, with the same skirmish as that above depicted in the background.

Henry Morgan

Probably the most famous buccaneer of them all, Henry Morgan was a larger-than-life figure, who plundered his way across the Spanish Main for the best part of a decade.

Pictures of Henry Morgan give the appearance of a Falstaff-type character. He was, in fact, a born leader, and showed great tactical skill, diplomacy, and business acumen during his career.

THE YOUNG MORGAN

We know little about his roots, but Morgan was probably born into a Welsh farming family around 1635. He came to the Caribbean as an indentured servant, but gained his freedom by 1655, when he appeared in Jamaica. He may well have joined the buccaneers operating out of Port Royal, but he first appeared in official records in 1662, by which time he was a Captain of Militia. Later that year he was awarded a privateering letter of marque, and began a new career as a buccaneer captain.

He probably sailed under the command of Sir Christopher Myngs, but by 1664 Morgan was named as a leading member of John Norris' expedition to Central America.

Henry Morgan, depicted during his assault on Panama early in 1671. The demoralized Spanish drew up in battle formation outside the city, but the buccaneers routed them with little difficulty.

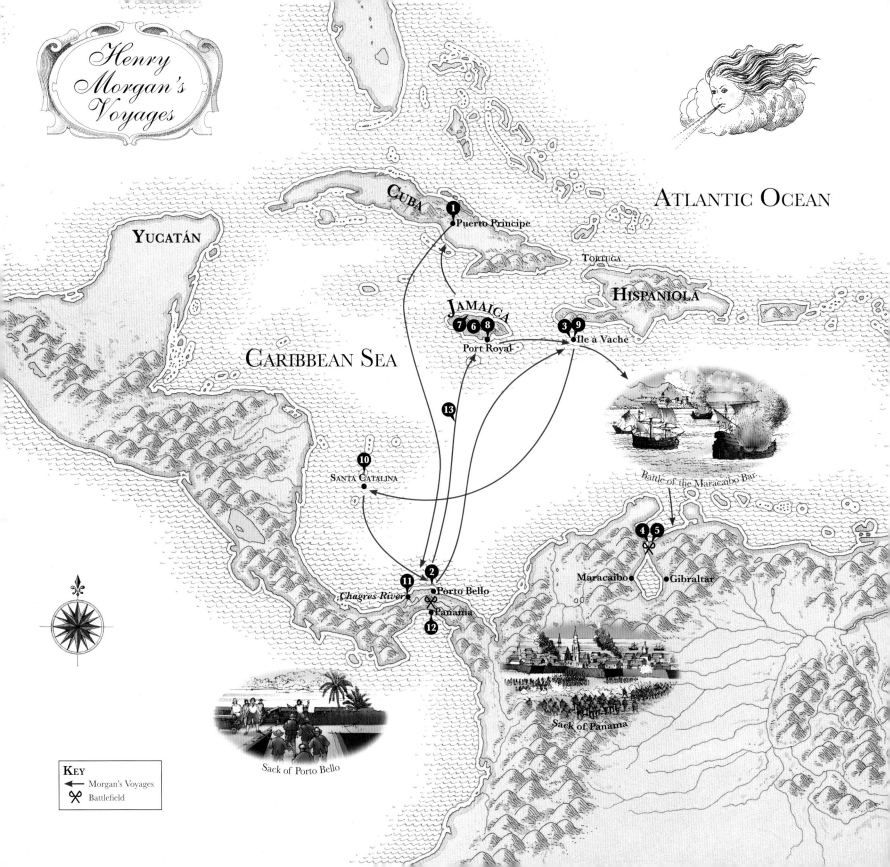

Henry Morgan's Voyages

ATLANTIC OCEAN

YUCATÁN

CUBA

1 ● Puerto Principe

TORTUGA

HISPANIOLA

JAMAICA

7 **6** **8**

● Port Royal

3 **9** ● Ile à Vache

CARIBBEAN SEA

13

Battle of the Maracaibo Bar

10

SANTA CATALINA ●

4 **5**

Maracaibo ● ● Gibraltar

11

Chagres River ● **2** ● Porto Bello

● Panama

12

Sack of Panama

KEY
→ Morgan's Voyages
✂ Battlefield

Sack of Porto Bello

The Voyages of England's Greatest Buccaneer, 1668–71

1 **April 1668** Morgan and his fellow Jamaican buccaneers sack Puerto Principe (now Camaguey) in Cuba.

2 **July 1668** Captures Porto Bello, and holds the port for ransom. He then defends it against a Spanish counter-attack and makes off with more than 250,000 pieces-of-eight.

3 **January 1669** Morgan calls a rendezvous of buccaneers on the Île à Vache (Cow Island). *HMS Oxford* is destroyed by an accidental explosion during the ensuing celebrations.

4 **March 1669** The buccaneers arrive in the Gulf of Maracaibo and capture the fort guarding its entrance. Morgan then goes on to sack Maracaibo and Gibraltar.

5 **April 1669** When the buccaneers find the exit to the Gulf it is blocked by a Spanish squadron. On April 27, Morgan launches a fireship against the Spanish, and then attacks their ships. The result is a spectacular victory for the buccaneers, and Morgan returns to Port Royal in triumph.

Port Royal

6 **June 1669** The Governor of Jamaica announces that peace has been declared with the Spanish.

7 **January 1670** A Spanish privateer raids Jamaica, giving the English an excuse to retaliate.

8 **August 1670** Morgan sails from Port Royal with 11 ships.

9 **September–October 1670** At Ile à Vache, he is joined by an even larger French force.

10 **December 1670** Morgan's fleet capture Santa Catalina, then continue on to the Isthmus of Panama.

11 **January 1671** An advanced party captures the fort guarding the mouth of the Chagres River. The buccaneers continue up the river in small boats, then complete their journey to Panama on foot.

12 **January 27, 1671** The Battle of Panama. Morgan's buccaneers arrive in front of Panama, and defeat the small Spanish army deployed to protect the city. Panama is captured by the buccaneers, who then hold the city for a month.

13 **March 1671** Morgan divides the plunder and returns to Port Royal with his loot.

On his return, he invested his share of the profits in land on Jamaica, buying the first of several plantations. He also married Mary, the daughter of his uncle, Sir Edward Morgan. He was now a man of substance, and a confidante of Sir Thomas Modyford, governor of Jamaica.

PORTO BELLO

Morgan then decided to attack Porto Bello, on the Isthmus of Panama. It was defended by three large stone forts, but Morgan and his men were undeterred. He anchored well up the coast and moved his men close to the city by canoe. On July 11, 1668, he launched a surprise dawn attack on the town from the west. The Spanish garrison took refuge in the forts, so Morgan had little option but to attack them, one after the other.

At the first fort—San Geronimo—he rounded up all the nuns and priests, and used them as a human shield. This trick allowed the buccaneers to reach the walls unscathed, and within minutes they had clambered up scaling ladders and fought their way inside. The buccaneers gave no mercy, massacring the entire garrison. After offering a token resistance, the garrisons of the remaining two forts surrendered, in return for more lenient treatment.

The buccaneers tortured their richer prisoners to make them reveal where they hid their personal possessions. Morgan also held Porto Bello to ransom, demanding money from the governor of Panama or he would burn the town to the ground. Instead the Spanish tried to attack the buccaneers, but Morgan's men ambushed them a few miles outside the town, leaving the governor with little option but to pay whatever Morgan asked for. By the time Morgan and his men returned to Port Royal, they had managed to garner over 250,000 pieces-of-eight as plunder.

The Puerto Principe Raid

In January 1668, Governor Modyford was concerned that the Spanish harbored plans to invade Jamaica. He ordered Morgan to raise a buccaneering force and use it to discover Spain's intentions. Morgan had 10 ships and 500 men under his command, and he was soon joined by another 2 ships and 200 buccaneers from Tortuga. This force was too small to attack any large Spanish port, so Morgan decided to attack Puerto Principe, 30 miles (48km) inland, in the center of Cuba. The unsuspecting townspeople were completely taken by surprise, but despite torturing prisoners and holding the town for ransom, the buccaneers could only raise 50,000 pieces-of-eight and no information of a plot. The disgruntled French contingent sailed off in search of more lucrative prizes, but Morgan decided to continue raiding.

Right: Henry Morgan's buccaneers storming the Cuban town of Puerto Principe (now called Camaguey) in early 1668.

Above: The Battle of Panama, fought on January 18, 1671, was the closest thing to a full-scale battle engagement between European troops that the Spanish Empire had seen, and involved over 5,000 men.

THE GREAT RAID ON PANAMA

Although Spain and England were at peace, Governor Modyford allowed Morgan to continue his lucrative raids. And so, in December 1670, Morgan arrived off the mouth of the Chagres River, near Porto Bello, where a landing party stormed the Spanish fort of San Lorenzo. Morgan then transferred about 1,800 of his men into canoes and set off upstream. After four days, his raiding force disembarked and cut through the Panamanian jungle to the road that linked Panama to Porto Bello. This meant he was covering the same ground as Francis Drake had, a century earlier.

The march was tough. Food and water were scarce, but the force of Morgan's personality, and their greed, drove the men on, until on January 19, 1671, they emerged from the jungle in front of the city of Panama on the Pacific coast. His men were too exhausted to launch an immediate attack, so Morgan let them rest. Then, the following morning, he advanced toward the city.

THE MARACAIBO RAID

By the end of the year, Morgan was ready to launch another attack. He arranged a rendezvous with the French buccaneers of Tortuga at the Île à Vache (Cow Island), off the southern coast of Hispaniola. On January 12, 1669, the two groups joined forces, although celebrations were marred when the firing of celebratory salvos led to a spark falling into the powder store of an English warship—*HMS Oxford*—which had been supplied by Governor Modyford. The *Oxford* blew up, taking 200 of her crew with her.

Morgan had just 500 men left—too few to attack a large city. Instead he repeated L'Olonnais' raid of two years before, and entered the Maracaibo Lagoon on the coast of Venezuela. The inhabitants of both Maracaibo and Gibraltar fled when the buccaneers appeared, leaving little for the buccaneers to plunder. However, when they headed for home, Morgan found his way blocked by a Spanish squadron that was lying across the narrow mouth of the lagoon. On April 27, Morgan attacked, sending a fireship ahead of him, which collided with the Spanish flagship. Both ships blew up. One of the other Spanish ships was boarded and captured and another driven ashore and burned. This little sea battle helped turn an unsuccessful raid into a profitable one; Morgan's ships returned to Port Royal with 125,000 pieces-of-eight in their holds.

Right: On April 27, 1669 Henry Morgan's buccaneering fleet fought and defeated a powerful blockading Spanish squadron off Maracaibo Bar.

Above: After the capture of Panama, Morgan and his men interrogated any Spaniards they captured, in an attempt to locate hidden valuables. Painting by Howard Pyle.

The Spanish had grouped in front of Panama, and had roughly as many men as the buccaneers. Although they were less skilled, the small army of Spaniards included some 400 cavalry. They also tried to stampede cattle into the buccaneer ranks, but the ploy misfired, and instead the cattle panicked and played havoc amid the Spanish lines.

Morgan's men then fired their muskets and charged, at which point the Spaniards broke and ran back into the city. The buccaneers gave chase, slaughtering about 500 of the Spaniards as they ran through the city. Somehow a

building caught fire, and by nightfall much of Panama was a smoking ruin.

To make matters worse, the Spanish had managed to load up most of the gold and silver in the city, and sailed just as the buccaneers were winning the battle. Deprived of their riches, the buccaneers looted what they could by torturing their prisoners to reveal hiding places, or stripping the churches and houses of whatever valuables they could find. In late February, Morgan headed home, but the spoils were meager—just 60,000 pieces-of-eight, to be shared between 2,000 men.

Governor Morgan

After his return, Morgan was ordered to London to stand trial for piracy. After all, he had attacked a Spanish city even though England and Spain were at peace. However, he had influential supporters, and not only was he acquitted, but Morgan was even knighted and then awarded the deputy governorship of Jamaica! He returned to the island in 1674 and spent the rest of his life looking after his extensive plantations, participating in island politics, and carousing with his old shipmates. Sir Henry Morgan finally died in 1688.

Buccaneers of the Pacific

After the buccaneers had looted their way around the Spanish Main, a few intrepid captains ventured into the Pacific, where they found there were substantial riches for the taking.

Above: English buccaneer William Dampier (1651–1715) was also a renowned author, explorer, and scientist. Portrait by Thomas Murray.

In December 1679, a group of English buccaneers led by Bartholomew Sharp, William Dampier, and others sacked Porto Bello, taking more than 36,000 pieces-of-eight from the Spaniards.

The First Sortie

Instead of returning to Porto Bello, the buccaneers crossed the Isthmus of Panama to the Pacific coast. There they seized local fishing boats and used them to capture larger Spanish ships. They then split up, one group electing to head south toward Cape Horn.

This group chose Captain Sharp to lead them, but he soon proved unpopular, and in April 1681 the band fragmented. Many went straight home the way they had come, but Sharp led the remainder south where he captured two lucrative prizes yielding 37,000 pieces-of-eight. He finally rounded Cape Horn and returned to the Caribbean in February 1682. This raid showed that the waters of America's Pacific coast were lucrative—and worth raiding.

Woodes Rogers

In August 1708, the buccaneer Woodes Rogers sailed from Bristol with two ships. He rounded Cape Horn and by February he was off the Juan Fernández Islands. There he rescued a castaway called Alexander Selkirk, a buccaneer who had been stranded for five years. His story later inspired Daniel Defoe to write *Robinson Crusoe*. Rogers raided the Ecuadorian port of Guayaquil, then after hiding in the Galapagos Islands until the Spanish had given up chasing him, he sailed north and in December 1709 captured one of the Manila galleons. He returned home by circumnavigating the globe, and in October 1711 his two ships arrived back in London. Their total haul was 1.6 million pieces-of-eight—over $140 million in today's money.

More Pacific Plundering

In August 1683 a small band of buccaneers led by John Cook returned to the Pacific. Cook died off the coast of Peru and so Edward Davis, captain of another ship they had fallen in with, took command of his ship. A third group led by Captain Charles Swan then arrived. Together they attacked the annual treasure fleet sailing from Peru to Panama, but were driven off.

Swan, accompanied by William Dampier, separated from the rest and sailed to the Philippines. There, Swan was so taken by the local women that he refused to leave. Dampier commandeered his ship and sailed home without him. Meanwhile, the buccaneers left behind launched raids along the Peruvian coast, which yielded 60,000 pieces-of-eight in plunder. Replete, they returned home to England with their loot. Dampier later wrote of his experiences, his book becoming a bestseller.

Below: Captain Swan and his men on the South American coast in 1684, in a contemporary mural by Frank Schoonover.

The French Filibusters

As strict laws and peace with the Spanish led to a decline in piracy in Jamaica, the French ports of Saint Dominique overtook them as the buccaneering centers of the Caribbean.

Peace with Spain had officially brought English buccaneering in the Caribbean to an end. However, the French still encouraged buccaneers to attack the Spanish.

THE CHEVALIER DE GRAMMONT

By developing the colony of St. Dominique (now Haiti) on the western side of Hispaniola, the French created the perfect haven for buccaneers, lying at the very heart of the Spanish Main. By the 1670s, Petit Goâve in southwestern St. Dominique had overtaken Tortuga as the center for French buccaneering, by which time their leader was a man called Michel de Grammont.

The origins of De Grammont are obscure, but according to the historian Exquemelin, he served in the French navy before arriving in the Caribbean around 1672 as a privateer. Unwelcome in the more regulated French colonies, he moved to Saint Dominique, and joined the "filibusters," or buccaneers, quickly rising to become their leader. At this point he gave himself the honorary title of Chevalier, the equivalent of the English "knight."

THE ISLAND OF THE BIRDS

In 1678, the Chevalier de Grammont led 1,200 French buccaneers in an attack on the Dutch island of Curaçao on the Spanish Main.

Howard Pyle's painting *Exacting Tribute from the Citizens* captures something of the brutality of a buccaneering raid. Here a town's leading Spanish citizen awaits his fate at the hands of a buccaneer captain.

Freebooters and Filibusters

While the French still called privateers "corsairs," they also used the term "buccaneer." However, by the 1670s the term *filibustier* had come into vogue, a name derived from the Spanish word *filibustero*, meaning "freebooter" or "pirate." Freebooter came from the Dutch word *vrijbuiter*, which was their word for a buccaneer. The French *filibustier* eventually became the English word "filibuster," which as well as being applied to buccaneers, became the term for American armed adventurers in the 19th century, and later politicians who obstructed the progress of legislation—a business known as "filibustering."

He joined forces with a French squadron, but this combined fleet was wrecked on a reef off the Isla de Aves ("Island of the Birds"), to the east of Curaçao. When the French admiral limped back to Martinique with his survivors, Grammont and his men plundered the shipwrecks. The filibusters still wanted to attack the Spanish, but with just six ships and 700 men left, Grammont's options were limited. He decided to raid the Maracaibo Lagoon, and that June he captured the newly built fort that guarded its mouth. Once inside the lagoon, the plunder was disappointingly sparse—the region had already been stripped bare by L'Olonnais and Morgan.

In the early summer of 1680, he seized La Guayra, the port of Caracas. Despite capturing the port's

Right: The "Chevalier" Michel de Grammont, as depicted in a 19th-century illustration.

governor and holding him for ransom, this daring venture yielded Grammont and his buccaneers very little plunder. However, the raid established him as one of the leading French buccaneers of his day.

In the summer of 1685, he joined forces with the Dutch *vrijbuiter* Laurens de Graff to raid Vera Cruz in Mexico, an assault which blithely ignored the fact that France was at war with Holland but at peace with Spain! In September 1686, Grammont was named as the "Royal Lieutenant" to the Governor of Saint Dominique. Grammond, however, decided that he wanted one last cruise before becoming respectable. He sailed off into the Caribbean, and was never seen again—the victim of a shipwreck or a hurricane.

THE SACK OF CARTAGENA

During the War of the League of Augsburg (1688–97), France found herself at war with the Dutch, the Spanish, and the English. As a result, all four nations issued privateering licenses to their buccaneers, but it was the French who would use these privateers to inflict a major blow on Spain's empire—by forming an alliance between the French navy and the filibusters of Saint Dominique.

In March 1689, a French Admiral, Baron Jean de Pointis, arrived off Petit Goâve with a squadron of 19 ships and 3,000 veteran troops. He was joined by 11 filibuster ships, commanded by Jean du Casse, the governor of the Saint Dominique colony. Du Casse's biggest job was preventing his *filibustiers* from leaving the expedition, as few were willing to tolerate the arrogance of the French Admiral. He managed to ease tensions by talking the Admiral into signing an agreement about plunder—when a Spanish port was attacked, the spoils would be shared equally between the buccaneers and the French crown.

By that time, Pointis and Casse had already selected their target. The port of Cartagena was well fortified but it was also reputedly the richest city in the Spanish Main. It was over a century since it had last been sacked by Drake, and it was hoped that by launching an attack at the right time, Cartagena would be filled with treasure waiting to be loaded on to the annual Terra Firme Flota. The city was built on a landlocked bay with one narrow entrance. Its well-defended inner harbor lay beyond the bay, protected by the guns of two forts.

The French arrived off Cartagena on April 13, and Casse persuaded the Admiral

Above: When the French landed near Cartagena in 1689, they besieged the port in conventional military fashion. Once the walls were breached by artillery, the buccaneers stormed into the city. This view, from the north, shows the breach being made in the center of the city wall. Late 17th-century French engraving.

to scout out the city and harbor before launching an assault. It was lucky he did so—the beach where Pointis planned to land his troops was fringed by a reef, which would have prevented his men from reaching the shore. In the end, the Frenchmen followed the example set by Drake a century before, and began by capturing the fort guarding the entrance to the outer harbor. Two other forts protected the inner harbor, but when the French approached they discovered one had been abandoned by its garrison. It was duly occupied by French soldiers. That left Fort San Lázaro, which remained in Spanish hands throughout the coming fight.

Siege guns were dragged into position, covering the landward approaches to the city, which were protected by an inlet, a causeway, and a fortified suburb. For a week the French guns pounded these defenses.

Then, on May 1, the buccaneers spearheaded an assault, and despite one repulse and heavy casualties, managed to fight their way across the bridge and into the city. The Spanish garrison finally surrendered on the evening of May 2.

THE DIVISION OF THE SPOILS

Then came the business of dividing the spoils. The looting of Cartagena was left to Pointis—the filibusters were kept outside the city. The trouble came when the Admiral transported all the plunder onto his own ships. Du Casse demanded the filibusters' share, but was astonished when the Admiral handed over just 40,000 livres—80,000 pieces-of-eight. For his part, Pointis argued it was a fair division, based on agreed French naval practice. The French fleet sailed two

days later, before the filibusters could find a way of causing trouble. Of course, instead of going home, they returned to Cartagena, which they plundered again. This time they weren't squeamish about torturing the inhabitants, and as a result Casse and his men raised another 2 million pieces-of-eight.

They also enjoyed a revenge of sorts over the French Admiral. Back in Paris, when King Louis XIV learned of the division of plunder, he ordered Pointis to pay the filibusters 400,000 gold livres rather than the 40,000 he had paid. Although very little of this extra money actually reached Saint Dominique, at least the filibusters had managed to extort their own plunder. A series of wars which lasted until 1713 also gave these filibusters ample opportunity for legal employment—as privateers in the service of their generous French monarch.

The Pirate Round

During the 17th century, English and Dutch ships made regular voyages to India and the East Indies, bringing back a fortune in spices. By the last decades of the century, pirates had begun to venture into the warm waters of the Indian Ocean.

Some of the richest prizes in the world—the ships belonging to India's Mughal rulers—could be found in these waters. It was a perfect hunting ground and was to become one of the most dangerous oceans in the world.

THE RICHEST SEAS

Indian and Arab ships sailed along the busy sea lanes between India's west Coast, the Red Sea, and the Persian Gulf, and while most contained mundane cargoes of produce, pilgrims, or manufactured goods, others were laden with a fortune in specie or spice, while the ships of the English and Dutch East India Companies were seen as highly lucrative targets because they carried the riches of the East to Europe.

It was this wealth of opportunity that made the Indian Ocean so attractive to pirates such as Henry Every, Thomas Tew, and William Kidd, and which encouraged the development of Madagascar as one of the most lively pirate havens in the world. Piracy was also rife on the Indian coast where the

Above: A well-armed British East Indiaman under full sail and flying the flag of the East India Company. Painting by Peter Monamy, c.1725.

local Angrian pirates established their own pirate kingdom. For more than three decades, from the mid-1690s onward, the Indian Ocean was regarded as one of the most dangerous pirate hot spots in the world.

THE PIRATE ROUNDSMEN

While many people have heard of the unfortunate Captain William Kidd, the exploits of other far more successful pirates are relatively unknown. However, while Kidd achieved little before he was caught and hanged, both Henry Every and Thomas Tew managed to capture spectacularly wealthy prizes. The wily Every even lived long enough to abscond with all his plunder, disappearing back into obscurity with his riches. The success of these early "roundsmen"—so named because they sailed around the Cape of Good Hope, a route known as the Pirate Round—encouraged others to venture into the same waters.

This in turn led to the development of Madagascar as a pirate paradise. Some writers claimed that the pirate base of St. Mary's Island was Libertaria—a pirate utopia where liberty and equality were practiced. The truth was altogether different. Despite its popularity, Madagascar remained a poor, underdeveloped backwater, where survival was more important than equality.

The Appeal of the Indian Ocean

During the age of sail, some of the richest ships afloat passed through the Indian Ocean. It is hardly surprising, then, that the area became an irresistible magnet for pirates in search of plunder.

Above: Europeans headed eastward in search of spice, which they found in abundance in the mythical Spice Islands of the East Indies.

The Indian Ocean had been a hunting ground for pirates long before the arrival of Europeans. Indian pirates operated off the coast of the subcontinent and in the busy sea lanes of the Red Sea and the Persian Gulf.

THE WATERS OF THE EMPEROR

Fortunately, there were also pirate hunters. Warships belonging to the Indian Mughal Empire patrolled the waters between the Indian coast and the Red Sea, while several Indian and Arabic ports also maintained their own local naval forces, patrolling their harbors and offering protection to passing shipping. Still, the sheer volume of Indian and Arab shipping in these waters meant that these patrols couldn't protect everyone, and therefore piracy was seen as a major threat—and big business.

THE COMING OF THE EUROPEANS

The situation facing the trading companies of Europe was very different. It was the Portuguese who first opened up a sea route between Europe and India at the end of the 15th century, and during the decades that followed, Portuguese trading colonies were established on the Indian coast. The Portuguese were soon followed by the Dutch and the English, and by the mid-17th century these Europeans had established a firm foothold in the region. These traders brought European cloth, manufactured goods, and precious metals to India in exchange for spices and silks.

While the English East India Company concentrated on trade with India itself, their Dutch counterparts developed markets in

The Angrian Pirate Dynasty

Kanhoji Angria was an African Muslim who established a string of pirate strongholds along India's western seaboard. Pirates and criminals flocked to join him and soon he controlled a miniature pirate kingdom. He forced ships to pay protection money and preyed on English vessels operating out of Bombay. In 1716, he even blockaded the port, forcing the East Indian Company to pay a humiliating ransom.

On his death in 1729, the pirate kingdom was divided between his sons, Sumbhaji and Mannaji, but it was Sumbhaji who emerged as the real pirate leader. He continued to lead one of the most successful pirate operations of the period until the East India Company sent in warships and troops to root out the pirates. By 1756, after almost four decades, the Angrian pirates were finally put out of business.

Above: An English East Indiaman makes her way through the English Channel in the mid-18th century. Although well-armed, these ships were primarily designed as merchantmen.

the East Indies and opened trade routes with China. By the end of the 17th century, the Portuguese had been replaced as the leading power in the region, while the English had surpassed the Dutch in terms of number of ships, and profit. By 1690, the ships—known as the "East Indiamen"—of the English East India Company were making regular voyages between London and Bombay, and their well-armed ships were powerful enough to deter all but the most ferocious of pirates.

A GOLDEN OPPORTUNITY

This period, during the late 17th century, was when the roundsmen appeared. The end of buccaneering in the Caribbean encouraged several pirates to venture further afield. The Portuguese monopoly of the West African coast had come to an end, and these African ports provided a springboard for both merchantmen and pirates alike, allowing them to reach the Indian Ocean more easily. The early success of Henry Every and Thomas Tew only served to encourage others to follow them.

This improved access to the Indian Ocean coincided with a series of internal disputes within the Indian Mughal Empire, and so resources that had once been spent on anti-piracy patrols were now diverted to counter rebellion and insurrection. This eventually led to the collapse of the Empire and the collapse of internal authority in large parts of India. For the pirates the timing was perfect. They were presented with a perfect opportunity to cruise rich, new waters, and for the next 25 years the waters of the Indian Ocean were plagued by pirates. During this period, the large island of Madagascar was turned into a pirate haven, and the roundsmen used this new-found base to prey on the ships of the East India Company.

Attacks on the East India Company's ships caused an outcry in Britain, and led to an increase in naval patrols and the introduction of convoys. In effect, the pirates were denied the opportunities they needed in order to flourish. By 1720, the pirate threat had passed and the British were able to divert their resources into countering the power of the Angrian pirates. Soon the waters of the Indian ocean were made safe again, and the East India Company could concentrate on the business of making money.

Thomas Tew

This pirate almost single-handedly created a pirate epidemic in the Indian Ocean. And his success inspired others to try their luck beyond the Cape of Good Hope.

In 1692, Captain Thomas Tew was granted a privateering letter of marque by the Governor of Bermuda. At that time, England was at war with France.

THE FIRST RED SEA PIRATE

Tew was the part owner of a sloop called the *Amity*, which he sailed across the Atlantic to the West African coast. Unable to find any French slavers, he decided to head south, sailing around the Cape of Good Hope to reach the Indian Ocean. This made him one of the first of the pirate roundsmen.

By June 1693, he had reached the Bab el Mandeb ("Gate of Tears"), which marked the eastern entrance to the Red Sea. There he came upon a well-armed warship owned by the Indian Mughal Emperor. Despite the disparity in size and crew, Tew boarded and captured the bigger ship, which turned out to be laden with plunder—gold, gems, ivory, spices, and silk. Tew and his crew had found their fortune. However, when Tew learned

The charismatic pirate Thomas Tew, left, courted the support of American colonial society, and even the Governor of New York, Benjamin Fletcher, was eager to hear the pirate recount his exploits.

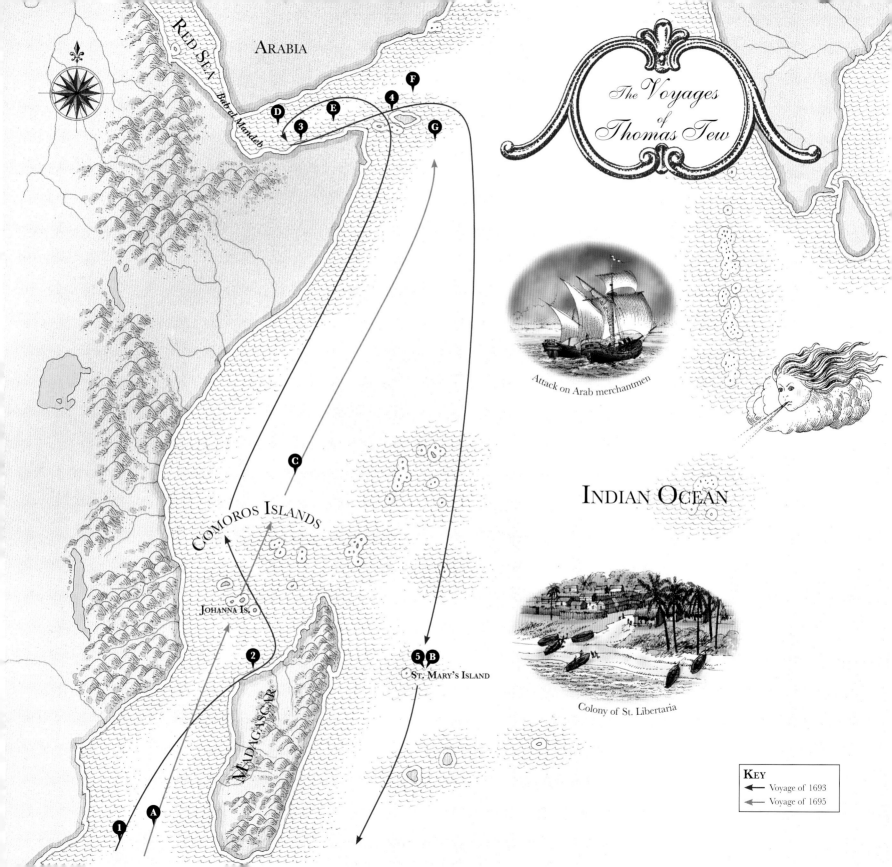

RED SEA

ARABIA

Bab el Mandeb

INDIAN OCEAN

COMOROS ISLANDS

JOHANNA IS.

MADAGASCAR

ST. MARY'S ISLAND

Attack on Arab merchantmen

The Voyages of Thomas Tew

Colony of St. Libertaria

KEY

← Voyage of 1693

← Voyage of 1695

Thomas Tew's Voyages in the Indian Ocean, 1693 and 1695

The Voyage of 1693

1 **May 1693** American colonial privateer Thomas Tew enters the Indian Ocean in the sloop *Amity*.

2 **June 1693** After taking on water on the coast of Madagascar, he sails north toward the Bab el Mandeb (Gate of Tears), where he hopes to intercept a rich Indian convoy.

3 **July 1693** Tew and his men capture a warship belonging to the Mughal Emperor of India, which yields a fortune in plunder.

4 Tew wants to continue to search for prizes, but his crew overrule him, and demand he return to the Americas.

5 He may well have put into St. Mary's Island on his return voyage, as it was later claimed he used the island as a temporary base.

The Voyage of 1695

A **May 1695** Tew returns to the Indian Ocean, and once again he heads toward the Bab el Mandeb.

B One source claimed Tew allied himself with pirates he encountered at St. Mary's Island. More likely he operated in agreement with other New England ships.

C Somewhere north of the Comoros Islands he encounters Henry Every, and the two join forces.

D **June 1695** Tew reaches the Bab el Mandeb, and cruises in search of prey.

E **July 1695** Tew and Every encounter two Indian ships: a warship and a merchantman. Although the merchantman *Ganj-i-Sawai* manages to escape, Tew decides to attack the warship *Fateh Mohammed* in the hope she is carrying treasure.

F In the battle that follows, the *Amity* comes alongside the *Fateh Mohammed*, but Tew is killed by a roundshot. With their captain dead the pirates surrender.

G Henry Every attacks the warship the following day, and rescues the survivors of Tew's crew. He then goes on to capture the Indian merchantman, a richly laden treasure ship.

there were other ships in the area he wanted to attack them, but his men overruled him. They didn't want to risk losing their plunder.

FRIENDS IN HIGH PLACES

Tew returned to his home port of Newport, Rhode Island, which he reached in April 1694. In theory, he had attacked a neutral ship, so Tew and his men should have been classed as pirates. But the Colonial Governor decided to view them as successful privateers, encouraged, according to rumor, by a healthy bribe. Tew was seen as something of a celebrity, and he even consorted with Governor Fletcher of New York, who was eager to hear about his success in the Red Sea. No doubt he was eager to back another expedition.

RETURN TO THE GATE OF TEARS

Tew returned to sea in November, this time sailing with three or four other ships, one of which was commanded by Henry Every. By June 1695, Tew was back in his old hunting ground of the Bab el Mandeb. It is highly likely that he knew what he was looking for, having learned that a Mughal treasure ship—the *Ganj-i-Sawai*—was due to sail past, escorted by a single warship, the *Fateh Mohammed*. While the accounts are a little vague, it seems that

Above: After taking the *Fateh Mohammed*, Every chased and captured the Mughal treasure ship *Ganj-i-Sawai*.

Tew attacked this powerful Indian warship. The attack was a blood-soaked failure—as the *Amity* came alongside, the Indian ship fired a full broadside and one shot struck Tew in the stomach. He died soon afterwards.

Thomas Tew had been a charismatic figure, and without him his men had no heart for the fight. They surrendered, throwing themselves on the mercy of the Indian captain. They were locked in the hold to await their fate at the hands of a vengeful emperor. Fate would intervene, however, and they would be spared the grim fate that awaited them in India.

Henry Every

Captain Henry Every was one of the few pirates who knew when to quit. He captured one of the richest pirate hauls in history—and then retired to live off his loot.

When Thomas Tew attacked the *Fateh Mohammed*, one of the other pirate ships supporting him was commanded by "Long Ben" Every, a former slave trader and privateer.

THE FATEH MOHAMMED

Born in Plymouth, England, and a sailor from his youth, Henry Every was part of a privateering crew that mutinied in 1694 off the West African coast. The men elected Every as their new captain and he immediately turned to piracy. The ship was renamed the *Fancy* (a popular pirate ship name), and Every began his cruise by capturing five English and Dutch ships off the Cape Verde Islands. There was now no turning back.

Every rounded the Cape of Good Hope and sailed north, landing in the Comoros Islands, which lie between the African continent and Madagascar. There he came upon a small French pirate ship, which he captured. By June he had met up with Thomas Tew, and was with him in the Bab el Mendeb when Tew was killed. Every was in the *Fancy* at the time, and he kept his distance from the Indian warship, shadowing her through the night. At dawn he made his move. He attacked the *Fateh Mohammed*, taking her by surprise. She might have been damaged in her fight against Tew, but in any event the Indian captain surrendered without putting up much of a fight. Every released the survivors of Tew's crew, massacred his Indian prisoners, and counted his loot. Every and his men were delighted—the plunder was later valued at over £50,000, the equivalent of $8.7 million today.

Left: Henry Every was the most successful of the Red Sea roundsmen. He earned a fortune in plunder when his pirate ship *Fancy* captured the Indian merchantman *Fateh Mohammed*.

Captain Every and the Treasure Ship, 1695

1 **Early 1695** After a mutiny in 1694, off the West African coast, Henry Every takes command of the English privateer and renames her the *Fancy*. He then sails her around the Cape of Good Hope into the Indian Ocean.

2 **Early June 1695** The pirates make their landfall at Johanna Island, in the Comoros Islands.

3 After careening his ship, Every captures and ransacks a French vessel, which also puts into the islands for water. Before releasing him and his ship, Every gives the French captain a letter, where he claims to be a law-abiding privateer, rather than a mutineer turned pirate.

4 **Late June 1695** Falls in with Thomas Tew, and together they decide to sail north to the Bab el Mandeb.

5 **July 1695** Tew and Every attack a lucrative Indian convoy, and Tew is killed when trying to capture the Indian warship *Fateh Mohammed*. The survivors of his crew are taken prisoner.

Pirate squadron

6 Every shadows the Indian warship, and attacks her at dawn. The *Fateh Mohammed* is captured, yielding a haul worth more than £50,000. From her crew, Every learns that the warship is escorting the *Ganj-i-Sawai*, a treasure ship belonging to the Mughal Emperor.

7 The pirates then shadow and attacked the *Ganj-i-Sawai*. A lucky shot brings down the Indian treasure ship's foremast, and Every brings the *Fancy* alongside and boards her. He captures the *Ganj-i-Sawai* after a brutal struggle.

8 Every sails to the French island colony of La Réunion, where he shares out the plunder between his crew. Each man is given the equivalent of £1,000 in coins, plus a handful of gems.

9 He then sails back into Atlantic and reaches the West Indies, where his crew disperse. The fate of Henry Every remains a mystery to this day.

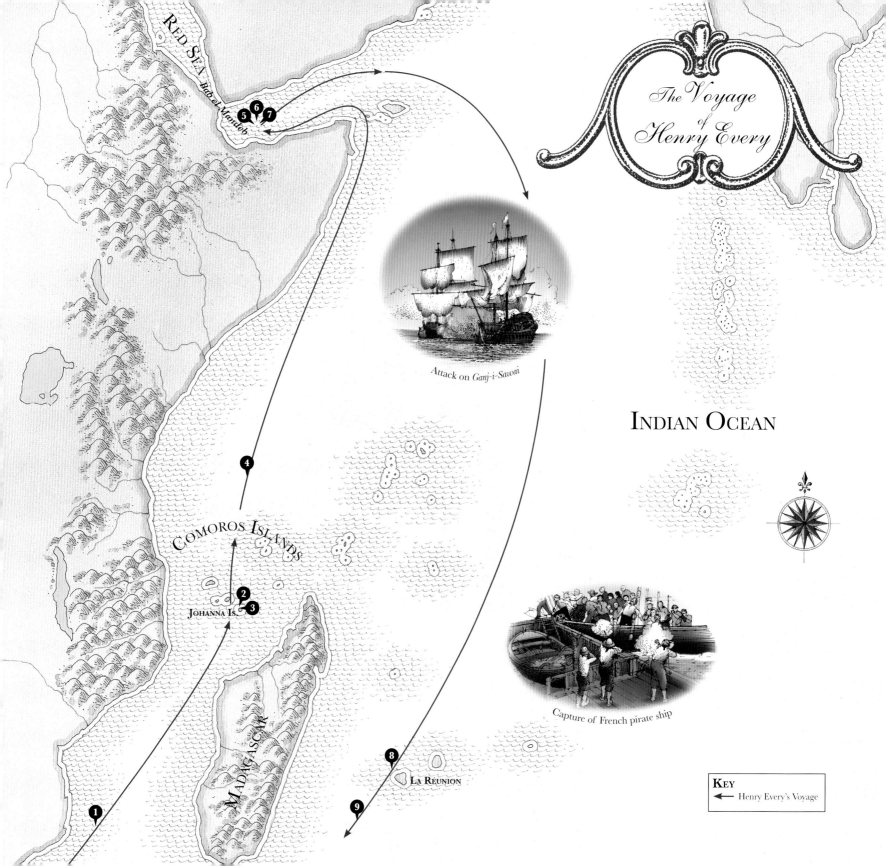

The Voyage
of
Henry Every

RED SEA
Bab el Mandeb

INDIAN OCEAN

Attack on *Ganj-i-Sawai*

Capture of French pirate ship

COMOROS ISLANDS

JOHANNA IS.

MADAGASCAR

LA RÉUNION

KEY
← Henry Every's Voyage

THE MUGHAL TREASURE SHIP

While this haul was impressive, Every abandoned his prize to hunt down a far richer one. After all, the warship was merely the convoy escort; the real plunder was on board the treasure ship *Ganj-i-Sawai*. She was known as a tough opponent, carrying 62 guns and more than 500 Mughal soldiers. However, the *Fancy* carried 46 guns and her 150-man crew had just been reinforced by Tew's survivors. He tracked down the treasure ship and attacked her. Every was lucky. A shot hit the Indian ship's mainmast, causing chaos on board. Every brought the

Fancy alongside the *Ganj-i-Sawai* and leaped aboard, followed by his men. The bitter hand-to-hand fight lasted for two hours but eventually the pirates emerged victorious.

Every knew that as the East India Company and the Mughal Emperor were allies, the attack would cause a major political storm. He quit the Indian ocean and sailed to the West Indies, where his crew dispersed. Henry Every then disappeared from the history books. It was later claimed he returned to England and ended his days as a country gentleman. Whatever his fate, he remains one of the few pirates to steal a fortune, and live to enjoy his ill-gotten gains.

Above: Pirates like Henry Every divided their plunder fairly among their crews. This is captured in Howard Pyle's painting *So the Treasure was Divided*.

The Treasure Haul

Following their victory over the *Ganj-i-Sawai*, Every and his men spent the next few days counting their loot, torturing or abusing their captives, and transferring the spoils to the *Fancy*. The haul was unimaginable—valued at around £350,000 ($64 million today). Every then headed for the island of La Réunion where the treasure was divided, each man receiving £1,000 in coins, plus a handful of gems. It remains one of the most successful pirate attacks in history—more so because the pirates lived to tell the tale.

Captain Kidd

William Kidd is known less for piratical success than for failure, and the price he paid for it. He was one of the most notorious, and unfortunate, pirates in history.

When Thomas Tew was visiting the Governor of New York, another sea captain, William Kidd, was living in the city, having earned a reputation as a daring privateer.

KIDD THE PRIVATEER

Born in Scotland, around 1654, Kidd spent some 20 years at sea before he gained command of his first ship in 1689, the privateer *Blessed William*. It was snatched by a mutinous crew who turned to piracy, but Kidd eventually captured a replacement from the French and returned to New York, where he helped defend the governor during an attempted coup. A hero, Kidd's reputation was now made.

In 1695, Kidd sailed to England, hoping to win a privateering contract. Instead he met Richard, Earl of Bellomont, who had just been appointed as the new governor of New York.

Left: Captain William Kidd, painted by Howard Pyle, shown on his privateer the *Adventure Galley*, with the city of New York in the background.

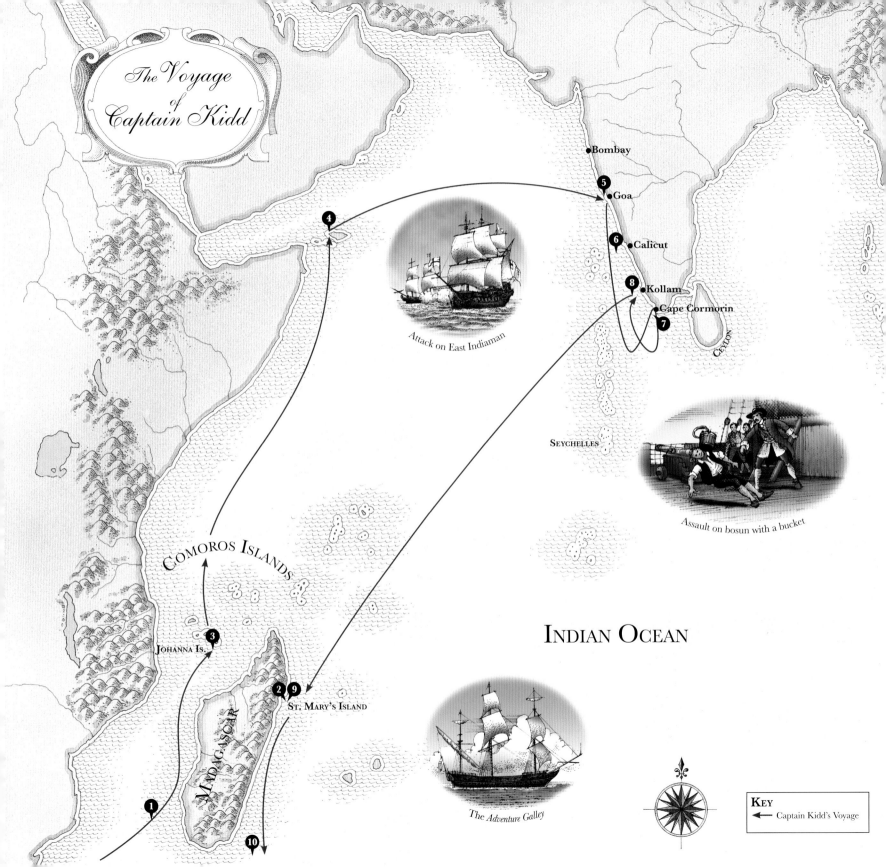

The Voyage of Captain Kidd

Bombay

5 Goa

6 Calicut

8 Kollam

Cape Cormorin

7

CEYLON

Attack on East Indiaman

Assault on bosun with a bucket

SEYCHELLES

4

COMOROS ISLANDS

INDIAN OCEAN

3

JOHANNA IS.

2 **9**

ST. MARY'S ISLAND

MADAGASCAR

1

10

The *Adventure Galley*

KEY
← Captain Kidd's Voyage

William Kidd's Disastrous Voyage, 1697–98

1 **January 1697** Captain Kidd, commanding the *Adventure Galley*, makes landfall on Madagascar, possibly on its western coast.

2 Plans to attack the pirate haven on St. Mary's Island, but decides he lacks the manpower he needs to guarantee success.

3 **March 1697** Takes on water on Johanna Island, in the Comoros Islands. There he encounters an East Indiaman, whose captain thinks Kidd is acting suspiciously. As many of his crew are sick, he remains in the islands for four months.

4 **August 1697** Kidd attacks an Indian convoy, but is driven off by the appearance of an East India Company warship. This is an act of piracy—he has stepped over the line.

5 Sails to the Malabar coast, and cruises off Goa in search of a prize. His only success is the capture of the small Dutch trading ship *Rupparell*, which he keeps.

6 **November 1697** Encounters two Portuguese warships, who attack him, rightly presuming the *Adventure Galley* is a pirate ship. However, Kidd manages to escape and resumes his cruise.

7 **January 30, 1698** Off Cape Cormorin, attacks and captures the *Queddah Merchant*, a rich Indian merchant ship. He uses the money raised to give his crew a share of the plunder.

Attack on the Queddah Merchant

8 **February 1698** Puts into the Dutch port of Quillon (now Kollam), where he sells some of the cargo taken from the *Queddah Merchant*. He remains in the port for a month.

9 **April 1698** Kidd puts in to the pirate haven of St. Mary's Island, where he abandons the *Adventure Galley*, which by then is badly rotted anyway. Many of his crew abandon him and join the pirates.

10 **June 1698** Now short of crew, Captain Kidd abandons his Dutch prize and sails home in the *Queddah Merchant*.

Left: Captain Kidd's privateering "letter of marque" of 1696, signed by King William III, has survived and is housed in London's National Archives.

The Earl talked Kidd into accepting the command of a newly built privateer—the 300-ton *Adventure Galley*, with 34 guns—a vessel that Bellomont and his backers hoped would yield a healthy profit. A letter of marque was arranged, and it might even have been implied that Kidd could attack Arab or Indian ships in an attempt to repeat Tew's great coup of three years before.

KIDD'S CRUISE

Captain Kidd sailed for New York in May 1696, where he recruited an experienced crew. He then crossed the Atlantic, rounded the Cape of Good Hope, and entered the Indian ocean. He made landfall in Madagscar in January 1697. He might have planned to attack the pirates of St. Mary's Island but he eventually continued on to the Comoros Islands, where he took on water and was viewed with suspicion by two passing East Indiamen. By this stage, Kidd had lost a third of his crew to disease.

By August, the *Adventure Galley* was in the Bab el Mandeb. Kidd later claimed that he was hunting for pirates, but it seems just as likely that he was looking for another Mughal treasure ship. He did attack one Indian convoy, but backed off when he discovered it was being escorted by an East India Company warship. Kidd was now desperate for success in any form.

He set course for India's Malabar Coast, where he hoped to find a rich Indian prize, but all he encountered was a small Arab merchantman and a Dutch vessel. By this stage his crew were mutinous, and Kidd seized on the suspected ringleader—his gunner William Moore—and beat him to

During an argument, Kidd hit his gunner with a bucket, which fractured his skull and killed him.

death with a wooden bucket. This drastic action might have staved off a mutiny but it would have serious repercussions later.

Kidd the Pirate

Kidd's big break came on January 30, 1698, while he was cruising off Cape Comorin, the southern tip of India. He encountered a large Indian merchantman, the *Queddah Merchant*, homeward bound from the Far East. Kidd ran up the French flag and forced her to surrender. Unfortunately her captain

Below: Captain Kidd buried his plunder on Gardiner's Island off Long Island, before sailing into New York. The treasure was later recovered by the authorities.

was English, which meant that Kidd could be identified. Technically, he had attacked a neutral ship, and was therefore a pirate.

The haul amounted to little more than £15,000 ($2.6 million today)—a far cry from the fortune won by Tew or Every. Kidd sold most of her cargo of silks and spices on the Indian coast, then sailed to St. Mary's Island where he abandoned the *Adventure Galley*. He shifted his cargo and crew onto the *Queddah Merchant* and sailed back to the Americas. Landing on Hispaniola, he learned he was regarded as a wanted pirate. Kidd left his ship and took passage north to New York, where he hoped his backer Lord Bellomont would make everything right.

A Political Pawn

As an insurance policy Kidd hid what remained of his plunder on Gardiner's Island, off Long Island, then tried to see Bellomont. However, the earl refused to meet Kidd, and five days later, in July 1699, the privateer-turned-pirate was arrested. He was forced to reveal where he had buried his plunder, and after a year in prison, Bellomont shipped Kidd to London to stand trial.

The political climate had changed while Kidd was away. The war with France was over and piracy was seen as a serious problem. The last thing Bellomont needed was a political scandal—and the fact that he had backed a pirate would have been exactly that. To avoid embarrassment, Kidd had to be tried, convicted, and executed before the truth could be exposed. Captain Kidd was abandoned to his fate by Bellomont.

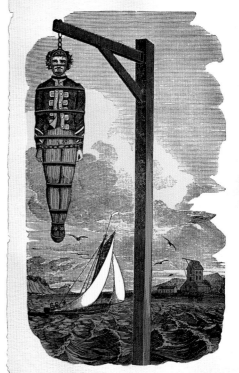

Pirate Hangings

Pirates were tried according to Admiralty law, and so executions traditionally took place on a waterfront, below the high water mark. After being hanged, Kidd's body met the grisly fate of many executed pirates—it was covered in tar and hung in a cage overlooking a busy shipping lane, as a deterrent to other would-be pirates. The body would remain there until there was nothing left of it but bleached bones.

Above: Kidd's dead body was tarred and suspended in an iron cage for 20 years over the River Thames, London, as a warning to those who would be pirates.

After his trial on May 8, 1701, damned by agents of the East India Company and condemned for murdering William Moore, Kidd was sentenced to death. On May 23, he was taken to Wapping and hanged by the banks of the River Thames—the traditional fate of condemned pirates.

Edward England

While most pirates of this time developed a reputation for ferocity, Edward England was kind hearted enough to free his prisoners.

Captain England did not believe in killing captives unless it was absolutely necessary. However, a great act of clemency would ultimately lead to his downfall.

ENGLAND THE IRISHMAN

Despite his name, England was an Irishman, whose original surname was probably Seegar. A privateer turned pirate when the Jamaican sloop he was serving on was captured by pirates, he eventually found himself in New Providence in the Bahamas. In 1718, he accepted a royal pardon from governor Rogers, but within a year was back to his old ways, operating off the coast of West Africa.

By the spring of 1720, England had reached Madagascar, by which time he had been elected as a pirate captain. He cruised in consort with a shipmate—John Taylor. When they captured a large merchantman, England took her as his 34-gun flagship, renaming her the *Fancy*. He now had a pirate ship large and powerful enough to take on most of the East India Company ships.

The pirate Edward England, pictured on Johanna Island, while his pirate ship *Fancy* takes on the East Indiaman *Cassandra*. The captain's leniency after his victory earned him the enmity of his crew.

THE FIGHT WITH THE *CASSANDRA*

In August 1720, the pirates put in to Johanna Island, where they planned to refill their water casks. Instead they found three ships at anchor—a Dutch merchantman and two British Indiamen. Two of these ships cut their anchor cables and fled, but Captain Macrae of the Indiaman *Cassandra* was made of sterner stuff. He sailed out to give battle. While Taylor chased the two fleeing ships, England steered for the *Cassandra*. A brutal contest followed, with the ships pounding at each other three times, by which time

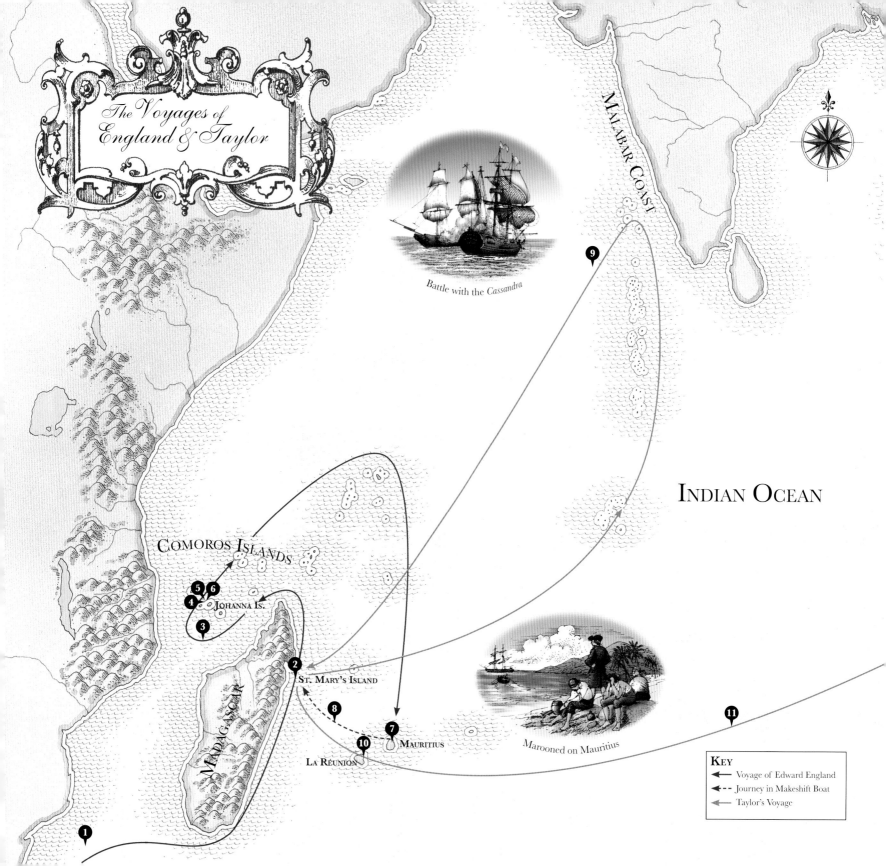

The Voyages of England & Taylor

MALABAR COAST

Battle with the *Cassandra*

INDIAN OCEAN

COMOROS ISLANDS

JOHANNA IS.

MADAGASCAR

ST. MARY'S ISLAND

LA RÉUNION

MAURITIUS

Marooned on Mauritius

KEY

⟵ Voyage of Edward England

◀--- Journey in Makeshift Boat

⟵ Taylor's Voyage

Edward England and John Taylor's Voyages, 1720–21

❶ Spring 1720 Edward England, commanding the sloop *Pearl*, arrives in the Indian Ocean together with a colleague, John Taylor, who commands the *Victory*.

❷ The pirates spend several months in port, enjoying the attention of local women. Most probably this takes place on the once busy pirate haven of St. Mary's Island. By 1720, the island is all but empty.

❸ July 1720 England and Taylor cruise the waters between Madagascar and the African coast, capturing several ships. England takes one of these for himself and renames her the *Fancy*.

❹ August 1720 The pirate ships head north, and on August 27, they make landfall at Johanna Island, in the Comoros Islands.

❺ There they encounter a Dutch ship, and two English East Indiamen. When two of them flee, Taylor gives chase and England engages the remaining vessel—the East Indiaman *Cassandra*. After a hard fight the *Cassandra* runs aground and is captured.

❻ England decides to free his prisoners, and allows them to sail to Bombay in the damaged *Fancy*. He keeps the *Cassandra* for himself.

❼ March 1721 England and Taylor resume their cruise, but eventually fall out over England's leniency to the prisoners. England and three supporters are duly marooned on the island of Mauritius.

❽ May 1721 England and his men build a boat and sail her to St. Mary's Island, making landfall there during the late summer. England dies on the island several months later, a beggar and destitute.

❾ June 1721 Taylor enjoyes a successful cruise off the Malabar Coast, then returns to St. Mary's Island, where he careens his ship.

Careening ship

❿ After joining forces with a French pirate, Taylor sailes to La Réunion, where he captures a rich Portuguese merchantman.

⓫ Rather than head back to Madagascar, Taylor elects to sail home via the Pacific Ocean, and reaches Panama. His crew then disperse, taking their plunder with them.

both the *Cassandra* and the *Fancy* were badly damaged. His ship foundering, Macrae decided to beach his vessel, and his crew scrambled ashore and hid on the island.

THE PRISONERS' LUCK

When Taylor returned, England got him to help tow the *Cassandra* off the beach. He began repairing the ship, turning her into his new flagship. After seven days, starvation forced Macrae and his men to surrender. Much to his surprise, and to Taylor's fury, England didn't execute his prisoners on the spot. Instead he granted them their freedom, allowing the Scottish captain and his men to sail away to safety in the battered *Fancy*.

As for England, his act of clemency lost him the respect of his pirate crew. Six months later, after an uneventful

John Taylor (Active 1719–21)

John Taylor continued his cruise after marooning his captain, capturing several lucrative prizes. At one stage, he even joined forces with the French pirate known as La Buse (The Buzzard). After capturing a plump Portuguese ship, the two pirate crews parted company, and by May 1723, Taylor was reported off Panama, on the far side of the Pacific. His fate after that is unknown.

cruise, England was deposed as captain and marooned on the island of Mauritius with three loyal crewmen. The four men managed to build a raft and sail it to St. Mary's Island, which they reached some time in 1724. England and his shipmates survived "on the charity of some of their brethren," and the pirate captain died in squalid poverty shortly afterwards.

Above: The atmospheric *Marooned* by Howard Pyle, 1909, captures the lonely fate of pirates abandoned by their fellows, as happened to Edward England and three of his crew members marooned on the island of Mauritius.

Madagascar

Lying beside the lucrative trade routes between the Cape of Good Hope and India, with its many secluded bays, Madagascar was the perfect location for a pirate haven.

For a quarter of a century Madagascar, and particularly the island of St. Mary's off its northeast coast, was one of the most notorious pirate strongholds in the world.

THE IDEAL LOCATION

Madagascar is more than 1,000 (1,600km) miles long, and 300 miles wide (480km), and lies in the Indian Ocean, some 250 miles (400km) off the East African coast. That placed it astride the major shipping lanes used by the English and Dutch East Indian Companies. The island contained numerous secluded bays where pirates could hide and if attacked, the hinterland was so vast that pursuit was all but impossible. Madagascar was also the first good watering place for ships after they'd rounded the Cape of Good Hope. Just as importantly, it was an easy sail with wind and tide to the pirate hunting ground at the mouth of the Red Sea.

A SAFE REFUGE

By the 1690s, pirates had started to use harbors on the eastern side of the island— Ranter Bay (now the Baie d'Antongil), St. Augustine's Bay, and St. Mary's Island (Île Sainte-Marie), which lay off the north-eastern side of Madagascar. Other popular pirate anchorages or rendezvous points in

Although this depiction of the pirate settlement on the tiny island of St. Mary's is probably inaccurate in terms of scale and proportions, it captures the makeshift nature of this active but ramshackle pirate den.

the Indian Ocean were Johanna Island in the Comoros Archipelago, and the islands of Mauritius and La Réunion to the east. St. Mary's Island was the most popular. In 1700, it was claimed that about 1,500 pirates used the island as a base, operating in 17 ships.

The heyday of Madagascar as a pirate base was short-lived, however. In 1705, the East Indian Company instituted a convoy system, which denied these pirates any rich and easy pickings. The waters of the Indian Ocean were also increasingly patrolled by the Royal Navy and by the East India Company, which maintained its own pirate-hunting squadron in the region. Denied the chance of plunder, most pirates drifted away, some seeking regular employment and others joining the Angrian pirates of the Indian coast. By 1711, it was reported that fewer than 60 or 70 pirates remained in Madagascar.

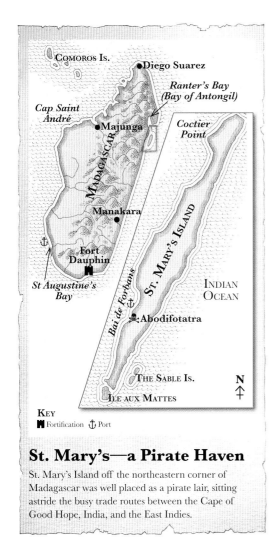

COMOROS IS.

Diego Suarez

Ranter's Bay
(Bay of Antongil)

Cap Saint
André

Coctier
Point

Majunga

MADAGASCAR

Manakara

ST. MARY'S ISLAND

Fort
Dauphin

INDIAN
OCEAN

St Augustine's
Bay

Bai de Forbans

Abodifotatra

THE SABLE IS.

N

ILE AUX MATTES

KEY
Fortification   Port

St. Mary's—a Pirate Haven

St. Mary's Island off the northeastern corner of Madagascar was well placed as a pirate lair, sitting astride the busy trade routes between the Cape of Good Hope, India, and the East Indies.

THE UTOPIA OF LIBERTARIA

In his 1724 *General History of the Pyrates*, Captain Johnson tells how a French pirate—James Misson—established an egalitarian pirate colony in Madagascar, where all property was held in common, slavery was abolished, and everyone was equal. Few people now believe such an idealistic community existed, but that the chapter about this pirate utopia was a thinly disguised political essay, extolling the virtues of ideals

Right: A pirate enjoying the comforts of Libertaria, while a colleague watches for passing ships.

first proposed by the Levellers during the English Civil War. It also reflects something of the feelings of injustice felt by seamen, and the way piracy was seen as offering some form of freedom from the restrictive rules and regulations of ordered society.

Misson's colony was supposed to have been called "Libertaria", and its principal settlement boasted stone houses, warehouses, and forts. The reality was very different. According to a report of life on St. Mary's Island in 1711, fewer than 70 former pirates remained on Madagascar, "the most of them very poor and despicable, even to the natives".

The idea of pirates conducting a social experiment in a tropical setting is appealing, but it flies in the face of what we know about pirates. In fact there are strong indications that pirate life in Madagascar was just as hierarchical as in any other criminal society. One pirate, Abraham Samuel, called himself the "King of Port Dolphin", while James Plantain set himself up as the "King of Ranter Bay."

THE LAST MADAGASCAN PIRATE

St. Mary's Island enjoyed a brief resurgence as a pirate haven in 1719, when the pirate Christopher Condent established a temporary base there. He found that a few pirates still lived on the island and used their knowledge of the seas to help him search for prey. In 1720, he captured a rich Arab merchantman off Bombay, yielding a fortune in plunder. Like Henry Every before him, Condent knew when to quit. He paid off his crew and sailed to La Réunion, where he accepted a French pardon.

By the time Edward England arrived at St. Mary's Island in 1724, the island had become little more than a derelict tropical backwater. However, traces of pirates still remain today. The island boasts a pirate cemetery, and in recent years maritime archaeologists have uncovered the remains of several wrecked and abandoned ships—one of which may well be Captain Kidd's *Adventure Galley*.

Below: The pirate cemetery on St. Mary's Island, one of several reminders of the island's pirate past.

The Golden Age: New Providence

Governments used privateers as a form of licensed pirate in times of war. However, not all of these men were happy to return to law-abiding work when the war ended and their activities were no longer authorized.

Above: Howard Pyle's *Who shall be Captain?* captures the drama of the Golden Age of Piracy.

During the War of the Spanish Succession (1701–13), Britain and Holland found themselves at war with France and Spain. Huge profits were made by privateers on both sides, and ports in the Caribbean became privateering centers. Then, in April 1713 the Treaty of Utrecht was signed, and the privateers were out of a job.

Many returned to regular employment, helped by the boom in maritime commerce, which was one of the benefits of the peace. But there were others who preferred to continue hunting down ships. As peace had been declared, this made these men pirates. In fact, the onset of peace led to a significant upsurge in piracy, first in the Caribbean, then along the Atlantic Seaboard of North America, and finally off the West African coast. This was the period that saw all the historical characters we associate with piracy during its heyday—Blackbeard, "Black Bart" Roberts, "Calico Jack" Rackam, "Black Sam" Bellamy, Charles Vane, Anne Bonny, Mary Read, and Howell Davis. For a few brief years, piracy was a scourge that threatened the fragile economy of the American colonies and played havoc with trade between Europe and the Caribbean.

This wave of piracy only lasted a decade or so. Historians have often claimed it lasted from about 1690 until 1730, a period that encompasses the end of the buccaneering era in the Spanish Main and the final crushing of mass piracy in the 1720s. In reality this era was even shorter, as before 1713 large-scale piracy was limited to the Indian Ocean. The real upsurge in piracy began after 1713 and lasted for a little over a decade.

Today, historians often call this period the "Golden Age of Piracy." While the phrase itself is a modern one, it does convey the fact that this is the era that incorporates all our modern notions of historical pirates. The fact it only lasted a decade shows just how influential the pirates of those days were, mainly because they provided material for all the pirate fiction writers, film directors, and biographers that followed.

The Golden Age

In truth, the "Golden Age" spanned little more than a decade, and it ended with the eradication of large-scale piracy during the 1720s.

The phrase "Golden Age of Piracy" was invented by historians who wanted to speak about the classic pirate era— the time of Blackbeard, "Black Bart" Roberts, and "Calico Jack" Rackam.

Piracy flourishes when legal employment is hard to find, and in safe havens beyond the reach of the authorities. This applies to a region like Somalia today, just as much as it did to the Bahamas in the early 18th century.

The significant outbreak of piracy during this time was due to several factors, one being the end of the buccaneering era and an increasingly anti-piratical policy by colonial authorities. The other was the peace that brought an end to legitimate privateering contracts. The end of the war created a glut of sailors skilled in the art of naval warfare. Thousands of former privateersmen were faced with the option of unemployment, poorly paid service in merchant ships, or turning to piracy. Many chose piracy, and flocked to the new pirate haven of New Providence in the Bahamas. Some former privateers, such as Benjamin Hornigold, tried to avoid attacking ships of their own nationality in an attempt to maintain an illusion of legitimacy. Others like Blackbeard and Charles Vane had no such scruples.

Why Was This Era Called the Golden Age of Piracy?

The origin of the phrase is a little difficult to track down. It was never used in the early 18th century, which means it was invented after the "Golden Age" came to an end. Robert Louis Stevenson never used it, and while most modern pirate historians have used the phrase, none of us invented it. The likely candidate is Rafael Sabatini (1875–1950), the British author who penned pirate novels such as *Captain Blood* (1922) and *The Black Swan* (1932), both of which were turned into Hollywood swashbuckling movies. In the end, the source of the phrase isn't really that important—it still serves as a useful shorthand for the classic era of piracy.

Above: An early 18th-century personification of America, threatened by the specter of piracy.

PARDONS AND EXECUTIONS

The Golden Age of Piracy came to an end when these pirates were hunted down and killed as part of a concerted anti-piracy campaign. The authorities used a number of powerful tools. One of the most effective was the offer of a royal pardon. The idea behind this was that many pirates didn't really want to be criminals but had been encouraged to cross the line into lawlessness. A pardon offered them a chance to step back from the brink and into legality. Royal pardons greatly reduced the number of active pirates, allowing the authorities to concentrate their resources on hunting down the most serious offenders.

Another method was to use the weight of the law as a means of intimidation. A series of high-profile pirate trials and executions took place, and in most cases the bodies of those executed were displayed as a deterrent to others. Charles Vane, "Calico Jack" Rackam, and Stede Bonnet were all executed in a glare of publicity designed to make others think twice about turning to piracy.

A VIOLENT AGE

As well as these measures, the hunting down of pirates was stepped up. Pirate-hunting warships made the waters of the Caribbean and the Atlantic seaboard unsafe for pirates, forcing those who remained to avoid well-patrolled waters such as the Bahamas or the east coast of America. A final deterrent was the string of successes that saw the death of some of the leading pirates of the day, including Blackbeard and Black Bart Roberts. Their deaths in battle helped demonstrate to others that the odds weren't stacked in the pirates' favor.

The phrase "Golden Age of Piracy" might sound romantic, but it fails to encompass the threat piracy posed at the time or the violent way these pirates carried out their attacks. These were desperate men, with few scruples. The truth was far removed from the romance and glamor of piracy as we see it today. During this so-called "Golden Age," the life of a pirate was hard, and inevitably ended in death at sword point or the end of a rope.

What Did These Pirates Plunder?

Unlike the pirates of fiction, the real pirates of this period rarely captured ships carrying treasure. Their prey was more likely to be the merchant ships that plied between Europe and the Caribbean or the American colonies, carrying mundane cargoes of sugar, timber, cloth, slaves, tobacco, wine, rum, or manufactured goods. The problem was that in order to make money the pirates had to sell the goods they plundered. To do this they needed a friendly port where merchants could buy the goods, which is why pirate havens such as New Providence were so important. Without such a market, pirates were unable to profit from their crimes. That meant the business of preventing piracy involved hunting them down on the high seas and denying them the use of friendly ports.

Right: This small two-masted bark is typical of the vessels that sailed the waters of the Americas during this period, and which regularly fell victim to pirates.

New Providence

For a brief period, the island of New Providence in the Bahamas was a bustling center of pirate activity. More importantly, the pirates who used it as a base included some of the most notorious characters in pirate history—and there was no law to stop them.

Above: The tranquil Bahamian harbor of Nassau on New Providence island, seen here in the 19th century, was once the most notorious pirate den in the Americas.

The story of the Bahamas as a pirate haven really began with a mass shipwreck. In June 1715, the returning Spanish treasure fleet was caught by a hurricane as it sailed north past the Bahamas. Most of its ships were wrecked on the Florida coast.

THE SPANISH TREASURE WRECKS

The Spanish sent a salvage expedition to recover the lost silver, but when news of the disaster spread, others had a similar idea. In November, some 300 British seamen attacked the salvage camp, and made off with over 60,000 pieces-of-eight. They were led by Captain Henry Jennings, a former privateer, who also managed to capture a Spanish merchantman laden with another haul of recovered treasure.

Jennings returned to the camp in January 1716, and this time his men seized more than

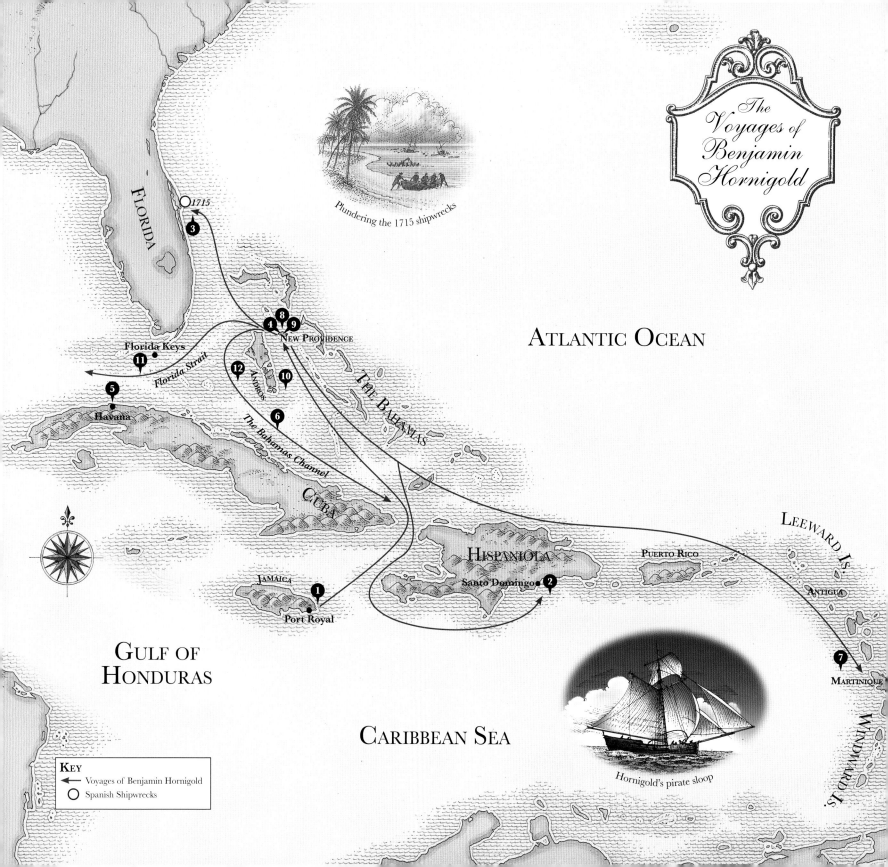

The Voyages of
Benjamin
Hornigold

Plundering the 1715 shipwrecks

ATLANTIC OCEAN

FLORIDA

○ 1715

❸

Florida Keys

⓫

Florida Strait

❹ ❽ ❾
NEW PROVIDENCE

⓬

ANDROS

⓾

THE BAHAMAS

❺

Havana

❻

The Bahamas Channel

CUBA

GULF OF
HONDURAS

JAMAICA

❶

Port Royal

HISPANIOLA

Santo Domingo ❷

PUERTO RICO

LEEWARD IS.

ANTIGUA

❼

MARTINIQUE

WINDWARD IS.

CARIBBEAN SEA

Hornigold's pirate sloop

KEY
→ Voyages of Benjamin Hornigold
○ Spanish Shipwrecks

Benjamin Hornigold, Pirate and Pirate Hunter, 1712–19

1 **1713** Benjamin Hornigold is a privateer, based in Port Royal, Jamaica. In May, word of a peace treaty reaches the island, and all privateering letters of marque are canceled.

2 **June 1714** Hornigold is mentioned by the Spanish governor of Santo Domingo, having attacked ships off the port.

3 **November 1715** Hornigold arrives in New Providence and trades with the locals. He is also associated with the plunder of Spanish treasure wrecks on the Florida coast.

4 **February 1716** Returns to New Providence, and establishes a base there. It soon develops into a pirate haven.

Waterfront of New Providence

5 **June 1716** It is reported that Hornigold is responsible for the capture of Spanish shipping off Havana, in the Florida Straits.

6 **August 1716** Hornigold cruises the waters of the Bahamas Channel, but limits his attacks to French and Spanish ships. During this period Blackbeard serves as one of his crew.

7 **Summer 1717** He is listed as being the ringleader of the New Providence pirates, and it is reported that he is operating off Martinique. Around this time Blackbeard leaves Hornigold, to forge his own career.

8 **December 1717** News of a royal pardon to pirates reaches the Bahamas, and Hornigold encourages his colleagues to accept the offer of clemency.

9 **July 1718** Hornigold signs the pardon and offers his support to Governor Woodes Rogers when he arrives in the Bahamas. He becomes a pirate hunter.

10 **September 1718** Hunts for the renegade pirate Charles Vane. Although he never finds Vane, off Andros he captures a pirate called Yeats, who was operating in Bahamian waters.

11 **January 1719** Hunts for pirates off the Florida Keys.

12 **Summer 1719** Hornigold and his sloop are overtaken by a hurricane in the Bahamas Channel and their ship founders. There are no survivors.

120,000 pieces-of-eight. The Spanish learned their lesson and fortified their camp until the salvage operation was completed. When they left, the British treasure hunters returned, sifting the sand for coins that the Spaniards might have missed. Technically, Florida was Spanish territory, and the British government closed their ports to the looters. Jennings and his men needed a friendly port—they chose New Providence in The Bahamas.

THE NEW PORT ROYAL

Merchants from Jamaica established trading posts there, while bars, brothels, gambling dens, and weapons shops sprang up virtually overnight. This gave pirates access to a friendly port, somewhere they could sell their stolen goods, recruit new crew members, repair their ships, and spend their ill-gotten gains. In effect it had become a smaller, more temporary version of Port Royal, the Jamaican town, in its buccaneering heyday. By the summer of 1716 colonial governors were complaining that pirates had taken over the Bahamas, and the islands were fast becoming a haven for criminals.

A Pirate Stronghold

In 1716, New Providence was already a small pirate haven, a shanty town that provided pirates with a small marketplace for stolen goods. In November 1715, the pirate Benjamin Hornigold arrived here and began to use the island as a base. The arrival of Henry Jennings and the treasure hunters six months later transformed the island settlement, and it rapidly grew into a bustling criminal den.

Right: This sign outside the town of Vero Beach, Florida, marks the site of the shipwrecks of the 1715 Spanish treasure fleet.

New Providence was the perfect location. The 60-square-mile (155sq km) island lay close to the shipping lanes between the Caribbean and the American colonies, and it was close to the Florida wreck sites. The island's harbor (now Nassau) was large enough to hold a hundred ships, while the island itself was well supplied with food and water. It even boasted a small fort that had been built by the island's original settlers. Best of all, while it was officially a British colony, there was no governor there to enforce the rule of law.

By the summer of 1717, more than 500 pirates were reportedly using the island as a base including Benjamin Hornigold, Charles Vane, Henry Jennings, Jack Rackam, Edward Teach (Blackbeard), and Sam Bellamy. The only form of law was imposed by the pirate captains themselves. Eventually the British authorities in London decided they had had enough. They appointed a governor— Woodes Rogers—whose orders were to drive the pirates from the Bahamas and to impose law and order on the region.

SITE OF SURVIVORS' AND SALVAGERS' CAMP THE 1715 FLEET

Woodes Rogers

In 1718, a new governor arrived in New Providence with orders to tame the Bahamas. What followed was one of the most dramatic showdowns in pirate history.

A former English privateer, Woodes Rogers was appointed by the British crown as royal governor of the Bahamas, with orders to clear the islands of pirates.

When the British government was looking for someone to tame the pirates of the Bahamas, Woodes Rogers was the ideal candidate—a man who had almost crossed the line into piracy himself. Leading a three-year privateering voyage against the Spanish, he had circumnavigated the globe, and on his return to Bristol in 1711, he had written a best-selling book about his experiences.

When Rogers arrived in New Providence, it was home to around 2,000 pirates, many of whom had no intention of taking orders from a royal official. Fortunately, Rogers was just one element of a greater anti-piracy campaign. Another was the offering of a royal pardon—issued originally by order of King Willaim III, and re-issued 15 years later by George I—which was sent to New Providence in December 1717.

THE DIE-HARDS' REFUSAL

The pirates of New Providence were divided into two groups: those led by Benjamin Hornigold who wanted to accept the pardon, and the rest, led by Charles Vane, who refused to surrender. A few months later, a British Royal Navy frigate arrived and her captain left with the names of more than 200 leading pirates eager to accept the king's offer. Many others, such as Blackbeard, had already left the island, never to return. However, that still left the die-hards, men like Charles Vane, who were unlikely to capitulate without a fight.

Woodes Rogers (c.1679–1732)

Rogers grew up in Bristol, England. His father was a shipowner who operated privateers during the War of the League of Augsburg (1688–97). His son learned the business from his father, and by the time the War of the Spanish Succession (1701–13) began, he was operating his own privateering vessels. In 1708, he commanded two ships—the *Duke* and the *Duchess*—and sailed them around Cape Horn and into the Pacific. He caused havoc to Spanish shipping, raided coastal settlements, and rescued the castaway Alexander Selkirk—the man on whom Daniel Defoe would later base his portrayal of Robinson Crusoe.

Above: The governor of the Bahamas, Woodes Rogers, and his family, as depicted by William Hogarth in 1729.

CHARLES VANE MAKES HIS EXIT

On July 26, 1718, Governor Rogers arrived off New Providence with several vessels, which included three small British warships. He anchored offshore and planned to make his entrance the following morning. That was when Charles Vane made his move. Under cover of darkness he sneaked his men on board his sloop the *Ranger*, then set course for the harbor entrance. He'd also stolen another ship and fitted it out as a fireship—a burning, blazing missile that he aimed at the nearest Royal Naval warship. While Rogers' ships were busy avoiding the fireship, Vane slipped past them, firing broadside as he went. The pirate sloop sailed on into the darkness, taking all of Vane's die-hard pirates with him. It was as dramatic an exit as any pirate could wish for.

ENTER BENJAMIN HORNIGOLD

More than 1,000 pirates remained on New Providence, and Rogers was greeted by some semblance of a welcoming ceremony when he eventually stepped ashore—with the charred wreckage of Vane's fireship smoldering behind him. Of these 1000 pirates, more than 600 were pardoned, while the remainder sneaked away over the next few weeks. Rogers realized he needed the help of Benjamin Hornigold and Henry Jennings, but Jennings wanted no part in government. He retired to Bermuda, along with the remains of his Spanish treasure.

Hornigold was given a commission as a pirate hunter, and while Rogers organized the island's defenses, the former pirate cleared the remainder of the pirates from Bahamian waters. The handful of pirates he caught were taken back to New Providence to stand trial. Their execution outside Fort Nassau was a tricky moment for Rogers, as he feared the pirates' former shipmates would stage a rescue, overthrowing his authority in the process. Fortunately, the execution went ahead as planned, the gallows guarded by Hornigold's pirate hunters.

That December a Spanish attack on New Providence was repulsed, but the threat it posed helped to unite the island behind its new governor. Gradually, order was restored over the Bahamas, despite the loss of Hornigold and his ship during a hurricane.

In 1721, Rogers returned to London to lobby for more resources. However, personally liable for the obligations he had contracted at Nassau, he was imprisoned for debt, and only released after a lengthy appeal. The government had withheld his salary but eventually he was paid and released. Rogers returned to the Bahamas and remained governor until his death in 1732. The archetypal pirate hunter of the Golden Age of Piracy, he was the man who single-handedly cleared the pirates from the Bahamas. In the process he denied them their one secure refuge in American waters, a mortal blow in the war against piracy.

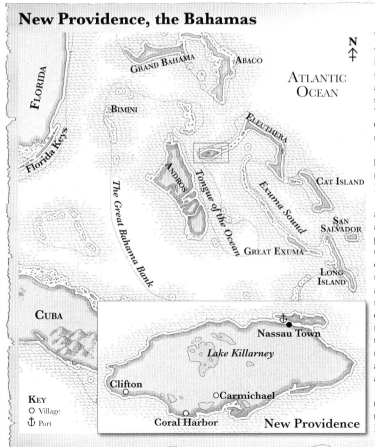

New Providence, the Bahamas

FLORIDA

GRAND BAHAMA · ABACO

ATLANTIC OCEAN

BIMINI

Florida Keys

ELEUTHERA

ANDROS

Tongue of the Ocean

CAT ISLAND

The Great Bahama Bank

Exuma Sound

SAN SALVADOR

GREAT EXUMA

LONG ISLAND

CUBA

Nassau Town

Lake Killarney

Clifton

Carmichael

KEY
O Village
⚓ Port

Coral Harbor

New Providence

The island of New Providence was first settled by Europeans in the late 17th century, drawn there by its fine natural harbor, and by its value as a source of sea salt. The settlement of Charles Town, named in honor of King Charles II, was founded beside the island's main anchorage in 1666. Less than three decades later it was renamed Nassau after the House of Orange-Nassau of King William III of England.

When the pirates first appeared in 1715 they were attracted by three things—the proximity of New Providence to the major shipping lanes of the Bahamas Channel and the Windward Passage, the availability of a marketplace to sell stolen goods, and the location of the island deep within the narrow channels and reefs of the Bahamas archipelago. That made the island difficult to attack, and a secure base. This all changed, however, when in 1718 Woodes Rogers arrived, to establish British control over the Bahamas and to clear New Providence of pirates.

Charles Vane

When the pirates of New Providence were offered a pardon if they gave up their life of crime, Charles Vane emerged as the leader of those who wanted nothing to do with the authorities.

Like many of the New Providence pirates, Charles Vane was a privateer who refused to stop attacking ships when his letter of marque expired, continuing to raid Spanish salvage ships off the coast of Florida.

Below: Charles Vane, the violent, hard-bitten leader of the die-hard New Providence pirates who refused to submit to royal authority in 1718.

Charles Vane was one of the crew of Henry Jennings when he attacked the Spanish salvage camp on the Florida coast in 1715, and he remained one of his followers during the years that followed. In the summer of 1717, Vane made his first independent cruise as a pirate captain, having gained command of his own sloop. He was moderately successful, and by that winter he had become one of the leading pirate captains of the Caribbean port.

OFF THE CAROLINAS

It was at this point that an offer of a royal pardon arrived, and despite Vane's protests, most of his fellow pirates wanted to accept the king's offer. Vane found himself the leader of the die-hard pirates who refused it, and so when Woodes Rogers appeared, he had no choice but to defy royal authority and make his dramatic exit.

After escaping from New Providence, Vane hovered off Charleston, where he preyed on shipping heading into the port. The South Carolina authorities fitted out two pirate-hunting sloops to chase Vane, but he managed to slip away before he was caught. Another pirate—Stede Bonnet— was less fortunate, and was trapped and captured by these sloops a few months later,

The Raids of New Providence Pirate Charles Vane, 1718–20

1 April 1718 Vane makes his first independent cruise, capturing two vessels off the coast of the Carolinas. He develops a reputation for cruelty.

2 July Vane and his so-called "die-hard" pirates fire on Governor Woodes Rogers as they make their dramatic exit from New Providence. The pirates successfully evade their pursuers.

3 August Cruises off Charles Town (now Charleston, South Carolina), capturing several ships. He successfully evades the pirate hunters sent to capture him.

4 September Vane and his crew meet up with Blackbeard and his men at Ocracoke Island, in the Outer Banks of the North Carolina colony. The pirates hold a week-long party by way of celebration.

Pirate party off Ocrakoke

5 October Operates off New York and Long Island, and captures a vessel off Long Island's eastern tip.

6 November Heads south for the winter, but encounters a French warship in the Windward Passage and flees. His crew are disgusted and replace him as captain. Vane and 16 supporters set off on their own, in a small captured sloop.

7 December Reaches the coast of Belize, then heads south to the Gulf of Honduras in search of prizes.

8 January 1719 Establishes a base on an unidentified island in the Gulf of Honduras called "Barnacko," and captures several logwood gathering vessels in Honduran waters.

9 February Shipwrecked during a hurricane— possibly on what is now Lighthouse Reef, off Belize. Vane is one of only two survivors.

10 April Vane is rescued, but is recognized as a pirate. He is taken to Jamaica to stand trial.

11 November Vane stands trial for piracy in Spanish Town, Jamaica. He is found guilty, and on March 22, 1720 he is hanged. His body is displayed as a warning to others.

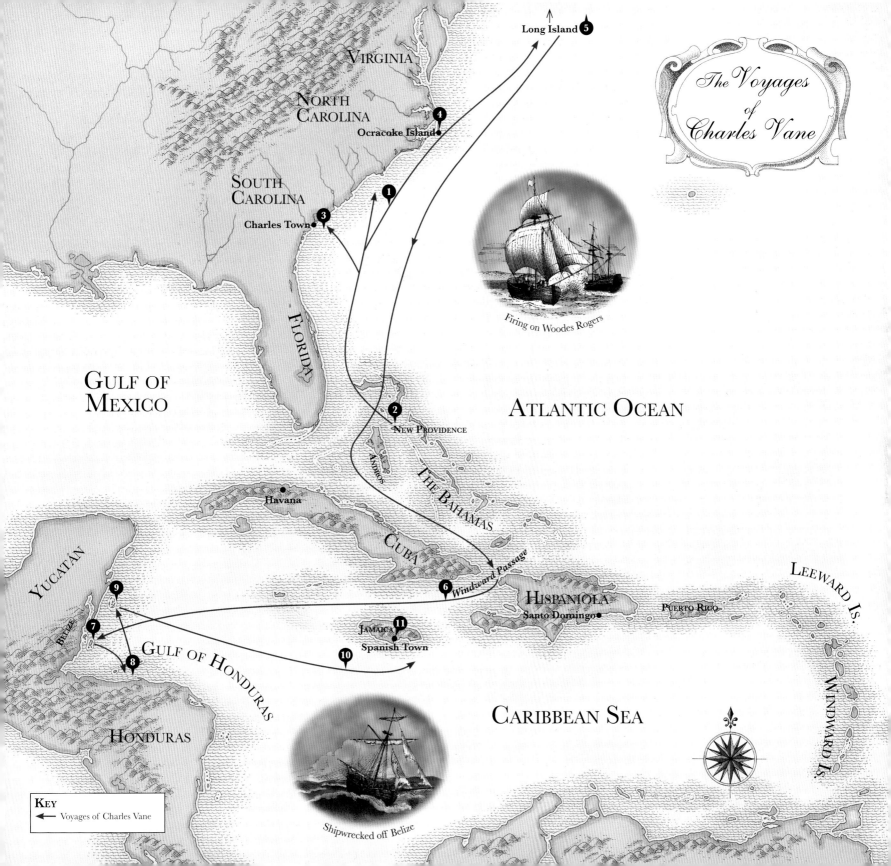

VIRGINIA

NORTH CAROLINA

Ocracoke Island ● ④

SOUTH CAROLINA

Charles Town ● ③

FLORIDA

GULF OF MEXICO

ATLANTIC OCEAN

Long Island ⑤

①

②

New Providence

Andros

THE BAHAMAS

Havana

CUBA

Windward Passage

⑥

HISPANIOLA

Santo Domingo ●

PUERTO RICO

LEEWARD IS.

YUCATÁN

⑨

⑦

BELIZE

⑧

GULF OF HONDURAS

HONDURAS

JAMAICA
Spanish Town ● ⑪

⑩

CARIBBEAN SEA

WINDWARD IS.

The Voyages
of
Charles Vane

Firing on Woodes Rogers

Shipwrecked off Belize

KEY
← Voyages of Charles Vane

Quartermaster Yeats

While Vane was loitering off Charleston, his quartermaster—a fellow pirate by the name of Yeats—was given command of a captured sloop. Yeats decided to go hunting alone, along with 15 crew members, but in the Bahamas they were intercepted by Benjamin Hornigold. The pirates were captured after a short fight and brought back to New Providence.

It was here that they were tried and executed—the first real test of Woodes Rogers' authority. The mass hanging took place without serious incident, demonstrating that the Bahamas were now closed to men like Vane.

at the mouth of the Cape Fear river. Vane meanwhile headed north, and by September his ship the *Ranger* was in North Carolina's Outer Banks. Here, Vane and his men spent a week partying with Blackbeard and his crew. News of this union filtered out and greatly alarmed the governors of Colonial America, who feared that the Outer Banks might become a new pirate den—a replacement for the Bahamas. However, Vane and Blackbeard had no intention of working together, so Vane headed north, spending a month cruising off New York before heading south into warmer waters.

In November, he encountered a French warship. He decided not to attack it, a decision that was interpreted as an act of cowardice by his crew. His new quartermaster was "Calico Jack" Rackam, who led a revolt, and ousted Vane as captain. While Rackam took over the *Ranger*, Vane and the 16 men who remained loyal to him were bundled into a small prize sloop, and sent on their way. Vane headed toward Honduras, making landfall off Belize in mid-December, 1718. He planned to raid the ships used by logwood cutters in the region, and he had some early success—until disaster struck. Vane's sloop was caught

In September 1718, the crews of Blackbeard and Vane met on Ocracoke Island, and held a week-long celebratory beach party.

Electing a Pirate Captain

Pirate captains were chosen from among the crew, and elected into their position of authority. The same was true of the quartermaster, who acted as the captain's deputy. If the crew decided that one of these officers wasn't doing his job properly, they could vote him out. This is exactly what happened to Charles Vane.

What this meant was that pirate captains needed to keep their crews supplied with plunder—particularly money and alcohol. Some pirate captains—most notably, Blackbeard—kept their men in check by intimidating them, so that nobody was willing to speak up against them. Others, such as Black Bart Roberts, did so by being extremely successful. Whichever way they did it, captains had to spend time and effort maintaining their authority, or risk losing it to a rival.

Above: A single-masted sloop, typical of the vessels favored by pirates of the early 18th century.

in a sudden storm and he was shipwrecked on a remote island off the coast of Belize. Vane was the only survivor.

A PIRATE MAROONED

The pirate spent several months on a desert island before a passing ship appeared. He was recognized, and the captain refused to take him on board. A few weeks later another ship arrived, and this time Vane was rescued. Unfortunately, he was identified, arrested, and transported to Jamaica to stand trial. In November 1719, he was thrown into jail, and the following March the pirate was put on trial. As he had fired on Woodes Rogers and defied royal authority, the outcome was never in any real doubt. He was taken to Gallows Point and hanged, and his body was then displayed in a cage as a warning

to others. Of course, Vane wasn't the last of the die-hard pirates. John Rackam, known as "Calico Jack," was still at large. And as long as he remained at sea, he represented a challenge to the authority of Woodes Rogers and the British crown.

Pirate Migration

During the Golden Age of Piracy, it was very common for pirates to cruise along the American seaboard as far north as Newfoundland during the summer. As soon as winter began, they tended to head south toward the warmer waters of the Caribbean. This also meant that they avoided the Caribbean during the hurricane season—a very sensible arrangement.

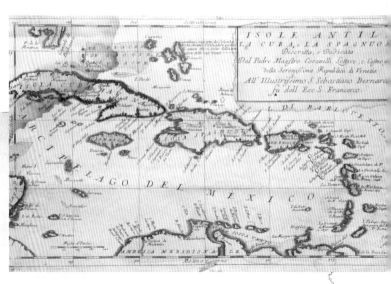

Above: The wind limited the ability of sailing ships to travel. Around Cuba, Hispaniola, and the West Indies, shown in this 18th-century chart, the prevailing wind was from the southeast.

"Calico Jack" and the Women Pirates

In 1720, the trial of Anne Bonny and Mary Read caused a sensation, for they had sailed as pirates alongside Captain Jack Rackam—an association that made him infamous.

The actions of Anne Bonny and Mary Read flew in the face of convention. For more than a year they had dressed as men, braved the high seas, and fought alongside the notorious pirate "Calico Jack" Rackam.

John Rackam, also known as "Calico Jack," was typical of the pirates who operated out of New Providence before 1718. A former privateer, he had turned to smuggling and piracy after the peace of 1713. By 1718, he had become the quartermaster on Charles Vane's sloop,

The Ranger, and was alongside Vane when he forced his way past Woodes Rogers' squadron in July 1718. Five months later, when Vane was accused of cowardice by his men, Rackam was elected captain. He took over Vanes' ship and his crew.

Why "Calico Jack"?

Calico is a textile made from unbleached cotton. It is finer than canvas, but cheaper than fully bleached and treated cotton. The cloth was named after the Indian port of Calicut (now Kozhikode), where it was produced. In 1700, the import of calico into the American colonies was banned in an attempt to prop up Britain's domestic textile industry. Therefore, it is thought that Calico Jack may have earned his nickname as one of the many men who smuggled the cloth into American or West Indian ports.

Right: "Calico" Jack Rackam, as depicted in an early illustration in Captain Johnson's *A General History of Pyrates* (1724).

The Voyages of Captain Rackam, with Anne Bonny and Mary Read, 1718–20

1718–19 voyage

1 **November 1718** When Charles Vane fails to attack a French warship in the Windward Channel his crew replace him as captain, and Rackam becomes the new leader of the so-called "die-hard" pirates.

2 **December** "Calico Jack" and the *Ranger* cruise the waters of the Leeward Islands, capturing a few small prizes.

3 **December** The pirates capture a ship laden with wine between Hispaniola and Jamaica, and spend two days drinking the cargo.

4 **Late December** He careens his ship somewhere on the north coast of Hispaniola. Christmas is celebrated by holding a beach party.

5 **Spring 1719** Rackam cruises in the Windward Passage but fails to capture any significant prize.

6 **May** Returns to the Bahamas and accepts a pardon from Governor Woodes Rogers. He spends the next year as a legitimate privateer.

1720 voyage

7 **August 22, 1720** Rackam and 13 followers steal the sloop *William* in Nassau Harbour, and sail off in her. His crew includes the two women pirates Anne Bonny and Mary Read.

8 **September** Rackam plunders a fleet of Bahamian fishing boats, then heads south to his old cruising ground of the Windward Passage.

9 **October** The pirates capture two sloops off the coast of Tortola, in the Virgin Islands, and then head south through the Windward Passage to search the northern coast of Jamaica.

10 **November 15** Rackam is anchored off the western tip of Jamaica. He is spotted by a pirate hunter, who attacks the *William*, and defeats the pirates after a sharp fight. Rackam and his surviving crew are taken to Spanish Town to stand trial.

11 **November 26** Rackam is found guilty of piracy, and hanged, along with 15 of his men. The two women pirates escape execution, as it is discovered that they are both with child. Mary Read dies in prison, still carrying her unborn child, while Anne Bonny and her child are eventually freed.

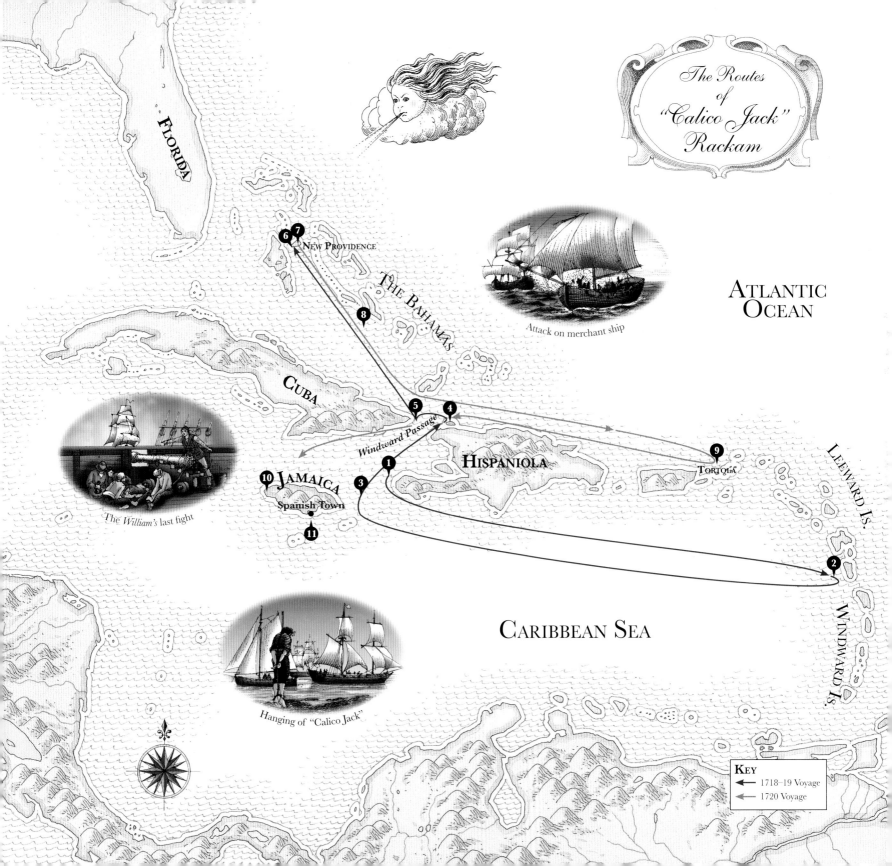

The Routes of "Calico Jack" Rackam

FLORIDA

ATLANTIC OCEAN

Attack on merchant ship

THE BAHAMAS

NEW PROVIDENCE

CUBA

Windward Passage

HISPANIOLA

LEEWARD IS.

TORTOLA

The William's last fight

JAMAICA

Spanish Town

CARIBBEAN SEA

WINDWARD IS.

Hanging of "Calico Jack"

KEY
1718–19 Voyage
1720 Voyage

Rackam's Cruise

After Rackam and Vane parted company, Rackam cruised the waters between Jamaica and the Leeward Islands. After that the records become a little confused. It seems that in December 1718, Britain and Spain went to war with each other, which is why New Providence was unsuccessfully attacked by the Spanish. Woodes Rogers needed privateers, so he offered another pardon to pirates willing to become legitimate privateers. In the end, the war only lasted until February 1720, but it was long enough for Rackam and his men to accept the offer. In May 1719, the die-hards surrendered and all were pardoned.

While he was in New Providence, Rackam met Anne Bonny, and the two became lovers. Bonny was already married, so when Rackam decided to return to piracy, she left her husband and sailed with him. In August 1720, the couple and a dozen other pirates stole the sloop *William,* and sailed her out of New Providence. Strangely enough, among the dozen-strong crew was another woman —Mary Read—who had disguised herself as a man. The actions of the two women would scandalize genteel 18th-century society.

Negril Point

Rackam's cruise was less than successful. On October 1, he captured two sloops off Tortola in the Virgin Islands, and then headed south through the Windward Passage. He captured a third prize off the northern coast of Jamaica, but the authorities learned of his activities and sent Captain Barnet and the pirate-hunting *Eagle* to intercept him. On

the evening of November 15, the *William* was lying off Negril Point—the westernmost tip of Jamaica—where they spent the night at anchor, drinking heavily.

That was where Barnet found them, catching the pirates unawares. Rackam cut his anchor cable and tried to run but he was quickly overhauled. Barnet's men swarmed

Anne Bonny and Mary Read

Most of what we know about these two women pirates comes from Captain Johnson, the author of *A General History of Pyrates*, published in 1724. He claimed that Anne Bonny was the illegitimate daughter of an Irish lawyer from South Carolina. She married a seaman, James Bonny, and ran off with him. The couple eventually ended up in New Providence, where she met "Calico Jack" Rackam.

While Johnson's account of Anne Bonny's life is reasonably believable, his biography of Mary Read was almost certainly made up. He claims she had been brought up as a boy so her father could claim an inheritance, which was only to be awarded if he had a male heir. She ran away to sea and then joined the army, still disguised as a boy. There she married a soldier, who died during a passage to the West Indies. She was subsequently captured by pirates and eventually landed up in New Providence, where she met Bonny and Rackam. In Johnson's account of Mary's life her activities spanned almost 30 years—which would have made her much too old to be a woman pirate!

Left: A bloodthirsty early 18th-century depiction of the two legendary women pirates, Anne Bonny and Mary Read.

they were overpowered. As they were tied up, they both cursed Rackam and their shipmates for being so inadequate.

The pirates were taken to Spanish Town near Port Royal to stand trial. The women became celebrities when it was revealed they had passed themselves off as men and had fought as pirates. Not only had they broken the law, but they had escaped the restrictions placed on women in contemporary society. In court it was reported that "they were both very profligate, cursing and swearing much, and very ready and willing to do anything." It was little wonder that the trial caused such a sensation!

On November 16, 1720, Rackam and nine of his crew were found guilty. The following day Calico Jack and four others were hanged on Gallows Point, followed the next day by the rest of his crew, who were executed outside Kingston. That left Anne Bonny and Mary Read. They had been found guilty, but were spared the noose when it was revealed they were both pregnant. Mary Read died in prison five months later, before her child could be born, but the fate of Anne Bonny is unknown. One rumor is that she was released just before she gave birth but ended her days as a beggar on the streets of Kingston.

Below: Idealized depiction of Anne Bonny revealing her identity as a woman to a vanquished foe.

aboard the *William*, but found that most of the crew were too drunk to put up much of a fight. The exception was the two women, who apparently fought like wildcats until

Pirate Flags

Pirate flags were designed to look threatening—a warning not to resist. And they were a symbol that told victims exactly who they were dealing with.

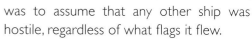

Above: The flag of Christopher Condent.

In the 17th century, most buccaneers flew their own national flags— English, Dutch, or French—although they also flew other symbols, designed to intimidate their victims.

THE JOLLY ROGER

The most common of these was an all-red flag, which meant that no quarter was expected or given—the buccaneers would fight to the death. The aim of the flag was to warn potential victims that any attempt to offer resistance would result in death. The same red flag was often flown by

Above: The flag of Christopher Moody.

privateers, who after all were nothing more than pirates or buccaneers with a license to attack enemy shipping.

These red flags were sometimes modified by adding symbols which had been invented by the buccaneering captain. The French gave these buccaneering flags the ironically harmless-sounding name "Jolie Rouge," meaning "pretty red." In English, this soon became the Jolly Roger. By 1700, the first black Jolly Roger was reported, flown by a small-time pirate called Emmanuel Wynne. His flag was black, with a white skull at its center, surmounting crossed bones and an hourglass. This was the skull and crossbones we have become so familiar with from pirate fiction. Over the next few decades this black flag would come to represent piracy. By 1714, it had become an immediately recognizable symbol—the flag of the pirate.

When the pirate Howell Davis turned to piracy, he didn't have a suitable flag, so he flew "a dirty tarpaulin, by way of black flag, they having no other." Charles Vane flew a British

Above: "Calico Jack" Rackam's flag.

Union flag and a pirate flag, while Edward England opted for a black flag on his mainmast, a red flag on his foremast, and the Union flag from his stern. The reason pirates still flew national flags is that they often tried to pass themselves off as law-abiding privateers. A wary captain would view any flag as suspect— a potential *ruse de guerre* (trick of war)—but the meaning of a black pirate flag was never in doubt. Whoever flew it was a fully-fledged pirate, and meant to cause harm to anyone who opposed him. Often the best policy for a merchant ship in time of war, or when sailing through pirate-infested waters, was to assume that any other ship was hostile, regardless of what flags it flew.

PIRATE SYMBOLS

Red buccaneering or black pirate flags were meant to intimidate. They became even more threatening when symbols were included on the flags, which underlined this sinister message of possible death and destruction. Although these symbols often varied, most followed a similar pattern. After all in the early 18th century, much of this symbolism was widely known.

A lot of it involved death or fate, which is why the skull and crossbones have long been associated with pirate flags. Other common images were skeletons, which also represented death; hourglasses, which showed time running out; or even bloodied weapons, meaning the pirates planned a bloody fight, with no quarter given. Blackbeard, for instance, flew a black flag which carried the image of a skeleton, stabbing

a blood-red heart with a spear. It was clear to any seaman who saw this flag run up the masthead of a ship that it didn't bode well for anyone apart from Blackbeard and his crew!

FLAGS OF DISTINCTION

Today, we tend to associate one particular flag—the skull and crossbones—with pirates. We know this design was flown by Edward England while he cruised the waters of the Indian Ocean. In fact, there were many variants of this basic design, as well as flags that used different symbols entirely. Roundsman Thomas Tew reputedly flew a black flag showing a white arm wielding a sword. Edward Low preferred a simple red skeleton, while "Calico Jack" Rackam replaced the crossbones with crossed swords. It seems that it was almost as important to have a distinctive flag as a threatening one. After all, with reputations like the ones enjoyed by Blackbeard or "Black Bart" Roberts, victims would surrender right away. In other words, it paid to fly your own flag!

Above: Edward Low's flag.

Left: The flag of Blackbeard.

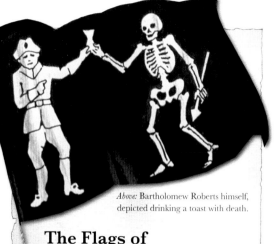

Above: Bartholomew Roberts himself, depicted drinking a toast with death.

The Flags of Bartholomew Roberts

Symbolism on pirate flags could sometimes take the form of a specific threat. For instance, the highly successful pirate "Black Bart" Roberts harbored a grudge against the governors of Barbados and Martinique, as both the British and the French officials had given orders to hunt him down. Therefore, when Roberts was cruising in the West Indies, he flew flags designed to intimidate anyone from these particular islands.

One of two flags associated with him was a black Jolly Roger, bearing the image of a pirate (presumably representing Roberts himself) standing on top of two skulls. One was labeled "ABH" to symbolize "A Barbadian's Head," the other skull labelled "AMH"—the head of someone from Martinique. The threat was implicit—he would spare no one he captured who hailed from those two islands. A second flag of his showed the same pirate, together with a skeleton. Both figures were holding an hourglass.

Right: Bartholomew Roberts, standing on the skulls of victims from Barbados and Martinique.

The Golden Age: The Atlantic Seaboard

With Woodes Rogers' pirate hunters patrolling the Bahamas, pirates moved to the Atlantic seaboard, and brought trade in the colonies to a standstill. Some of them —Blackbeard and Sam Bellamy, for example—became particularly notorious.

While the threat posed by the pirates of New Providence was serious enough, for the most part these men were small-time criminals whose activities were a nuisance but rarely had any impact on trade.

From the summer of 1718 onward, this began to change. Denied a secure base in the Bahamas, the pirates ventured further afield—deep into the Caribbean, or northward up the American seaboard, as far as Newfoundland and the fisheries of the Grand Banks. This put the pirates astride the major shipping lanes that linked ports such as Boston, New York, and Philadelphia, with their principal marketplace in Britain.

Pirates like Stede Bonnet operated off the Carolinas, Sam Bellamy cruised the waters of New England, and other lesser pirates did what they could to make their mark. With the exception of Bonnet, all of these posed a marked threat. Then Blackbeard appeared. At first he seemed little different from the dozen other pirates that operated

Left: The brutal and final fight of Blackbeard in 1718, as depicted by the early 20th-century American artist Frank Schoonover.

in American waters at the time. He preyed on ships off the coast of Virginia, Delaware, and New York, and then moved south when winter came. He ranged across the full breadth of the Caribbean, hunting down prizes off Martinique and the Leeward Islands, and causing mayhem among the ships that belonged to the logwood cutters who operated along the coast of Honduras. Then he headed north again, which is when he really made his mark.

In 1718, Blackbeard blockaded Charles Town, and brought the busy trade of the South Carolina colony to a complete standstill. For a few brief weeks, he commanded a more powerful squadron of ships than anything the Royal Navy had under its command in American waters. When he sailed away, the merchant communities of the colonies held their breath. Would he appear off the Virginia Capes, or the Delaware River? Williamsburg, Virginia, and New York were protected by warships, but would they be powerful enough to fight this powerful pirate squadron? While what he did next was something of an anticlimax, after Blackbeard nobody took pirates for granted again.

Blackbeard *the most notorious pirate of them all*

Probably the most recognizable, fearsome character from pirate history, Blackbeard shook the very foundations of British colonial rule in the Americas.

Above: Blackbeard, from a contemporary illustration, shown here armed with a cutlass, and "three brace of pistols."

Blackbeard used his ferocious appearance and notorious reputation as weapons to achieve his ends. They have also helped establish his position as the archetypal pirate of the Golden Age ever since.

THE RISE OF BLACKBEARD

For such an important piratical figure, we know little about Blackbeard's early life. According to Captain Johnson in his book *A General History of Pyrates*, the English pirate's real name was Edward Teach, and he was born in Bristol around 1680. Johnson claims that Teach served as a privateer based in Port Royal, where he distinguished himself for his bravery during the War of the Spanish Succession. After peace was declared in 1713, he gravitated to the pirate den of New Providence where he joined the crew of Benjamin Hornigold. The old pirate recognized potential when he saw it and became Teach's mentor, eventually raising him to the command of his own pirate sloop.

Teach first appears in the historical records in March 1717, when a merchant captain reported that a "Captain Thatch" was operating out of New Providence, in a six-gun pirate ship crewed by 70 men. He was still sailing in consort with Hornigold but by September had set off on his own, probably around the time Hornigold was deposed by his crew for refusing to attack British ships. Hornigold and his men returned to New Providence but Teach continued his cruise along the Virginia and Delaware coasts. Every time he captured a ship, he asked for volunteers to join his crew; in this way he gradually built up his pirate band. That October, he also fell in with the "gentleman pirate" Stede Bonnet, who remained an involuntary guest of Blackbeard until the following summer. To add insult to injury, Teach ordered another pirate to command Bonnet's sloop the *Revenge*.

THE *QUEEN ANNE'S REVENGE*

The onset of winter encouraged Teach to head south toward the warmer waters of the West Indies. On November 17, 1717, the

Above: A drawing of a French slave ship of the time, very similar in appearance to Blackbeard's *Queen Anne's Revenge.*

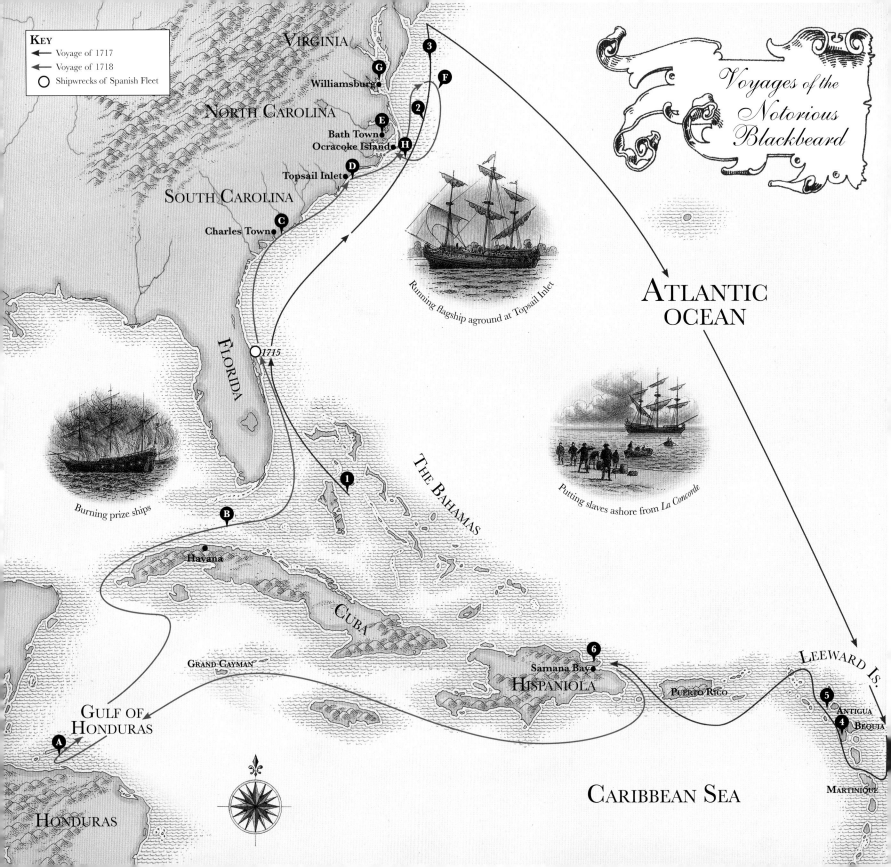

VIRGINIA

G

Williamsburg

NORTH CAROLINA

F

2

E

Bath Town

Ocracoke Island

H

D

Topsail Inlet

SOUTH CAROLINA

C

Charles Town

FLORIDA

1715

3

Running flagship aground at Topsail Inlet

ATLANTIC
OCEAN

Burning prize ships

1

THE BAHAMAS

Putting slaves ashore from La Concorde

B

Havana

CUBA

GRAND CAYMAN

6

Samana Bay

HISPANIOLA

PUERTO RICO

LEEWARD IS.

5

ANTIGUA

4

BEQUIA

GULF OF
HONDURAS

A

CARIBBEAN SEA

HONDURAS

MARTINIQUE

*Voyages of the
Notorious
Blackbeard*

Blackbeard's Reign of Terror at Sea, 1717–18

1717

1 **March 1717** Blackbeard's first independent cruise in the Bahamas Channel.

2 **September** Cruises off the Virginia Capes and the Delaware River.

3 **October** Falls in with Stede Bonnet, and forces the "gentleman pirate" to sail in consort with him. After cruising as far as New Jersey, he heads south.

4 **November 17** Captures the French slave ship *La Concorde* off Martinique. He takes her to Bequia, where he converts her into his new flagship—*Queen Anne's Revenge*.

5 **November–December** Cruises the waters of the Leeward Islands, capturing four sloops.

6 **December** Blackbeard careens his ship in Samana Bay, on the eastern coast of Hispaniola.

1718

A **March 1718** Blackbeard sails to the Gulf of Honduras with two ships—the *Queen Anne's Revenge* and the sloop *Revenge*. He spends a month there, capturing and burning several ships.

B **April** Captures a Spanish sloop off Havana, and plunders the shipwrecks of the 1715 treasure fleet off the Florida coast.

C **May 22** Arrives off Charles Town (now Charleston) South Carolina, and blockades the port, capturing ships and holding the town to ransom.

D **June** Arrives at Topsail Inlet (near Beaufort, North Carolina). The *Queen Anne's Revenge* runs aground. Bonnet is sent to Bath Town, to negotiate a pardon, while Blackbeard sails off on his own, taking his plunder with him.

E **July** Accepts a pardon from Governor Eden. While he spends much of his time at Bath Town, he also establishes a base on Ocracoke Island.

F **September** Captures two French merchantmen off the Delaware coast—a covert return to piracy.

G **November** Governor Spotswood of Virginia sends two sloops to hunt down Blackbeard, supported by a land force, sent to seize plunder at Bath Town.

H **November 22** Blackbeard is attacked by Lt. Maynard's two sloops, and is killed in the ensuing battle. The surviving pirates are taken to Williamsburg to stand trial.

two pirate sloops were off Martinique when they spotted an approaching merchantman. She was quickly captured, and turned out to be *La Concorde*, a 200-ton French slave ship from Nantes. Teach took her as a prize, landed the slaves and crew, and set about converting her into his new flagship. She was transformed into a powerful 40-gun ship, and renamed the *Queen Anne's Revenge*.

He then cruised the Leeward Islands, capturing several vessels. The captain of one of these later described the pirate as "a tall spare man with a very black beard which he wore very long." The newspapers of the day soon transformed the unknown Teach into "Blackbeard"—a nickname that remained with him for the rest of his days, and beyond.

By March 1718, the pirates had moved to the Gulf of Honduras, where Blackbeard attacked ships gathering to pick up logwood—a valuable commodity used as a dye.

The Blockade of Charleston

In April, Blackbeard sailed north again, stopping off on the eastern coast of Florida where his men spent a few days picking through the remains of the wrecked treasure fleet of 1715 before moving on toward Charles Town (now Charleston), in the colony of South Carolina. He arrived at the port on May 22, 1718, and immediately blockaded it, capturing any ships that tried to enter or leave. This was an extremely

The Wreck of the *Queen Anne's Revenge*

In 1996 the remains of the *Queen Anne's Revenge* were discovered off Beaufort, North Carolina. The wreck site has been undergoing excavation ever since, revealing a wealth of information about Blackbeard and his world. So far, archaeologists have recovered guns, domestic items, some plunder, and even a syringe, which possibly once formed part of the medicine chest acquired by Blackbeard from the citizens of Charles Town. These priceless artifacts are now on display in the North Carolina Maritime Museum, located on the seafront at Beaufort.

A selection of objects recovered from the wreck of the *Queen Anne's Revenge*, including silver coins, a perfume pitcher, an ornate crucifix, cast iron genadoes (grenades), and a brass urethral syringe—this last object may have once formed part of the chest of medical supplies Blackbeard demanded from the citizens of Charles Town, South Carolina.

Blackbeard's Demonic Appearance

Blackbeard's name derived from the long beard he sported, which gave him a particularly ferocious appearance. He enhanced this by decorating his beard, and in time of action he even wore lengths of burning slow match under his hat, like lighted tapers.

Here's how Captain Johnson described him, in his *A General History of Pyrates* (1724).

"So our hero, Captain Teach, assumed the cognomen of Blackbeard from that large quantity of hair which, like a frightful meteor, covered his whole face and frightened America more than any comet that has appeared there a long time. The beard was black, which he suffered to grow of an extravagant length; as to breadth it came up to his eyes. He was accustomed to twist it with ribbons, in small tails, after the manner of our Ramillies wigs, and turn them about his ears.

In time of Action, he wore a Sling over his Shoulders, with three brace of Pistols, hanging from Holsters like Bandoliers; he wore a Fur-Cap, and stuck a lighted Match on each Side, under it, which appearing on each side of his Face, his Eyes naturally looking Fierce and Wild, made him altogether such a Figure, that Imagination cannot form an idea of a Fury, from hell, to look more frightful … If he had the look of a fury, his humours and passions were suitable to it."

Above: Blackbeard was easily identified by his long braided beard, tied with small strips of ribbon.

Rght: When Teach blockaded Charleston in 1718, the town was fortified, but its guns were unable to reach the mouth of the harbor, which lay five miles to the east.

audacious act because it threatened the very wellbeing of one of Colonial America's busiest ports.

Blackbeard spent a week off Charleston, but before he left he demanded a ransom. He didn't want money—preferring instead a chest of medicines. After all, these pirates had no recourse to medical attention, so goods of this kind would have been priceless. It has also been suggested that Blackbeard and his men needed the medicine to help treat an outbreak of venereal disease among the crew.

LORD OF THE OUTER BANKS

Blackbeard's next act was even more daring. He realized the *Queen Anne's Revenge* had become a liability as she was too large to hide in America's coastal waters. He "accidentally" ran her aground at Topsail Inlet, near the modern town of Beaufort, North Carolina. Another sloop went aground with her, leaving the pirates with just a small Spanish prize and Bonnet's *Revenge*.

Blackbeard suggested that Bonnet journey north to seek a pardon for the pirates from Governor Eden of North Carolina. Bonnet eagerly agreed but while he was away Blackbeard transferred all the plunder into the small sloop, stripped the *Revenge* of everything he could, then sailed away leaving most of his crew stranded on the beach. When Bonnet returned, he swore revenge,

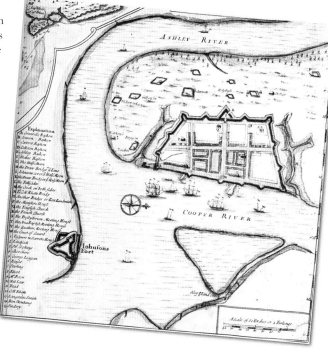

but he never managed to catch up with the wily Blackbeard. Blackbeard, on the other hand, arranged his own pardon and spent the summer in North Carolina. While he based himself in the small settlement of Bath Town, he maintained a lair on Ocracoke Island in the Outer Banks, the long string of barrier islands off the coast of North Carolina.

BLACKBEARD'S LAST BATTLE

The end came in November 1718. Unlike his counterpart in North Carolina, Governor Spotswood of Virginia wasn't convinced that Blackbeard had mended his ways. When rumors of fresh attacks began to circulate, Spotswood took the law into his own hands. Two British warships lay at anchor in Virginia's James River, and the governor ordered them to deal with Blackbeard once and for all. Two small sloops were hired, manned by naval volunteers, and sent south to Ocracoke inlet, under the command of Lieutenant Robert Maynard of the Royal Navy. The two craft sailed to Ocracoke.

Maynard launched his attack at dawn on November 22. Blackbeard had just 25 men on board his sloop, the *Adventure*, but she was armed with eight guns. Maynard's sloops—the *Ranger* and the *Jane*—had no guns, but were crewed by 50 well-armed veteran sailors. As the sloops approached the *Adventure* they were both racked by gunfire, which killed several crewmen, and forced the *Jane* to drop out of the fray. Blackbeard

Alexander Spotswood (c.1676–1740)

Unlike his counterpart in the neighboring colony of North Carolina, Governor Spotswood of Virginia had no time for pirates, pardoned or otherwise. He suspected North Carolina's Governor Eden of colluding with Blackbeard, and so decided to deal with the pirate himself.

Left: The wily Lieutenant Maynard lured Blackbeard into boarding his vessel—the sloop *Ranger*. Once the pirates were committed to the fight, Maynard ordered his crew to spring from their hiding place in the hold, taking the pirates by surprise.

Inset: After the battle, Blackbeard's head was hung from the bowsprit of the *Ranger*, a grisly trophy of Maynard's celebrated victory.

taunted his enemies, and he must have been convinced he could defeat Maynard. However, by the time the two ships collided Maynard had hidden most of his men below decks. They surged up out of the hold, taking the pirates completely by surprise.

A furious hand-to-hand battle followed, during which Blackbeard and Maynard sought each other out. Maynard wounded Blackbeard twice with his pistols, but the pirate got the better of the sword duel that followed. Then, just as Blackbeard was about to deliver a killer blow, a seaman slashed at him with his cutlass, cutting the pirate's throat. With his next stroke he severed Blackbeard's head from his body. With their captain dead the pirate crew quickly surrendered and Maynard was victorious. He returned to Virginia in triumph, with Blackbeard's severed head hanging from the bowsprit of his sloop.

Stede Bonnet
the gentleman pirate

Stede Bonnet was an exception among the typical pirates of the day—a gentleman, who decided on a life of piracy to escape from the constraints of polite society!

Above: Stede Bonnet was clearly not cut out to be a pirate—he was a gentleman, he bought his own ship, and he even hired a pirate crew.

Most pirates were lowly seamen, who took to piracy as a means of escaping harsh conditions and poor prospects. Stede Bonnet, however, came from a very different background.

Stede Bonnet was described by a contemporary as "a gentleman of good reputation in the island of Barbados, [who] was master of a plentiful fortune, and had the advantage of a liberal education." He owned a wealthy sugar plantation on the island, he was married into island society, and even held the rank of major in the local militia. In other words, Bonnet was a highly unlikely candidate for piracy.

Many reasons have been given for his break with the law—a shrewish wife, a scandal, and a mid-life crisis were all cited, but at the time his landowning neighbors described it as a "disorder of the mind." Whatever the reason, in the spring of 1717 he bought a 10-gun sloop that he called the *Revenge*, hired a 70-man crew from the waterfront of Bridgetown, and set off in search of piratical adventure. In fact, Bonnet could even be described as the first victim of the romanticism that surrounded piracy!

Voyages of the "Gentleman Pirate," 1717–18

1717

A **Spring 1717** Stede Bonnet begins his piratical career cruising off the Virginia Capes, where he captures four merchantmen.

B **October** Bonnet and his sloop *Revenge* fall in with Blackbeard, who commandeers the *Revenge*, and treats Bonnet as his "guest." For the next eight months, Bonnet accompanies Blackbeard on his voyages.

1718

1 **June 1718** Blackbeard arrives at Topsail Inlet (near Beaufort, North Carolina), and his flagship *Queen Anne's Revenge* runs aground. Bonnet is sent to Bath Town to arrange a pardon with Governor Eden. Meanwhile, Blackbeard absconds with all the plunder.

2 **July** Bonnet returns to Topsail Inlet, to find Blackbeard has betrayed him. He sets off in pursuit. He fails to catch Blackbeard, so instead resumes his piratical activities.

3 **Late July** Cruises off the Virginia Capes and Delaware Bay, capturing nine small vessels. He then heads south.

4 **August** Puts in to the Cape Fear River, and careens and repaired his ship just below the site of Wilmington, North Carolina. The *Revenge* is also re-named the *Royal James*.

5 **Early September** After the pirate Charles Vane appears off Charles Town (Charleston), the colony's governor sends two pirate-hunting sloops in pursuit.

6 **September 26** Colonel Rhett's sloops *Henry* and *Sea Nymph* arrive at the mouth of the river, and spot the *Royal James* and two prizes. Rhett decides to attack the following morning.

7 **September 27** At dawn, Bonnet tries to force his way past the two sloops blocking his way. Instead, he runs aground, and after a five-hour fight he surrenders the *Royal James*. The pirates are taken back to Charles Town to stand trial.

8 **October** Bonnet is treated as a gentleman, but he breaches the trust put on him by trying to escape. He is captured, and hauled back to jail, with 29 of his men. On November 8 most of his crew are hanged for piracy, with Bonnet and the remaining 5 crewmen going to the gallows five days later, on November 13.

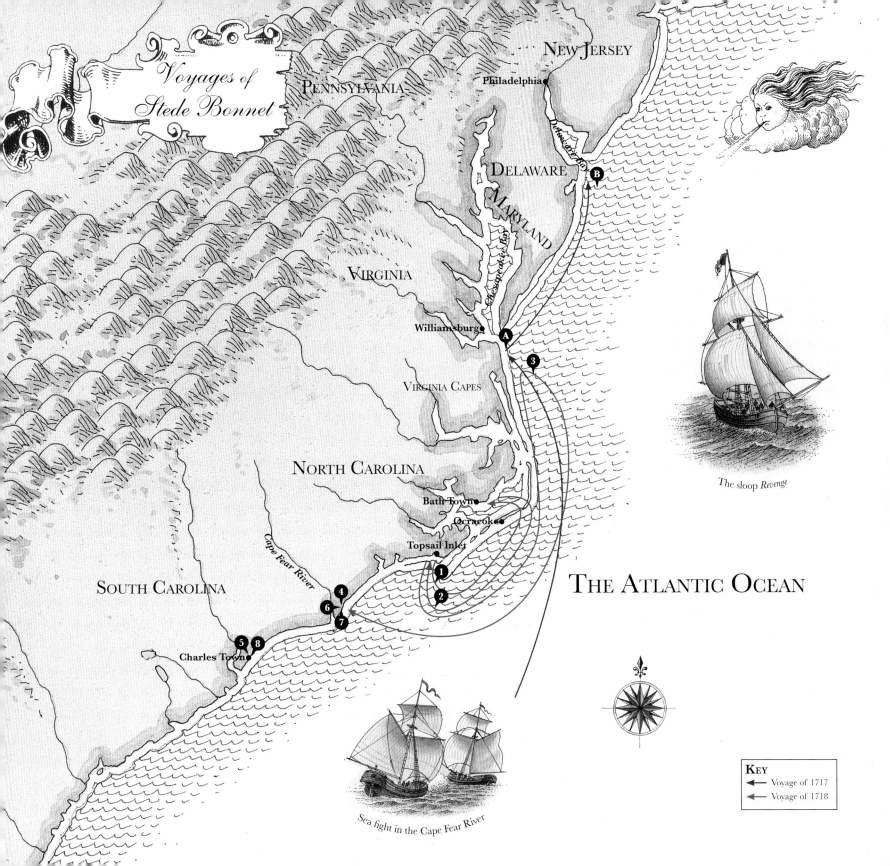

Voyages of Stede Bonnet

NEW JERSEY

Philadelphia

PENNSYLVANIA

DELAWARE

MARYLAND

B

VIRGINIA

Williamsburg

A

3

VIRGINIA CAPES

The sloop *Revenge*

NORTH CAROLINA

Bath Town

Ocracoke

Topsail Inlet

1

SOUTH CAROLINA

Cape Fear River

4

6

2

THE ATLANTIC OCEAN

7

5 **8**

Charles Town

Sea fight in the Cape Fear River

KEY

← Voyage of 1717
← Voyage of 1718

A Matter of Education

As a gentleman, Stede Bonnet was an exception—most pirates were common seamen, with little or no education. A few knew how to navigate a ship, a skill that required a working knowledge of mathematics. Reading and writing were less important to a pirate captain, although as former privateersmen many had needed these skills in order to cope with government prize agents and the authorities. While pirates elected their own captain, a man like Bonnet had learning, which partly made up for his lack of piratical experience.

BONNET'S FIRST CRUISE

Sensibly enough for his first cruise as a pirate, Bonnet avoided his home waters of the West Indies. Instead, he set course for the Atlantic seaboard of the American colonies, arriving off the Virginia Capes in the early summer of 1717. He captured four merchantmen, including one from Barbados, which he burned to hide the evidence. By September he was operating in Delaware Bay—the maritime gateway to Philadelphia. Instead of merchantmen, he ran into Blackbeard, who "invited" Bonnet to sail in company with him. In fact, Blackbeard took over the *Revenge* and Bonnet became little more than a prisoner on board his own ship.

BLACKBEARD'S GUEST

Bonnet remained Blackbeard's "guest" throughout Blackbeard's cruise into the Caribbean and subsequent blockade of Charles Town, and was still with him when he ran his ship, the *Queen Anne's Revenge*, aground on the Outer Banks near Beaufort. When Blackbeard suggested that Bonnet visit the local governor and accept a pardon, the gentleman seized the opportunity. However, when he returned he found that Blackbeard had stripped the *Revenge*, and sailed off with Bonnet's share of the summer's plunder, leaving his men (and most of Blackbeard's former crew) stranded on the beach.

Bonnet swore revenge, and set off in pursuit. But he never caught up with Blackbeard and returned to pirating, capturing several vessels off the Virginia coast and as far north as Delaware. This meant his chances of a pardon had evaporated. In July 1718, he decided that as the navy were actively looking for him, he needed to find a safe place to hide and to repair the *Revenge*. He chose the Cape Fear River, in the colony of North Carolina, not far from the modern-day city of Wilmington.

BATTLE IN THE CAPE FEAR RIVER

While his sloop was being repaired, the pirate-hunting sloops *Henry* and *Sea Nymph* left Charles Town under the command

Above: The battle at Cape Fear River between Bonnet and Colonel Rhett became a farce when both sides ran aground on sandbars. It was Rhett's two lighter ships that refloated first, and Bonnet was forced to surrender.

of Colonel Rhett. His real targets were Blackbeard and Charles Vane, but on September 26, as he approached the mouth of the Cape Fear River, he came upon Stede Bonnet. By that time the *Revenge*—now renamed the *Royal James*—was ready for sea, and as it was dusk, both sides prepared for a battle the following morning.

Colonel Rhett

Colonel William Rhett was an Englishman who moved to the South Carolina colony in 1698, where he established a rice plantation. He was also given a commission in the colony's militia. In 1706 he helped defend Charles Town against an attack by a Franco-Spanish squadron, and so in 1718 he was the obvious choice to lead a pirate-hunting expedition.

Above: Colonel William Rhett, the pirate-hunter.

Bonnet was outnumbered, so he hoped to surprise the enemy, race past them with guns blazing, and head out into the open sea. Unfortunately, just as the *Royal James* came within range of the two pirate-hunting sloops, she ran aground on a sandbank. Then, when the *Henry* and *the Sea Nymph* moved in for the kill, they both ran aground as well. All three ships were stranded within musket range of each other, exchanging fire while waiting for the tide to come in. This strange battle lasted five hours, but it was the *Henry* that was the first to float free. With her guns threatening to sweep the decks of the *Royal James*, Bonnet had little choice but to surrender.

THE TRIAL

Bonnet's men were thrown into Charles Town jail on October 3, 1718, although as a gentleman, Bonnet was housed in a private house. Three weeks later, and on the eve of their trial, Bonnet and another prisoner tried to escape, but were recaptured a few days later. This time there was no leniency, and the gentleman pirate was thrown in jail alongside his men.

On November 7, 29 of Bonnet's crew were sentenced to death, and all but five of them were hanged the following day at

Above: Stede Bonnet was hanged on the waterfront of Charles Town, manacled, and clutching a nosegay of wildflowers as a symbol of repentance.

White Point. Two days later, Bonnet himself was tried. There was never any doubt about the outcome and he was sentenced to death. While in prison, Bonnet sent a letter to the Governor for forgiveness and promising reform, but he was eventually hanged for his crimes on November 13, in the company of the last of his crew.

Sam Bellamy and the *Whydah*

Next to Blackbeard, one of the most successful of the former Bahamian pirates was "Black Sam" Bellamy, who was the scourge of the New England coast until disaster overtook him.

Though his career as a pirate captain was short-lived, Samuel Bellamy was a formidable pirate. He captained numerous ships, including his flagship the *Whydah*, which was also to bring him fame posthumously

BELLAMY BECOMES A PIRATE

Sam Bellamy was born in Devon, England, around 1689. Legend had it that he fell in love with a Massachusetts girl but that as a sailor he was considered a poor match by her parents. He determined to make his fortune—by fair means or foul. In any event, by 1716 he was in New Providence serving under Benjamin Hornigold. Hornigold gave Bellamy command of a prize sloop, and the younger pirate captain set off on his own. He soon teamed up with the French pirate "La Buse" (The Buzzard) and spent the winter hunting for prey off the Virgin Islands.

Young "Black Sam" proved himself to be a skilled captain, and he soon swapped his original sloop—the *Mary Anne*—for a larger square-rigged ship that he renamed the *Sultana*. In February 1717, he captured the British slave ship *Whydah Merchant* in the Bahamas Channel, laden with a valuable cargo of rum, gold dust, and money, valued at over £20,000—the equivalent of $2.9 million today. He also transferred from the *Sultana* into the larger *Whydah*, which he armed with 28 guns—while graciously presenting the *Sultana* to the *Whydah*'s old crew.

Left: Sam Bellamy began his career as a pirate captain in the sloop *Mary Anne*, a vessel very similar to the one shown here, being pursued by a British warship. During this period, the sloop was the piratical vessel of choice.

The Short-Lived but Formidable Career of Sam Bellamy, 1716–17

1716

1 **August 1716** Benjamin Hornigold gives Bellamy command of his own ship—a captured sloop called the *Mary Anne*. Soon afterwards Hornigold and Bellamy part company.

2 **September** Bellamy cruises the waters around the Virgin Islands, in the company of the French pirate Olivier Le Vasseur (La Buse). Several prizes are captured and taken back to New Providence.

3 **November** Captures the British merchantman *Sultana*, probably in the Windward Passage, and converts her into his flagship. He gives command of the *Mary Anne* to his quartermaster, Paul Williams.

1717

A **February 1717** Captures the British slave ship *Whydah* in The Bahamas Channel and turns her into his new flagship. He sets his prisoners free, giving them the *Sultana*.

B **March** In the *Whydah*, he is accompanied by the sloop *Mary Anne*. The two ships capture four merchantmen off the Virginia Capes. It is here that—according to Captain Johnson—Bellamy delivers a spirited tirade against ship owners.

C **Early April** Bellamy is caught in a storm off the coast of Virginia, and is driven north into the waters of New England. The *Whydah* and the *Mary Anne* become separated.

D It is later claimed that Bellamy planned to establish a base on Roberts Island, off the coast of Maine.

E **Mid-April** The *Whydah* may have captured another ship off Nantucket Island, a vessel carrying a cargo of wine. Their subsequent drunkenness has been cited as a reason why Bellamy's men couldn't weather the storm.

F **April 26** Bellamy in the *Whydah* is off Cape Cod when he encounters another hurricane-force storm. The *Whydah* strikes a sandbar off Cape Cod, and all but two of her crew drown. Bellamy goes down with his ship. The fate of Paul Williams is unclear, but it has been suggested that after Bellamy's death he and his men gave up piracy.

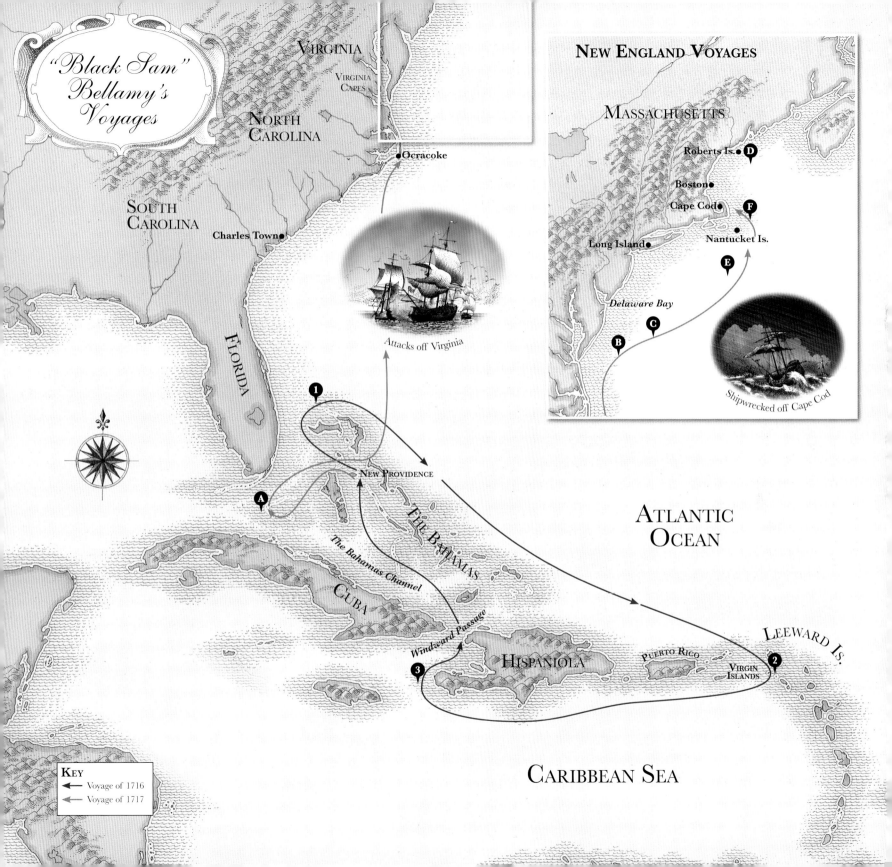

"Black Sam" Bellamy's Voyages

VIRGINIA

VIRGINIA CAPES

NORTH CAROLINA

Ocracoke

SOUTH CAROLINA

Charles Town

FLORIDA

① NEW PROVIDENCE

Attacks off Virginia

Ⓐ

The Bahamas Channel

THE BAHAMAS

CUBA

Windward Passage

③

HISPANIOLA

PUERTO RICO

VIRGIN ISLANDS

② LEEWARD IS.

ATLANTIC OCEAN

CARIBBEAN SEA

NEW ENGLAND VOYAGES

MASSACHUSETTS

Roberts Is. Ⓓ

Boston

Cape Cod Ⓕ

Long Island   Nantucket Is.

Ⓔ

Delaware Bay

Ⓒ

Ⓑ

Shipwrecked off Cape Cod

KEY
← Voyage of 1716
← Voyage of 1717

Disaster off Cape Cod

In April 1717, off the coast of Virginia, the *Whydah* and two prize sloops were overtaken by a storm, which drove her northward toward Cape Cod. On April 26, Bellamy and his crew were caught by a second storm, this time blowing from the southeast on to the rocky coast. While the sloops managed to fight their way out to sea, the *Whydah* was less fortunate. It was even claimed that her crew were drunk, having captured a Nantucket ship laden with wine a few days before. The *Whydah* struck a sandbar and capsized, throwing 146 pirates into the sea. There were only two survivors, both of whom were rounded up by the authorities. Samuel Bellamy went down with his ship.

In 1994, the wreck of the *Whydah* was rediscovered by wreck hunter Barry Clifford, and relics recovered from the seabed are now on display in a purpose-built museum in Provincetown, Massachusetts. There visitors can see the *Whydah*'s bell, the slave shackles used by her former owners, her weapons, and even some of the plunder that for a few months made Sam Bellamy one of the richest pirates in the Americas.

Gold and silver recovered from the wreck of Sam Bellamy's pirate ship the *Whydah*.

"Black Sam" the Libertarian

By March 1717, Bellamy had captured four more ships off the coast of Virginia. According to Captain Johnson, he gave an impassioned speech to some of his prisoners, railing against the injustices of shipowners. When the merchantmen refused to join him, "Black Sam" reputedly answered: "You are a devilish conscience rascal, I am a free prince, and I have as much authority to make war on the whole world, as he who has a hundred sail of ships at sea, and an army of 100,000 men in the field; and this my conscience tells me: but there is no arguing with such sniveling puppies, who allow superiors to kick them about deck at pleasure."

Above: Bellamy's libertarian views worried the colonial authorities, who feared pirates could seize a port like Charles Town, and incite insurrection or hold it for ransom. Illustration by Frank Schoonover.

George Lowther and Edward Low

George Lowther

Edward Low

Not all of the pirates recorded in Captain Johnson's *A General History of Pyrates* were of the caliber of Blackbeard or "Black Sam" Bellamy.

The English pirates George Lowther and Edward Low were certainly vicious, but they lacked the skills of their more celebrated counterparts.

GEORGE LOWTHER

In May 1721, George Lowther was a mate on board the slaver *Gambia Castle*. One night he mutinied, took over the ship, and renamed her *Happy Deliverance*. Lowther then sailed to the West Indies where he captured his first prize off Barbados. After wintering in the Cayman Islands, he headed to Honduras where he earned a reputation for wanton cruelty, torturing prisoners for sport. In fact, this may well have been the actions of his quartermaster, Edward Low.

Lowther lost the *Happy Deliverance* when she was burned in an attack by natives, but he captured another brig and headed north toward Virginia. He and Low parted company that summer, then Lowther came off worse in a fight with a feisty merchantman and spent the winter repairing his ship. By the spring of 1723, he was at sea again, ranging from Newfoundland in the north to the coast of Venezuela in the south. In

September, he put into an island off the South American coast and was careening his ship when he was attacked by a pirate hunter. His ship was destroyed, and most of the defenseless pirates were shipped off to stand trial, but Lowther was never captured. It was later claimed he took his own life.

EDWARD LOW

A former London pickpocket, Edward Low emigrated to Boston in his teens, and by 1721 was a seaman serving on a sloop in the Gulf of Honduras. He led a mutiny but it went awry, and he and his supporters were forced

Below: Edward Low and his men, torturing a prisoner on board a prize. Low enjoyed torturing those he captured and almost always the sadistic practice ended in death for the unfortunate prisoner.

Voyage of 1721–22
Voyage of 1723

The Voyages of George Lowther

VIRGINIA

VIRGINIA CAPES

NORTH CAROLINA

SOUTH CAROLINA

Charles Town

FLORIDA

GULF OF MEXICO

ATLANTIC OCEAN

THE BAHAMAS

CUBA

Lowther and Low's pirates join forces

CAYMAN ISLANDS

GULF OF HONDURAS

HONDURAS

BELIZE

Capture of the *Ranger*

HISPANIOLA

PUERTO RICO

CARIBBEAN SEA

LEEWARD IS.

WINDWARD IS.

ST. LUCIA

BLANCO

George Lowther's Infamous Voyages, 1721–23

1721–22

1 **December 1721** George Lowther arrives off the Cayman Islands in his ship the *Happy Deliverance*. He encounters another pirate crew, led by Edward Low. The two join forces.

2 **January 1722** Lowther captures the *Greyhound* of Boston off the coast of Belize. The crew are tortured.

3 In the Gulf of Honduras the pirates capture six more vessels, of which three are burned.

4 **February** Lowther careens the *Happy Deliverance* on the coast of Honduras but the camp is overrun by Indians, and the ship destroyed. Lowther and Low are left with two sloops. Lowther commands the *Ranger*.

5 **April** The pirates cruise the waters of the West Indies, but after capturing and destroying a brig off Guadeloupe, they learn that warships are looking for them. They therefore head north.

6 **May** Low and Lowther arrive off the Virginia Capes, but they soon disagree, and go their separate ways.

7 **June** Lowther captures and loots a ship off Long Island. He then heads south again as Low is reputedly causing havoc to the north.

8 **August** Lowther attacks a merchantman off South Carolina but runs aground and is almost captured. He limps north to repair his ship.

9 **Winter** Lowther careens and repairs his ship, and passes the winter in a camp, probably set up beside the Cape Fear River.

1723

A **Spring and Early Summer 1723** Lowther heads north to the fishing grounds off Newfoundland, where he captures several small vessels.

B **July** Lowther decides to return to the West Indies. In August, he captures a brig off St. Lucia.

C **September** Lowther needs to careen his ship, and puts in to Blanco, off the Venezuelan coast. There he is surprised by a pirate-hunter, and the *Ranger* is captured. Lowther is never found, and it is assumed he died at his own hand on the remote island.

to escape in a small boat. They steered for the Cayman Islands, where they encountered George Lowther. Low accepted an offer to serve as Lowther's quartermaster and cruised with him until the following summer. By that stage the two men had fallen out and so, in May 1722, Lowther gave Low a prize brigantine and sent him on his way.

By the end of the year, Low was off Brazil, where he reputedly tortured prisoners, cutting off their lips before killing them. By March 1723 he was back off Honduras, where he massacred over 60 Spanish prisoners before fleeing northward. More atrocities followed off the Carolinas and in the West Indies. In July, he crossed the Atlantic again, this time in a captured 34-gun ship, and the last report of him was in 1724, off the West African coast. It is rumored that he was captured but there aren't any historical records to support this. It's more likely that this sadistic captain was quietly marooned—or murdered by his shipmates!

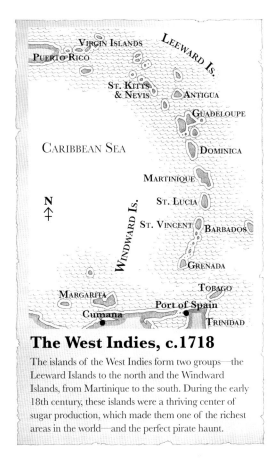

The West Indies, c.1718

The islands of the West Indies form two groups—the Leeward Islands to the north and the Windward Islands, from Martinique to the south. During the early 18th century, these islands were a thriving center of sugar production, which made them one of the richest areas in the world—and the perfect pirate haunt.

Below: Pirates "sweating" an unlucky captive—prodding him to dance until he dropped from exhaustion.

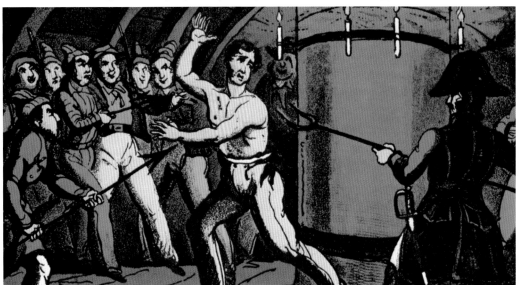

Pirate Ships

Although a few pirates like Blackbeard or "Black Bart" Roberts operated in large, well-armed ships, most pirates preferred much smaller craft.

There were several types of pirate vessel available, but for the pirates of the Golden Age the craft of choice was a sloop. They were fast, maneuverable, and ideally suited to the business of piracy.

THE PERFECT PIRATE SHIP

A sloop was a small, fast-sailing vessel, with one mast—little bigger than some of the larger racing yachts of today. Technically, most of them were "gaff-rigged," which meant they had a trapezoidal mainsail, stretched between a gaff (spar) at the top, and a boom at the bottom. A square foresail and a topsail above it provided additional sail power, as did one or more jib sheets, attached to the bowsprit. This meant that these small vessels—often little more than 35–80 feet (11–24m) long—packed a lot of canvas compared to their size and weight. This, together with the narrow, sleek lines of their hull made them very fast—able to outpace larger pursuers.

The best sloops were supposed to come from Bermuda, but both Jamaica and the

Above: Pirates attacking a warship, from a late 17th-century painting. Such engagements were rare—pirates usually avoided fighting men-of-war. Instead they preyed on more lucrative and less well-armed merchantmen.

Bahamas were also known for their sloops. These craft were nimble and able to take full advantage of the wind, which again gave them an edge when overhauling larger ships. Finally, they had a very shallow draft, which allowed them to sail in waters that were too shallow for larger ships. For pirates, this meant they could use places like the shallow waters of the Bahamas to escape. Most pirate sloops of the Golden Age of Piracy displaced less than 100 tons, were armed with up to ten guns, and carried a crew of about 50–70 men. However, some sloops were known to have carried double this number of men.

OTHER POPULAR CRAFT

Of course, pirates used other types of sailing vessels too. The next most common type was the brigantine, or brig, which had two masts, with a combination of square and fore-and-aft rigged sails. These vessels could carry as

Finally, there were the big pirate flagships, large fast ships that had been captured, then converted to suit the needs of their new owners. Ships like the *Queen Anne's Revenge* and the *Whydah* both started off as slave ships, which were known for their speed. That made them very suitable as pirate flagships. Most of these larger ships were three-masted—and in the language of the Age of Sail they could be described as ships (if "ship-rigged," with square sails) or barques (later called barks), with a greater predominance of fore-and-aft rigged sails. A pirate of this era could instantly identify a vessel by her sail plan, or "the cut of her jib."

The business of converting them often included the lowering of her superstructure, to create a better fighting platform, the piercing of her hull to accommodate more guns, and the opening up of the cabins into one open, more egalitarian space. Then all that was left was to hoist the black flag, and set off in search of fresh prey.

Naming the Ship

Almost every pirate renamed their ship when they first captured it. Certain names were more popular than others. For instance, many pirates often favored names like *Revenge*, *Fortune*, or *Fancy*. Others were named as a protest against the existing government. For instance, Stede Bonnet renamed his sloop the *Royal James*, suggesting a link to the Jacobite "pretender" to the British throne. Bartholomew Roberts renamed a succession of his ships either *Fortune*, *Good Fortune*, or *Royal Fortune*, while others preferred more egalitarian names—like Thomas Tew's *Liberty*. Finally, there were the exotic, like William Moody's *Rising Sun* or Christopher Condent's *Flying Dragon*.

Of course, changing names was also a way of trying to avoid being identified. The changing of a ship's original name to a pirate one was therefore a means of camouflage. This was almost certainly the reason behind Bonnet's name change, and may explain why pirates didn't seem particularly willing to stick to one ship name throughout their careers.

many as 16 guns, which meant they traded the speed of a sloop for a greater level of firepower or size of crew.

Another popular small vessel of the time was the schooner—a new form of fast two-masted vessel that appeared in Colonial American waters during the 18th century. However, its appearance largely postdates the Golden Age of Piracy.

Right: A pirate schooner (right) closing in on its prey— a three-masted merchant ship. The first mention of a pirate schooner was in 1717, after which they became increasingly popular in American waters.

The Golden Age: The Great Voyage

The colorful Howell Davis, and his successor Bartholomew Roberts —"Black Bart"—were the two men who led one of the longest and most spectacular pirate sprees in history.

One of the most dramatic pirate voyages of the Golden Age of Piracy began in September 1718, when two small sloops dropped anchor off the coast of Hispaniola.

The crews of these sloops were mostly former pirates from New Providence—men who had accepted Woodes Rogers' pardon just two months before. On the first evening at anchor the crews mutinied, and the ringleaders—Howell Davis among them—took over the two vessels.

So began a voyage that would take these pirates to West Africa, Brazil, Newfoundland, Scotland, and the Caribbean, and would involve murder, ambush, betrayal, and one mass-hanging on the African coast. It would also produce a man who was arguably the most successful pirate of the Golden Age of Piracy, and involve the capture, burning, or sinking of hundreds of ships. It would take the

Above: Pirates boarding a merchant ship—a dramatic 19th-century depiction of an attack that took place off the West African coast.

best part of five years to complete, even though few of the original mutineers managed to live to see its end.

While Woodes Rogers did well to drive pirates from the Bahamas, his actions seemed to have a detrimental effect elsewhere. For instance, while Blackbeard and Charles Vane were operating off the coast of America's Atlantic seaboard, Howell Davis, his shipmates, and his successors were playing havoc with shipping off the West African coast. Thanks to the slave trade, this was one of the busiest and most lucrative shipping regions of the world in the early 18th century. For a few brief years, after 1718, this became the new pirate hot-spot, where as many as a dozen pirate crews hunted for prey.

By the time the "great voyage" had run its course, the Golden Age of Piracy had come to an end. One of the most important contributing factors to its suppression was the mass-hanging of many of Howell Davis' old crew. Another was that due to the activities of Bartholomew Roberts, the British authorities diverted extra resources into the war against the pirates. This not only dealt with Roberts, but led to the widespread eradication of piracy on both sides of the Atlantic.

Howell Davis

The first of the pirate captains of the "Great Voyage," Davis was a charming, intelligent pirate who had an exciting, albeit brief, career.

Captain Howell Davis was known as a master of deception and subterfuge. In the end, though, he was the one who fell victim to a ruse.

According to Captain Johnson in his 1724 *History of Pyrates*, Howell Davis was born in Milford Haven, Pembrokeshire, in Wales. In 1718, he was serving as the mate on a slaver, the *Cadogan* of Bristol, when it was captured by Edward England off Sierra Leone. Davis joined the pirates, and was given the *Cadogan* as a prize. He tried to sail her to Brazil, where he planned to sell her human cargo, but his law-abiding shipmates refused, and instead sailed the *Cadogan* to Barbados where Davis was imprisoned.

He was only held for a few months and on his release went to New Providence,

hoping to join a pirate crew. Instead, he found that Governor Woodes Rogers had arrived, and the pirates there had all accepted a pardon. He decided to sign on as a crewman on the sloop *Buck* until he could return to his chosen profession. He didn't have to wait long. His chance came in September 1718, during their first night at anchor off Hispaniola, when the crews mutinied. Howell Davis was elected captain.

THE SLAVE COAST

Davis now commanded a 10-gun sloop and 60 pirates. He captured a few prizes in the Caribbean, and then crossed the Atlantic to

Above: The Welsh-born pirate Howell Davis, from a melodramatic 19th-century engraving. During his brief career, he proved a skilled master of deception.

the Cape Verde Islands, off the West African coast. He persuaded the local Portuguese governor that he was a law-abiding English privateer, and spent a month in the islands, before he broke his cover and captured a large merchantman, which he re-named *Royal James*. His next stop was the mouth of the Gambia River, where he repeated the deception, convincing the local governor he was a law-abiding captain. As a result he managed to seize the local town, its fort, and a slave ship. Here he met other pirates, and together they headed south into the Bight of Africa, in search of more rich pickings.

The African Bight

The "bight" (a broad bay) was the area of West Africa where most early 18th-century slave ships picked up their human cargo, either through established trading posts—many of them operated by the Royal African Company or by the Portuguese—or else by dealing directly with the African rulers in towns such as Whydah (Ouidah) and Calabar. Pirates considered the area a rich hunting ground.

Left: A 17th-century chart of the West Coast of Africa—a lucrative hunting ground for pirates like Davis and Roberts.

Cape Verde Islands

1
2

3
●Gallassee

DAHOMEY

SIERRA
LEONE

OYO

ASANTE

IBO

4

Anambu
6

Calabar●
7

5
IVORY COAST

GOLD COAST

SLAVE COAST

8

PRÍNCIPE

The
Voyage of
Howell Davis

ATLANTIC
OCEAN

SÃO TOMÉ

Loading provisions

Capture of slave ship

KEY
⟵ Howell Davis' Voyage

Howell Davis' Expedition to the African Coast, 1719

1 January 1719 The pirate Howell Davis arrives in the Cape Verde Islands in the sloop *Buck*, after a transatlantic voyage. He convinces the Portuguese governor that he is a pirate-hunter. The pirates spend a month in the islands, enjoying the local hospitality.

2 February Davis reveals his identity when he raids the harbor of Porto Inglé, and captures the merchantman *Loyal Merchant*. She is renamed *Royal James* and the *Buck* is abandoned.

3 Late February–March Arrives at Gallassee on the African coast (now Serrekunda/Banjul in Gambia). He uses trickery to seize the local guard ship, fort, and town. Davis is then joined by the French pirate Olivier Le Vasseur. The two crews spend a week celebrating.

4 April The two pirate crews capture six merchantmen off Sierra Leone, before going their separate ways.

5 May Davis captures two slave ships off the Ivory Coast (now Ghana). He keeps one for himself, renaming her *Royal Rover*.

6 June Davis and his men arrive off the slaving port of Anambu (now Anomabu in Ghana), 13 miles (21km) from the British stronghold at Cape Coast Castle. The pirates capture three slave ships at anchor, and encourage several seamen to join them. One of these recruits is Bartholomew Roberts.

7 Late June The leaking *Royal James* is abandoned near Calabar, and the pirates crowd onto their remaining vessel, the *Royal Rover*. Davis decides to head to the Portuguese island of Principe.

8 July In Príncipe, Davis pretends he and his men are pirate-hunters. Unfortunately, a prisoner escapes and warns the Portuguese governor, who lays a trap. Davis and his officers are invited ashore, where they are ambushed and Davis is killed. The survivors of Davis' crew escape to the safety of the *Royal Rover*. The pirates then bombard the town, and sail away, leaving the dead body of their captain behind.

Skirmish on Príncipe

Deception and Death

Davis captured several more ships, recruiting more crew as he went. One such recruit was the pirate Bartholomew Roberts (see page 164). Davis also switched ships, taking her over as a prize and renaming her *Royal Rover*. Finally, in July 1719, he arrived in Príncipe, a Portuguese island 250 miles (402km) off the coast of Guinea. Once again, he cleverly pretended he was a British privateer, and asked for water and supplies. At first, the local governor believed him, but then a Portuguese prisoner escaped from the pirate ship and told the governor the truth. Davis and his officers were duly invited ashore, but were ambushed, and in the skirmish that followed Davis was shot and killed.

Above: West African slave-hunters, who brought captives to the coast for the European slavers to transport and sell overseas.

Below: A 19th-century depiction of a meeting between slavers and a delegation of African slave-hunters.

Bartholomew Roberts

Bartholomew Roberts—"Black Bart"—was probably the most successful pirate of the "Golden Age," capturing more than 200 ships on both sides of the Atlantic and amassing a fortune.

Left: Bartholomew Roberts was known as a pirate who liked to wear finery, including a richly decorated silk coat and jewelery plundered from his victims.

When Howell Davis was killed, the survivors of his crew held another election, to decide who would be their new captain. Despite tough competition from Davis' original shipmates, the crew elected a relative newcomer—Bartholomew Roberts.

A New Captain

Like Davis, Roberts was born in South Wales. In June 1719, he was the mate of the slave ship *Princess*, which Davis captured. He joined the pirate crew and just six weeks later was elected their captain.

Roberts spent the next two months in the Bight of Africa, capturing several ships, one of which yielded 50 pounds (23kg) of gold dust. Then he crossed the Atlantic to Brazil. where he spent nine weeks without capturing anything. Then, as he approached the port of Bahia (now Salvador), he saw the anchorage was filled with the ships of the Lisbon fleet—Portugal's answer to the Spanish treasure fleets. He sneaked into

Bartholomew Roberts: Admiral of the Leeward Islands, 1719–20.

1 **November 1719** Bartholomew Roberts is anchored at the Île du Diable with three vessels, including a Portuguese treasure galleon. When a sail appears Roberts gives chase. His deputy Walter Kennedy grabs the opportunity to sail away with the treasure.

2 **Abandoned** by Kennedy, Roberts sails to Tobago, where he captures a sloop.

3 **February 1720** He then captures three more vessels off Barbados. Roberts encounters the French pirate Montigny La Palisse, but on February 21 they are driven from the area by Barbadian pirate hunters.

4 **March** Roberts careens his sloop in Dominica, and evades Martiniquan pirate hunters.

5 **May** Roberts heads north toward Newfoundland.

6 **June 21** The pirates attack the fishing station of Trepassey in Newfoundland, capturing a ship, and destroying over 22 more.

7 **July** After being rejoined by La Palisse, Roberts cruises the Grand Banks, capturing several more prizes before sailing southward again.

8 **Late August** Captures a sloop off South Carolina.

9 **Early September** Returns to the West Indies, putting in to La Désirade (then Carriacou) where he careens his ship.

10 **Late September** Roberts is joined by La Palisse, and together they attack Basseterre, destroying the town and capturing two ships. They then raid the French island of St. Barthelemy.

11 Roberts renames his ship *Royal Fortune*, and adopts the title "Admiral of the Leeward Islands." By early October, Roberts is operating in the Virgin Islands, where he captures a brig, which becomes his new *Royal Fortune*.

12 **Late October** Off Dominica the pirates capture a large Dutch merchantman, which becomes the third *Royal Fortune*. Roberts pillages and destroys 15 more ships in the island's anchorage.

13 **November** Realizing the Royal Navy are looking for him, Roberts quits the Caribbean, and sails north to Bermuda, before beginning a transatlantic voyage to fresh hunting grounds off the West African coast.

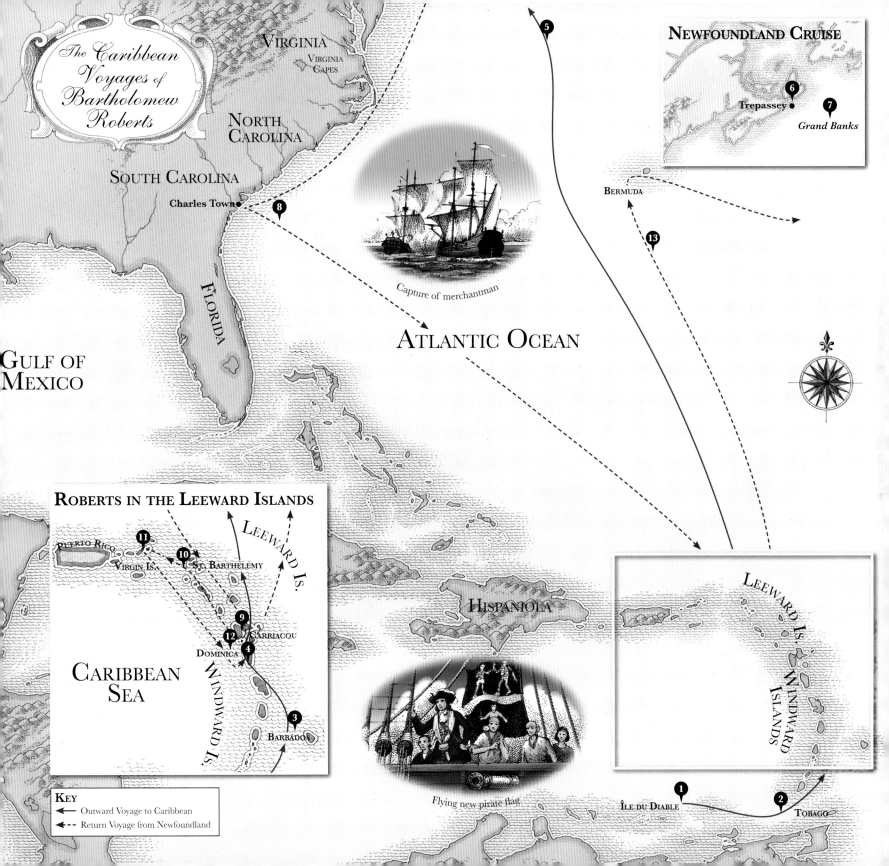

The Caribbean Voyages of Bartholomew Roberts

VIRGINIA

VIRGINIA CAPES

NORTH CAROLINA

SOUTH CAROLINA

Charles Town

FLORIDA

GULF OF MEXICO

ATLANTIC OCEAN

5

8

Capture of merchantman

NEWFOUNDLAND CRUISE

Trepassey **6**

7 *Grand Banks*

BERMUDA

13

ROBERTS IN THE LEEWARD ISLANDS

PUERTO RICO

VIRGIN IS.

11

10 ST. BARTHELEMY

LEEWARD IS.

9

12 SARRIACOU

DOMINICA **4**

CARIBBEAN SEA

WINDWARD IS.

3

BARBADOS

HISPANIOLA

LEEWARD IS.

WINDWARD ISLANDS

Flying new pirate flag

1 ÎLE DU DIABLE

2 TOBAGO

KEY

→ Outward Voyage to Caribbean

⇢ Return Voyage from Newfoundland

Above: Bartholomew Roberts, pictured with his ships the *Great Ranger* and the *Royal Fortune*, shown in the background entering the busy anchorage at Whydah. Roberts' flagship is depicted flying his own version of the "Jolly Roger." He captured a fleet of 11 slave ships, lying at anchor in the harbor.

the anchorage under cover of darkness, and overpowered the crew of the richest ship in the fleet. The hold of the treasure galleon *Sagrada Familia* was filled with plunder—the equivalent of 240,000 pieces-of-eight. Roberts and his crew were now wealthy men.

It was now November 1719. While anchored off the coast of Venezuela, Roberts spotted a sail. He took a captured sloop and gave chase, leaving Walter Kennedy in charge of his remaining ships, and the treasure. While he was gone, Kennedy absconded with the

ships—and the loot. Undeterred, Roberts sailed to the West Indies, where he wreaked a trail of destruction, capturing several ships, and evading the pirate hunters sent from Barbados and Martinique to track him down. He even had the temerity to order a new

A. The Habit of ye Fishermen. B. The Line. C. The manner of Fishing. D. The Dressers of ye Fish. E. The Trough into which they throw ye Cod when Dressed. F. Salt Boxes. G. The manner of Carrying ye Cod. H. The Cleansing ye Cod. I. A Press extract ye Oyl from ye Cods Livers. K. Casks to receive ye Water & Blood that comes from ye Livers. L. Another Cask to receive ye Oyl. M. The manner of Drying ye Cod.

flag made, designed to intimidate the inhabitants of the two islands by way of revenge. Still, by the start of the following summer it was clear that the West Indies were becoming dangerous and so he headed north to a new cruising ground.

MORE GOOD FORTUNE

The summer of 1720 was spent off Newfoundland, where Roberts preyed on the fishing fleets gathered off the Grand Banks. He even attacked a Newfoundland fishing station, capturing a new ship which he claimed for himself, renaming her *Good Fortune* in the process. That summer he captured more than 40 vessels, not counting small fishing boats. By September, he was back in the West Indies, where he attacked several small French settlements and captured yet more merchantmen. He also captured a ship for his own, calling her the *Royal Fortune*,

Right: The HMS *Swallow*, shown firing at the *Royal Fortune*, brought Roberts' legendary career to an end.

Left: The undefended Newfoundland fisheries offered pirates like Roberts the opportunity for easy plunder.

a name he would give to two more ships in as many months. According to the newspapers, Roberts described himself as "the Admiral of the Windward Islands." However, by the time the paper was printed, Roberts was on the far side of the Atlantic, in yet another *Royal Fortune*.

THE LAST BATTLE

In April 1721, Roberts reached the West African coast. He embarked on a leisurely rampage, capturing several slavers, including the 40-gun Royal African Company ship

Onslow which, naturally, he renamed *Royal Fortune*. Another prize was also turned into a pirate ship, which he called the *Great Ranger*. He was still off the West African coast the following January when he captured 11 more slavers at the port of Whydah (Ouidah). It was then that Black Bart's luck finally ran out.

On February 5, a ship appeared off Whydah, and Roberts sent the *Great Ranger* out to intercept her. The newcomer fled over the horizon and the pirate ship gave chase. However, once out of sight of land the stranger turned about and gave battle. She turned out to be the 50-gun warship HMS *Swallow*, commanded by Captain Challoner Ogle. The *Swallow* captured the *Great Ranger* after a two-hour battle, by which time the pirate ship was a shattered wreck. Ogle then set course for Whydah again.

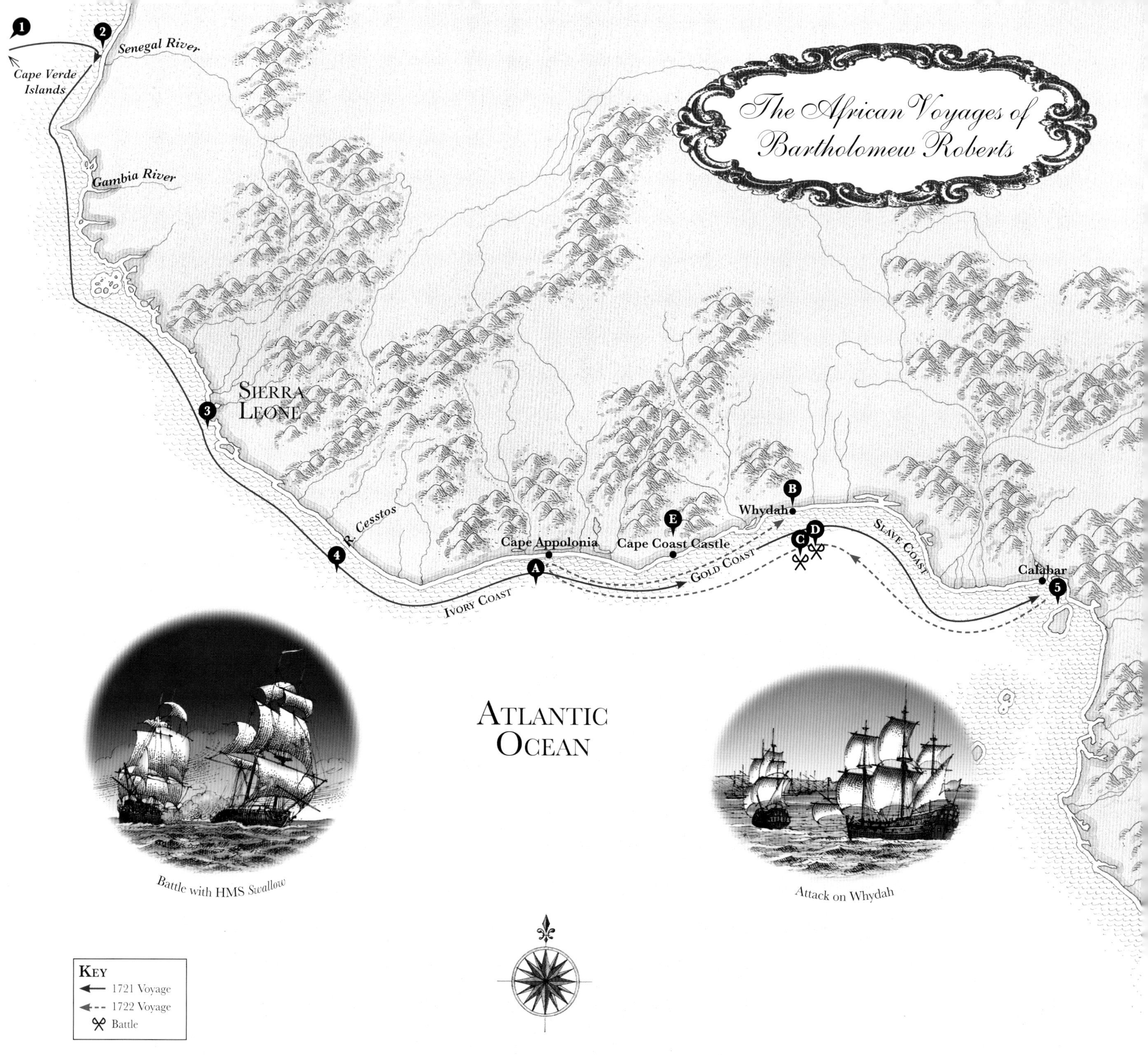

The African Voyages of Bartholomew Roberts
1
2
Cape Verde Islands
Senegal River
Gambia River
Sierra Leone
3
4
R. Cesstos
Ivory Coast
A
Cape Appolonia
E
Cape Coast Castle
Gold Coast
B
Whydah
C
D
Slave Coast
Calabar
5
Atlantic Ocean
Key
1721 Voyage
1722 Voyage
Battle

Battle with HMS *Swallow*

Attack on Whydah

Bartholomew Roberts off the African Coast, 1721–22

1721

1 **Late May 1721** Bartholomew Roberts arrives in the Cape Verde Islands, where he takes on water and provisions.

2 **June** The *Royal Fortune* makes an African landfall off the Senegal River, where two French sloops are captured. One of them is renamed *Ranger*.

The Royal Fortune

3 **Late June** Roberts and his men spend six weeks of the coast of Sierra Leone, careening their ship and carousing on shore.

4 **August** Roberts arrives off the River Cesstos, where he encounters and captures the Royal African Company ship *Onslow*. Roberts names her his fourth, and last, *Royal Fortune*.

5 **October** The two pirate ships reach Calabar, where they capture three slave ships from Bristol. They attempt to careen their ships, but local hostility forces the pirates to head back toward the west.

1722

A **Early January 1722** Roberts captures two more slave ships off Cape Appolonia on the Ivory Coast, .

B **January 11** Roberts appears off Whydah (Ouidah) on the Slave Coast, where he captures 11 slave ships. One of them is renamed the *Great Ranger*, while the sloop *Ranger* becomes *Little Ranger*. All the merchant captains offer him protection money, save one. Roberts retaliates by burning the *Porcupine* to the waterline, while her human cargo is still on board.

C **February 5** HMS *Swallow* appears off Whydah, and thinking her a slave ship, Roberts sends the *Great Ranger* in pursuit. Once out of sight of land Captain Ogle attacks the pirate ship, capturing her after a two-hour fight.

D **February 10** The *Swallow* reappears off Whydah, and Roberts sails the *Royal Fortune* out to give battle. He is killed during the first exchange; after a brief fight his ship is captured.

E **April 1722** Bartholomew Roberts' crew are tried for piracy at Cape Coast Castle—54 of them are sentenced and hanged.

When the *Swallow* reappeared on February 10, Roberts dressed in his finest clothes and sailed out of the harbor in the *Royal Fortune*, to do battle. The *Swallow* fired first and the conspicuous Roberts was killed in the first broadside. His men threw the body over the side and kept fighting, but they were no match for Ogle's well-trained gunners.

Within an hour the pirates surrendered. Of *Royal Fortune*'s 152 crew members, 52 were found to be Africans—all former slaves. They were sold back into slavery while their shipmates were thrown into the cells of Cape Coast Castle. They were eventually put on trial, and in late April 1722, some 54 of them were sentenced to death, and hanged in a line of gallows erected along the shore. Thirty-seven more were sentenced to servitude as indentured servants and were shipped to the plantations of the West Indies—a death sentence in all but name. More than 70 more were acquitted because they managed to prove they had been abducted against their will. This mass hanging marked the end of the Golden Age of Piracy. All that remained was to tie up the many loose ends.

"Black Bart" and His Sense of Style

Bartholomew Roberts soon acquired the nickname "Black Bart" (or "Black Barty"). Apparently it stemmed from his dark complexion rather than from any particularly sinister streak he possessed. By all accounts Roberts was also regarded as good-looking—at least by the standards of the day. Later, he became known as a snappy dresser, too, and according to Captain Johnson in his history of piracy, on the day of his death Roberts wore: "A rich crimson damask waistcoat and breeches, a red feather in his hat, a gold chain around his neck, with a diamond cross hanging to it, a sword in his hand, and two pairs of pistols hanging at the end of a silk sling slung over his shoulders."

Above: Roberts was killed during the first exchange of broadsides between the *Royal Fortune* and HMS *Swallow*. His dispirited crew dumped his body over the side to prevent it becoming a macabre trophy for Captain Ogle.

Walter Kennedy and the Pirate Lords

During the Great Voyage two groups of pirates abandoned Bartholomew Roberts and forged their own brief careers. They were led by Walter Kennedy and Thomas Anstis.

Above: Merchantman being pursued by a larger and more powerful pirate ship, similar to Kennedy's *Royal Rover*.

Walter Kennedy and Thomas Anstis, represent the two loose ends of the story of the Great Voyage. Known as "Pirate Lords" for being ringleaders in the mutiny of September 1718, both served under Captain Howell Davis and then Bartholomew Roberts.

WALTER KENNEDY

The first of these Pirate Lords was Walter Kennedy, an Irishman and former pickpocket. In November 1719, he deserted Bartholomew Roberts, and sailed away with his treasure, and his flagship, the *Royal Rover*.

The Piratical Adventures of Walter Kennedy, 1719–20

1 **In November 1719**, Walter Kennedy is Bartholomew Roberts' deputy. The pirates lie at anchor off Île du Diable on the Venezuelan coast. Their force consists of a sloop, the brig *Royal Rover*, and the *Sagrada Familia*, a rich Portuguese treasure ship. When Roberts sets off in the sloop to chase a prize, Kennedy absconds with the treasure.

2 Somewhere off the Leeward Islands Kennedy moves the Portuguese treasure on to the *Royal Rover* and hands the galleon over to one of his prisoners, who sails her into Antigua.

3 **December 15** Kennedy captures the merchantman *Sea Nymph* off Barbados. After a week he releases the ship, unloading some of his disaffected crew on to her. He then sails north.

4 **January 1720** Cruises off the Virginia Capes, but only captures a single small prize. When he releases his prize, eight more of his crew defect.

5 **February** Captures the New York merchantman the *Eagle* off the Bahamas, which carries a cargo of rum. While the bulk of his men drink the plunder, Kennedy absconds again in the *Eagle*, with 48 loyal crewmen.

6 The *Royal Rover* anchors off the Dutch island of St. Thomas, but is captured by pirate-hunters when the crew is ashore. She founders on the voyage to Nevis.

St. Thomas

7 **March** Kennedy sails the *Eagle* across the Atlantic, hoping to make landfall in Ireland.

8 **May** Instead, the pirates encounter a storm off the north of Ireland, and are shipwrecked on the coast of Argyll, Scotland.

9 **June** While Kennedy heads to London, most of his crew arrive in Edinburgh, where their free-spending causes suspicion. They are eventually arrested.

10 **December** The majority of Kennedy's crew are hanged in Edinburgh.

11 **July 1721** Kennedy is arrested for theft in London, whereupon he is identified and tried. On July 19, he is hanged at Execution Dock, Wapping.

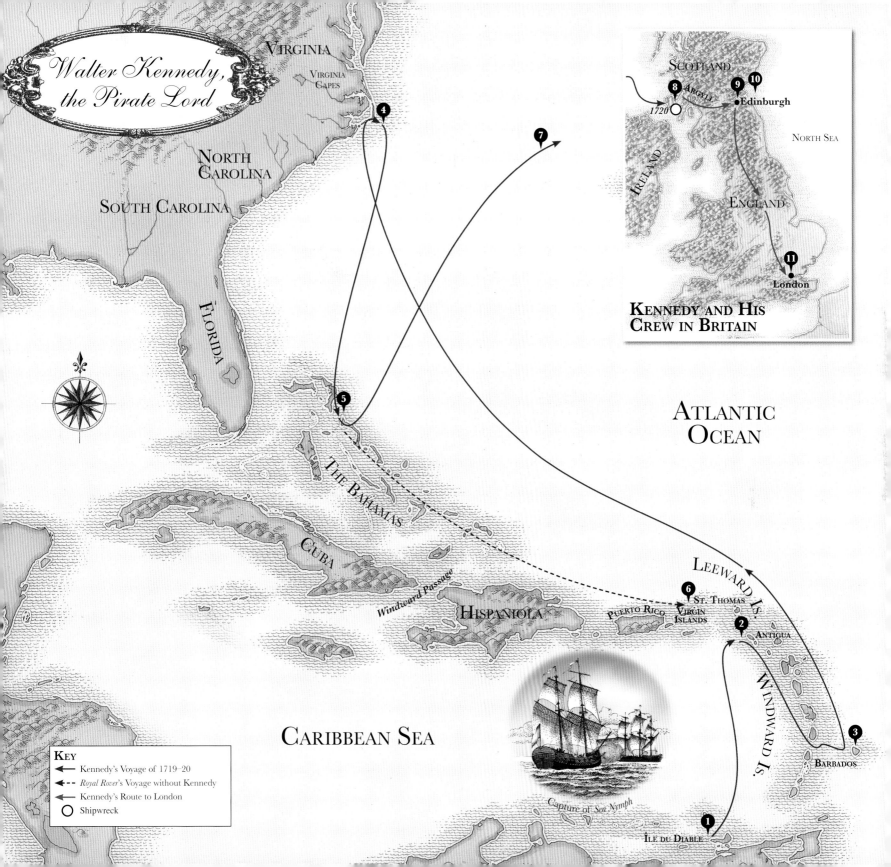

Walter Kennedy, the Pirate Lord

VIRGINIA CAPES

NORTH CAROLINA

SOUTH CAROLINA

FLORIDA

4

7

5

THE BAHAMAS

CUBA

Windward Passage

HISPANIOLA

PUERTO RICO

VIRGIN ISLANDS

ST. THOMAS

6

ANTIGUA

2

LEEWARD IS.

WINDWARD IS.

BARBADOS

3

ATLANTIC OCEAN

CARIBBEAN SEA

Capture of Sea Nymph

1

ÎLE DU DIABLE

SCOTLAND

ARGYLL

8

9

10

1720

Edinburgh

IRELAND

ENGLAND

NORTH SEA

11

London

KENNEDY AND HIS CREW IN BRITAIN

KEY

→ Kennedy's Voyage of 1719–20

--→ *Royal Rover*'s Voyage without Kennedy

→ Kennedy's Route to London

○ Shipwreck

After a brief foray into the West Indies, Kennedy headed north to Virginia. He was an indifferent navigator and an unpopular leader—and each time he captured a prize, more of his men deserted. Therefore, in February 1720, when Kennedy captured the sloop *Eagle*, he transferred the bulk of the Bahia treasure to her and abandoned the rest of his crew in the *Royal Rover*. The latter later foundered off Saint Croix in the Virgin Islands.

Kennedy planned to sail the *Eagle* to his native Ireland. However, his sloop was overtaken by a storm and was driven on to the coast of Argyll in Scotland. Several pirates were later arrested in Edinburgh, after spending Portuguese gold. They were put on trial and nine of them were hanged in December 1720. Kennedy himself made it as far as London, but he was arrested—possibly for theft—and identified by one of his former victims. He was put on trial, convicted, and on July 19, 1721, he was hanged at Wapping's Execution Dock.

THOMAS ANSTIS

Another of the Pirate Lords, Thomas Anstis, was with Bartholomew Roberts when Walter Kennedy deserted him in November 1719.

He remained a trusted lieutenant to Roberts until April 1721, when Anstis in his 18-gun brig *Good Fortune* became separated from Roberts during a mid-Atlantic storm. Anstis spent the next year cruising the waters of the Caribbean, but despite gaining a reputation for violence he wasn't a particularly successful pirate, and gathered very little in the way of plunder.

By the following spring, Anstis had been deposed as captain. The pirates attempted to secure a pardon, spending the summer loitering on the Cuban coast, hoping for clemency that never came. In August 1722, they returned to sea, by which time John Finn had become the new captain. They continued southward along the West Indies chain until they reached Tobago.

Finn decided to careen the *Good Fortune* in a secluded bay, but on May 17, 1723, the 40-gun HMS *Winchelsea* appeared. Anstis and a skeleton crew were still on board the pirate ship and they escaped, leaving Finn and their shipmates behind to be captured. As for Anstis, his crew had had enough of him. They shot him as he was sleeping, and took the ship into the Dutch colony of Curaçao, where they asked for clemency. Some were acquitted, but most were tried and hanged.

Right: To amuse themselves, Anstis' men held a mock pirate trial during their stay in Cuba—where the pirate judge and jury willingly sentenced their shipmates to death!

The Pirate Code

Although pirates operated outside the law, they frequently established their own codes of conduct.

These articles of agreement were designed to prevent disputes over the division of rum or plunder, and some even provided for the needs of pirates who were wounded in battle. The example shown was drawn up by Bartholomew Roberts and his men in 1721, and they swore on the Bible to uphold the codes.

I *Every man has a Vote in Affairs of Moment, has equal Tide to the fresh Provisions, or strong Liquors, at any Time seized, & use them at pleasure, unless a Scarcity make it necessary, for the good of all, to Vote a Retrenchment.*

II *Every man to be called fairly in rum, by List, on Board of Prizes, because they were on these Occasions allow'd a Shift of Cloaths: Bur if they defrauded the Company to the Value of a Dollar, in Plate, Jewels, or Money, MAROONING was their punishment.*

III *No Person to game at Cards or Dice for Money.*

IV *The Lights & Candles to be put out at eight o' clock at Night. If any of the Crew, after that Hour, still remained inclined for Drinking, they were to do it on the open Deck.*

V *To Keep their Piece, Pistols, & Cutlass clean, & fit for Service.*

VI *No Boy or Woman to be allow'd amongst them. If any Man were found seducing any of the latter Sex, and carried her to Sea, disguised, he was to suffer Death.*

VII *To Desert the Ship, or their Quarters in Battle, was punished with Death, or Marooning*

VIII *No striking one another on Board, but every Man's Quarrels to be ended on shore, at Sword & Pistol, thus: The Quarter-Master of the Ship, when the Parties will not come to any Reconciliation, accompanies them on Shore with what Assistance he thinks proper, & turns the Disputants Back to Back, at so many Paces, Distance. At the Word of Command, they turn and fire immediately, (or else the Piece is knocked out of their Hands). If both miss, they come to their Cutlasses, and then he is declared Victor who draws the first Blood.*

IX *No Man to talk of breaking up their Way of Living, till each has shared £1000. If in order to this, any Man shall lose a Limb, or become a Cripple in their Service, he was to have 800 Dollars, out of pub lick Stock, and for lesser Hurts, proportionably.*

X *The Captain and Quarter-Master to receive two Share of a Prize: the Master, Boatswain, & gunner, one Share and a half, and other Officers, one and a Quarter.*

XI *The Musicians to have Rest on the Sabbath Day, but the other six Days and Nights, none without special Favour.*

The Privateers

Privateering is often called licensed piracy—the only difference being that privateers were encouraged to attack their victims, and were used as legitimate tools of war. During the Age of Sail it became a highly lucrative business.

From the Middle Ages onward, privateers acted like pirates, with one important difference—their attacks were perfectly legal, a well-regulated and fully recognized extension of warfare. As long as the privateer's country was at war, the ship he attacked belonged to an enemy, and he held a letter of marque, then these activities were perfectly lawful.

Privateering really came into its own during the wars of the 18th century, when Britain and France seemed rarely at peace with one other. Both countries made extensive use of privateers, as did the American colonists, whose vessels were turned against the British during the American wars of independence. During this period, hundreds of letters of marque were issued, and shipowners hurried to build purpose-built privateering ships.

The profits that could be made were immense. One or two rich prizes could pay for the building of a ship, and earn the captain and the shipowners a small fortune. A string of successes also often allowed the shipowner to convert the best of these prizes into more privateering vessels. In other words, as a war dragged on, the threat posed by privateers tended to increase—except when the coastline of a country was blockaded by an enemy navy, as happened to America in its two wars with Britain, or France and Spain during the French revolutionary wars. In these situations enterprising privateering captains made extensive use of neutral or foreign ports, particularly in places like the Caribbean, the Indian Ocean, or the Pacific.

Governments earned money from privateering too—an average of 10 percent of the value of any ship captured. For them, privateering was a cheap and effective tool to use against a rival power. The problem was that when a war ended, some privateers were tempted to turn to piracy rather than to less lucrative occupations.

Left: Privateering existed long before its 18th-century heyday. This painting by Van Wieringen, c.1625, depicts an English privateer off La Rochelle, France.

The Business of Privateering

Privateering was essentially piracy legitimized by the privateer's government in time of war. The issue of a privateering license meant that privateers were supported by the weight of the law.

Above: An 18th-century privateer depicted in action, causing havoc to a French mercantile convoy—*Commodore Walker's Action: the privateer "Boscawen" engaging a fleet of French ships*, May 1745, by Charles Brooking.

The whole business of privateering was scrupulously regulated in order to avoid any accusations of piracy, and licensed by a letter of marque.

THE LETTER OF MARQUE

A letter of marque could be issued to a privateer captain and his crew in time of war, authorizing him to plunder enemy shipping. The system first originated in the Middle Ages when "letters of reprisal" gave official sanction to a sea captain who wanted to seek revenge for the loss of a ship at the hands of the enemy. From the late 17th century onward, "letters of reprisal" had become known as "letters of marque," and were issued to anyone with the means to furnish a privately armed warship, or privateer, and who was willing to pay the government a deposit to guarantee their good conduct. These letters were all-important. If a

A Privateering Letter of Marque, Issued by the U.S. President in 1800

John Adams, President of the United States of America, presents greeting.

Know ye, that in pursuance of an Act of Congress of the United States in this case provided, passed on 9th July 1798, I have commissioned, and by these presents do commission the private armed ship called the Herald *of the burden of 325 tons, or thereabouts, owned by Ebenezer Preble and Samuel Jackman of Boston, Merchants, and Nathaniel Silsbee of Salem, Mariner, all in the State of Massachusetts, mounting ten guns and navigated by 30 men… to subdue, sieze or take any armed French vessel which shall be found within the jurisdictional limits of the United States, or elsewhere on the high seas.*

privateer was captured and was unable to produce his letter of marque, he was liable to be tried and hanged as a pirate.

In effect, the government had entered into a business contract with the ship owners and captain. These people put up a bond as a guarantee of good behavior (in 1812, up to $10,000 in the USA; £3,000 in Britain/Canada). In addition, the government imposed restrictions on the privateers, usually in the form of a set of instructions, like the one shown right, which dates from the American Revolution (1775–83).

In return for agreeing to the instructions, the government regulated the sale of captured vessels, which was meant to take place in a friendly port, and earned a 10 percent stake in the profits. This made the business of privateering highly profitable— except of course for the ship owners and captains whose ships were taken.

Below: British sailors "cutting out" a French privateer during the French Revolutionary War, while she lies anchored in front of a French battery.

IN CONGRESS – WEDNESDAY, APRIL 3, 1776

INSTRUCTIONS to the COMMANDERS of Private Ships or Vessels of War, which shall have Commissions or Letters of Marque and Reprisal, authorizing them to make Captures of British Vessels and Cargoes.

I You may, by Force of Arms, attack, subdue, and take all ships and other Vessels belonging to the Inhabitants of Great-Britain, on the High Seas, between high-water and low-water marks, except Ships and Vessels bringing Persons who intend to settle and reside in the United Colonies, or bringing Arms, Ammunition, and War-like Stores to the said Colonies, for the use of such Inhabitants thereof that are Friends to the American Cause, which you shall suffer to pass unmolested, the Commanders thereof permitting a peaceable Search, and giving satisfactory Information of the Contents of the Landings, and Destination of the Voyages.

II You may, by Force of Arms, attack, subdue, and take all Ships and their Vessels whatsoever carrying Soldiers, Arms, Gun-powder, Ammunition, Provisions, or any other contraband Goods, to any of the British Armies or Ships of War employed against these Colonies.

III You shall bring such Ships and Vessels you shall take, with their Guns, Rigging, Tackle, Apparel, Furniture, and Landings to some convenient Port or Ports of the United Colonies, that Proceedings may thereupon be had in due Form before the Courts which are or shall be there appointed to hear and determine Causes civil and maritime.

IV You or one of your Chief Officers shall bring or send the master and Pilot and one or more principal Person or persons of the Company of every Ship or Vessel by you taken, as soon after the Capture as may be, to the judge or judges of such Court aforesaid.

V You shall keep and preserve every Ship or Vessel and Cargo by you taken, until they shall by Sentence of a Court properly authorized be adjudged lawful Prize, not selling, spoiling, wasting, or diminishing the same, or breaking the Bulk thereof, nor suffering any such Thing to be done.

VI If you, or any of your Officers and Crew shall, in cold Blood, kill or maim, or, by Torture or otherwise, cruelly, inhumanely, and contrary to common Usage and the Practice of civilized nations in War, treat any person or persons surprised in the Ship or Vessel you shall take, the Offender shall be severely punished.

By Order of Congress,
John Hancock PRESIDENT

America's Rebel Privateers

When the American colonists rebelled against British rule, they had no navy and few ships. Privateering was one way that American sailors could play their part in the struggle for liberty.

When the American Revolution began in 1775, America had no purpose-built warships, and those that were built or commissioned were used as commerce raiders.

American ship owners quickly took advantage of the conflict to turn their vessels into privateers. By the time the war ended, almost 800 letters of marque had been issued by the Continental Congress or by individual colonies. The majority of these went to shipowners and captains from the ports of New England. Philadelphia was another privateers' center, while a few operated farther south from the ports of Baltimore, Annapolis, Wilmington, and Charleston.

The first prizes were captured during the summer of 1775, and by that winter American privateers had become a serious menace to British shipping in American waters, particularly off New England and the middle colonies. By April 1776, some 30 British or loyalist ships had been captured off Boston alone, which forced the Royal Navy to divert valuable ships to patrol the American coast. Some of the earliest attacks were made by small longboats. For instance, in April 1775, rebel whaling boats captured a British schooner off Martha's Vineyard.

Left: An American naval officer is portrayed attempting to enforce discipline on his unruly crew of former privateersmen, c.1776.

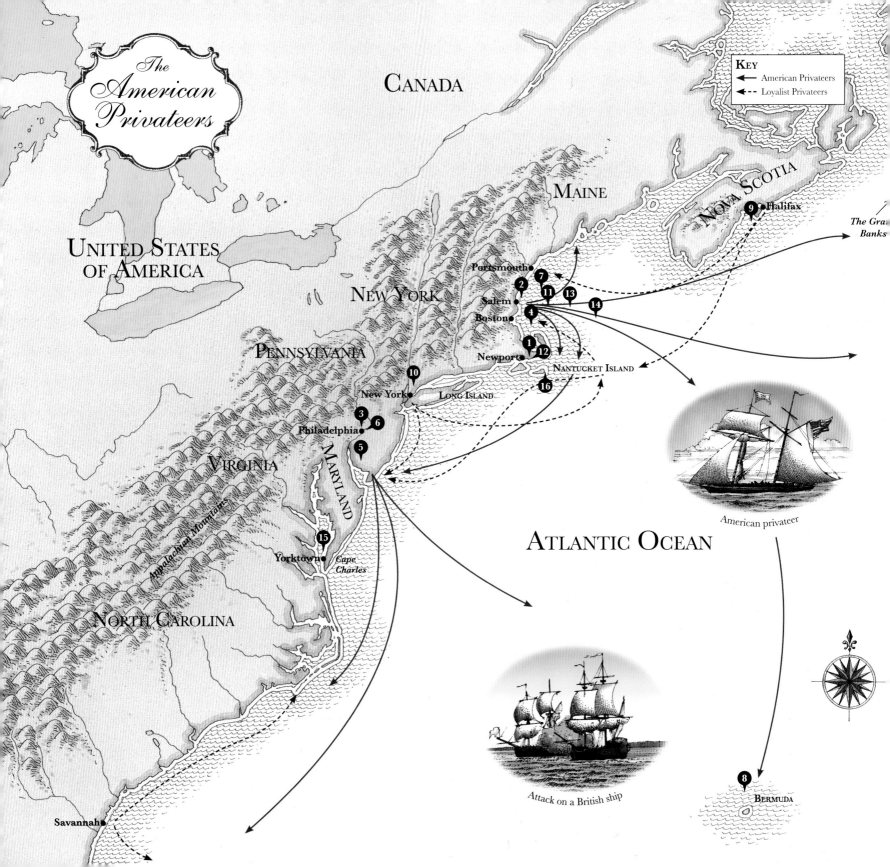

The American Privateers

CANADA

UNITED STATES OF AMERICA

MAINE

NOVA SCOTIA

KEY
→ American Privateers
⇢ Loyalist Privateers

● **9** Halifax

The Grand Banks

NEW YORK

Portsmouth ● **7**
2
Salem ●
Boston ● **4** **11** **13** **14**

PENNSYLVANIA

1 **12**
Newport ●

Nantucket Island

10

16

New York ●

LONG ISLAND

3 **6**

Philadelphia ●

5

VIRGINIA

MARYLAND

Appalachian Mountains

15

Yorktown ●

Cape Charles

NORTH CAROLINA

ATLANTIC OCEAN

American privateer

Attack on a British ship

8

BERMUDA

Savannah ●

The Pirates and Privateers of the American Revolution, 1775–82

1775

1 April The first "spider boat"—a longboat crewed by privateersmen—attacks British merchant shipping in the harbor of Newport, Rhode Island. Technically, this attack wasn't sanctioned by a government, so it constituted an act of piracy.

2 Early Summer Following the example of Rhode Island, the legislature of Massachusetts, based in Salem, issues its first privateering letter of marque.

3 October Foundations of United States Navy seen when Congress, based in Philadelphia, authorizes the building of the first purpose-built American warship.

4 November British vessels are captured by American privateers off Boston.

5 December Commissioning of first U.S. warships in Delaware River.

1776

6 March The Continental Congress in Philadelphia authorizes privateering, and issues the first United States letters of marque.

7 June The privateer *Yankee Hero* is captured by the frigate HMS *Melford* off Newburyport, Massachusetts. Their spirited defense against a superior foe earns her crew widespread acclaim.

8 July Captain Fiske, commanding the *Tyrannicide* of Salem, captures several British merchant ships off Bermuda.

9 August The first Loyalist American privateering prize is brought in to Halifax, Nova Scotia.

10 August American privateers attack British transports and warships in the Hudson River, above New York.

1777–82

11 Spring 1777 Salem becomes the busiest privateering port in the Americas. It is claimed the harbor is filled with captured British shipping.

12 1778 American privateers help the French launch their abortive attack against Newport, Rhode Island, which is held by a British garrison and fleet.

13 Spring 1780 The purpose-built privateers *General Washington* and *General Pickering*, both of Salem, begin their first highly successful cruises.

14 Summer 1781 The privateer *Rattlesnake* enters service in Salem, Massachussets. She is the largest purpose-built privateer of the war.

15 October 1781 British army surrenders at Yorktown, Virginia

16 Spring 1782 Loyalists attack Nantucket, in the last large-scale privateering action of the war.

However, by early 1776 larger and better-armed privateers were operating far out into the Atlantic or the Caribbean. This left the smaller privateers to concentrate on harassing the British and Canadian fishing fleets off Newfoundland. Captured British ships often provided much-needed weapons and ammunition, which were then used against their former owners.

In 1777, a total of 73 American ships were registered as privateers. By 1781, this had grown to 449 vessels—a whole fleet of privately owned warships. By the end of the war many of these ships were large, purpose-built vessels, carrying 20 guns or more. During the war these privateers captured over 3,000 British merchant ships.

Americans weren't the only ones to benefit from privateering. British, American Loyalist, and Canadian privateers were also granted letters of marque by the British crown, and both Halifax in Nova Scotia and British-held New York became thriving privateering ports. When France and Spain, became involved, the possibilities offered to British privateers increased dramatically. More than 2,500 French, Spanish, or American ships had been captured by the time the war ended.

The Profits of Privateering

Privateersmen received no regular pay, so their only source of income was prize money. Typically, an American sailor could earn over $500 each time his ship captured a prize. This was the equivalent of ten years of seaman's wages. Huge profits were there for the taking. For instance, the American privateer *Rattlesnake* of Salem, Massachusetts, took prizes worth more than a million dollars in a single cruise. For a few short years ports like Salem, Boston, and Baltimore became "boom towns," funded by this form of legitimized piracy.

Above: The Americans had no privateering monopoly—the British, Canadians, and American Loyalists also used sloops like this to prey on American merchantmen. *The Privateer "Fly" and Other Vessels*, by Francis Holman.

John Paul Jones

A hero to Americans, and a privateer who crossed the line to the British, John Paul Jones was the founder of the U.S. Navy during the American Revolution.

Above: John Paul Jones may have been the founder of the United States Navy, but the British regarded him as little more than a pirate.

While Americans viewed John Paul Jones as a national hero, their first well-known naval fighter, the British saw him as a privateer who had strayed over the line into common robbery and piracy.

THE YOUNG JOHN PAUL

John Paul Jones was born in 1747 as the son of a gardener in southwest Scotland. In fact his surname was Paul—the Jones was added later. He became a sailor when he was 13, serving as an apprentice on board the *Friendship*, and for the next decade he served aboard several British merchant ships, becoming a captain in 1770. In 1773, he killed one of his crewmen during a dispute,

and fled to America. It was at this stage he adopted the surname Jones. In 1775, when the rebellion against British rule began, Jones made his way to Philadelphia to offer his services. He was commissioned into the fledgling U.S. Navy, and for the next year he served as second-in-command of the USS *Alfred*, an improvised warship based on the Delaware River. He continually lobbied for his own command, and in June 1777 he was given the 18-gun brig USS *Ranger*.

THE CRUISE OF THE RANGER

Captain Jones sailed from Portsmouth, New Hampshire, in November 1777, and arrived in France less than a month later, having captured two British merchant ships on the way. It was there, in Quiberon Bay, that his ship was saluted by the French fleet—the first official salute given to the new American flag. In early April, he resumed his cruise, heading into the Irish Sea. He captured two prizes, then led a raid on the small coastal town of Whitehaven in the north of England. Jones spiked the guns of a shore battery, burned the small vessels in the harbor, and then sailed away.

His next raid was even more audacious. He landed on the Scottish coast near Kirkcudbright—in his home county—and seized the house of the leading landowner in the area, the Earl of Selkirk. The Earl was away when the Americans arrived and so, denied a lucrative kidnap victim, the sailors ransacked the house before they left.

Jones resumed his cruise, and on April 24, he encountered the British brig HMS *Drake*

Below: John Paul Jones boarding HMS *Drake* in 1777. The artist has emphasized Jones' roots by giving him a Scottish soldiers' bonnet.

off Carrickfergus in Northern Ireland. Jones captured her after an hour-long fight. The *Drake* was then safely brought back to Brest as a prize by Jones' lieutenant.

BATTLE OF FLAMBOROUGH HEAD

In 1779, Jones was given the command of a new warship—a former French merchantman that he renamed the USS *Bonhomme Richard*. He set sail in August, accompanied by a small flotilla of French warships and privateers. This force captured three prizes in the Irish Sea, then Jones steered north around Scotland, to enter the North Sea. On September 23, he was passing Flamborough Head on the Yorkshire coast. There he encountered a British convoy returning from the Baltic, escorted by two warships. Jones gave battle, and steered his ship toward the 50-gun warship HMS *Serapis*.

Jones knew that the gunnery of the British ship would be superior to his own, so he decided to board the British ship. However, the boarding attempt failed, and so the two ships lay alongside each other, exchanging broadsides at point-blank range. At one point the American colors were shot away. Captain Pearson of the *Serapis* hailed the

Above: The Battle of Flamborough Head, fought on September 13, 1779. The battle saw John Paul Jones in the USS *Bonhomme Richard* capture HMS *Serapis* after a particularly hard-fought duel.

American, asking him, "Has your ship struck?" Jones replied "I have not yet begun to fight," and the bloodletting continued.

Finally, a hand grenade detonated in *Serapis'* magazine, causing the explosion of a large quantity of gunpowder and crippling the British ship. Captain Pearson had no choice but to surrender. By that time both ships were shattered—the *Bonhomme Richard* sank soon afterwards, after Jones had transferred to the crippled *Serapis*. He limped back to France, and into the history books as America's first naval hero.

A CAPTAIN FOR HIRE

In France, Jones was feted for his victory, and his deeds were honored by a song, which described him as an "American pirate." When the war ended in 1783, Jones spent another five years in France before gaining employment in the Russian Navy. He served with distinction but returned to France two years later and died there in 1792. In 1905, his body was exhumed and returned to America, to be buried in the chapel of the U.S. Naval Academy in Annapolis.

The French Privateers

During the age of sailing warfare the French fleet were rarely able to stand up to the British at sea, and consequently relied heavily on privateers.

The French privateers fought what they called "the little war"—meaning the war on commerce—by attacking British merchant ships and damaging her trade activity.

PRIVATEERS IN THE AMERICAS

During the buccaneering heyday of the mid- to late 17th century, the French had made extensive use of privateers, based first on Tortuga and then Saint Dominique (now Haiti). Then came a succession of wars against Britain, from the War of the Grand Alliance (1688–97) and the War of the Spanish Succession (1701–14), through to the American Revolution (1775–83—France

involved from 1778), and the French Revolutionary War (1793–1802). This last conflict led directly to the Napoleonic Wars (1803–15). Given the number of French and British islands in the Caribbean, and the general lack of large naval forces, the region became a privateering haven, with places like Martinique became bustling centers.

The Treaty of Whitehall signed between France and England in 1686 stipulated that any minor clash in the New World would not lead to a war between the two countries. The aim was to prevent border clashes erupting into anything serious, but in effect it also blurred the line between piracy and privateering in American and Caribbean waters. In war the French embraced privateering with a passion, particularly as legitimate trade between France and its overseas colonies was disrupted. Privateering became a lucrative alternative to commerce.

Above: This painting by Samuel Drummond shows the crew of the British sloop *Windsor Castle* overpowering the French privateers who attacked them in 1807.

The French islands of the Lesser Antilles developed into major privateering bases during the War of the Austrian Succession (1739–48), and French privateers operating out of bases in Canada preyed on British shipping off Newfoundland and the American coast. Privateering had become big business. During the period from 1739

The Corsair Jean Bart

One of the most successful French privateers of the late 17th century was Jean Bart (1651–1702), the son of a fisherman who became a Dunkirk-based privateering captain. During the 1670s, he operated against the Dutch in the Mediterranean, and during the War of the Grand Alliance he preyed on shipping off the British coast. In 1691, he even led a raid on the Scottish coast, and three years later he captured a large Dutch grain fleet, which he sailed up the River Seine to help feed the poorly fed population of Paris.

Right: Despite his lowly birth, Jean Bart became an officer in the French navy. Here he is depicted threatening to blow up his ship, rather than allow its demoralized crew to surrender.

to 1783, more than 3,500 British ships were captured by French privateers—almost a tenth of the British mercantile and fishing fleets of the time.

During the Seven Years War the French reliance on privateering reached new levels, and hundreds of letters of marque were issued, both by the government in Paris and by French colonial governors. As a result, the British diverted precious resources to capture the privateering havens of Louisburg, Martinique, Guadeloupe, and Dominica. French privateers were also active during the American Revolution, when an under-strength and poorly maintained Royal Navy was hard-pressed to cope with a simultaneous naval war against America, France, Holland, and Spain. The British learned their lesson and so during the French Revolutionary War they maintained a strong presence in the Caribbean, forcing French privateers like Robert Surcouf to hunt further afield. Still, French privateers remained a serious threat to British interests throughout the period, and British warships that could be used elsewhere were tied down, protecting convoys.

EUROPEAN PRIVATEERS

On the other side of the Atlantic the French ports of La Rochelle, Nantes Bayonne, St. Malo, and Dunkirk all developed into thriving privateering ports during the 18th century. Privateering crews tended to avoid Brest, Cherbourg, and Toulon, which as French naval ports were heavily blockaded by the British in times of war. During the American Revolution many of these French privateering ports provided facilities to American privateers, who often cruised in consort with the French. By the time of the French Revolution, Dunkirk and St. Malo were effectively closed down as privateering bases by British blockading squadrons, but Nantes, La Rochelle, and Bayonne on the Bay of Biscay continued to operate as privateering havens.

Below: In 1811, HMS *Hermes* rammed the French privateer *La Mouche* off Boulogne, leaving no survivors.

Robert Surcouf:
King of the Corsairs

The most successful French privateer of the 18th and early 19th century was Robert Surcouf, whose exploits earned him the nickname "King of the Corsairs."

During his privateering career, Robert Surcouf became a legend in France and a public enemy in Britain. He was renowned by both countries for his gallantry and chivalry.

The privateering achievements of Robert Surcouf made him a hero in France.

THE YOUNG ADVENTURER

Robert Surcouf was born in 1773 in the port of St. Malo in Brittany, traditionally a privateering stronghold. At the age of 15 he became a sailor, serving on board a slave ship bound for the Indian Ocean. He spent five years as a slaver, before returning to St. Malo in 1792—the year the French Revolution began. Surcouf returned to sea, and was in the Île de France (now Mauritius) in the Indian Ocean early the following year when Britain declared war on France. He helped drive off two British blockading warships, which made him a local hero, a success he repeated in the summer of 1794 when he captured another British warship. By this time he had command of his own ship, but was still denied a letter of marque by the local governor, and therefore a share in the cargo. He decided to return to France, determined to acquire his privateering license.

SCOURGE OF THE INDIAN OCEAN

Surcouf duly became a properly authorized privateer, and in August 1798, he made his first independent cruise in the 18-gun *Clarisse* of Nantes. He captured ten ships

The "King of the Corsairs" in the Indian Ocean

1793–94

1 **Robert Surcouf** begins his career as a privateer, operating from the Île de France (now Mauritius).

2 **June 1794** While in command of the tiny sloop *La Créole*, Surcouf captures a convoy of three English ships carrying food, thereby bringing much-need supplies to the people of the island.

3 **August 1794** An argument with the governor over the issuing of a letter of marque forces Surcouf to quit the island; he returns to France.

1799

4 Returns to the Indian Ocean in his privateer *Clarisse* and cruises as far east as Sumatra, where he captures two ships.

5 **November** Surcouf captures the small East India Company warship *Auspicious* off Ceylon (now Sri Lanka), with a lucrative cargo on board.

6 **December** Surcouf returns to the Île de France.

1800–1

A **March** He begins a new cruise, and in two months he captures several prizes off the coast of Madagascar.

B **May** Surcouf gains command of a more powerful privateer—the *Confiance*, which has just completed repairs in the Île de France.

C **June** He returns to sea, and captures several more prizes off the west coast of India.

D **October** Surcouf encounters the East Indiaman *Kent* in the Bay of Bengal, and captures her after a particularly hard-fought engagement. Her cargo is valued at over 5 million francs.

E **February 1801** The privateer returns to France with his plunder.

1807

I **June** Surcouf returns to the Île de France in his new vessel, *La Revenant*, breaking through the loose British blockade of the island, and shepherding in several prizes.

II **August** He begins a seven-month cruise, ranging throughout the Indian Ocean, and captures 20 British ships.

III When the governor seizes his ship to help defend the island, a disgusted Surcouf takes the governor's ship and returns to France.

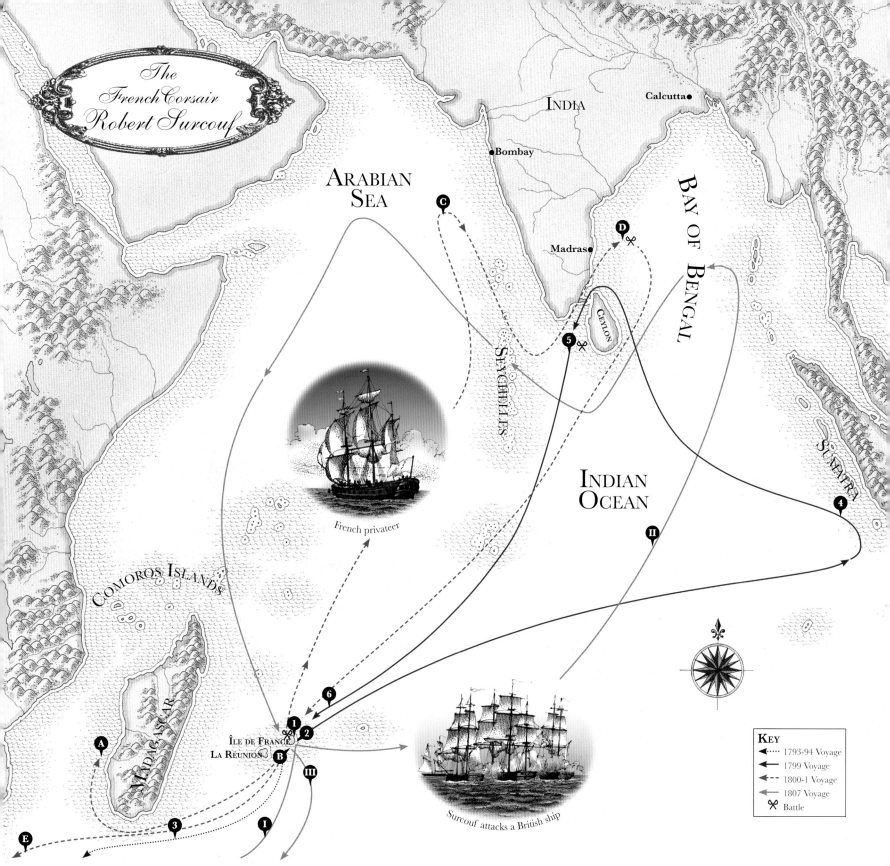

The French Corsair
Robert Surcouf

INDIA

Calcutta

Bombay

ARABIAN
SEA

Madras

BAY OF
BENGAL

C

D

CEYLON

5

SEYCHELLES

SUMATRA

French privateer

INDIAN
OCEAN

4

II

COMOROS ISLANDS

6

1
2

ÎLE DE FRANCE
LA RÉUNION

B

III

MADAGASCAR

A

Surcouf attacks a British ship

E

3

I

KEY
1793-94 Voyage
1799 Voyage
1800-1 Voyage
1807 Voyage
Battle

Above: Robert Surcouf's greatest triumph came in 1800 when he captured the East Indiaman *Kent*.

Below: The crew of Surcouf's privateer *Confiance* captured the British East Indiaman *Kent* after a hard-fought boarding action.

in the South Atlantic and the Indian Ocean before returning to the Île de France as a successful privateer.

In May 1800, Surcouf took command of a new ship—the 18-gun *Confiance*—and sailed the Indian Ocean in search of prey. He captured ten British ships off India, and on October 17, he captured the 38-gun East Indiaman *Kent* in the Bay of Bengal, one of the richest privateering prizes of the war. It also made Surcouf a national hero. He evaded British patrols and returned to France in April 1801. The sale of his plunder made him an extremely wealthy man, and he went to live in St. Malo, where with the coming of peace in early 1802, he established himself as a shipowner and businessman.

NAPOLEON'S CORSAIR

During the Napoleonic Wars (1803–15) Surcouf sent 14 privateers to the Indian Ocean, where they met with mixed success. In 1807, he returned to sea in his own purpose-built privateer, which captured 20 British ships during a year-long cruise. After his ship was commandeered by the Governor of the Île de France he seized one of the governor's own frigates and returned to France. He was subsequently ennobled as a Baron by the Emperor Napoleon and finally decided to return to St. Malo to retire.

Surcouf's Way of War

During his career, Robert Surcouf was known for his humane treatment of prisoners, and for the discipline of his men. He was also a gifted tactician. For instance, he used deception and speed to bring his small ship alongside a larger enemy before her guns could inflict much damage. He then relied on specially trained marines and large numbers of boarders to overwhelm an enemy.

Right: This bronze statue of Surcouf stands on the waterfront of his native town and privateering base of St. Malo in Brittany.

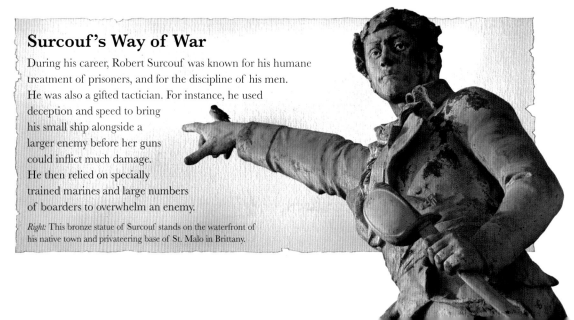

The Privateers of 1812

In the summer of 1812, an unnecessary war broke out between Britain and the United States. Once again, American privateers put to sea in search of British prey.

Above: Crowninshield Wharf in Salem, Massachusetts, in 1806. Several privateers are shown here, including the *America*, *Fame*, and *Prudent*. Painting by George Ropes Jr.

Despite its name, the "War of 1812" between the United States and the British Empire lasted for three years. In theory, the war was fought to resolve a few minor issues—British trade restrictions, the pressing of American seamen into the Royal Navy, and territorial disputes involving the dominion of Canada.

PRESIDENT MADISON'S WAR

For the most part, the war on land was limited to clashes along the Canadian border, but at sea American commerce raiders and privateers ranged far afield, and caused widespread disruption to British trade. Britain was already at war with France, and it took time to divert the ships needed to blockade American ports. In the meantime, American privateers were fitted out and sent to sea in large numbers.

Letters of marque were issued in large numbers. More than 517 privateering contracts had been signed by President Madison before the war finally came to an end in January 1815, by which time over 1,300 British merchant ships had been captured.

Left: In January 1813, HMS *Surprise* attacked the American 12-gun privateer *Decatur* off the Leeward Islands, capturing her after a short, sharp fight.

THE COURSE OF THE WAR

At first, the American privateers scored some remarkable successes. One Liverpool captain was captured three times during the war, and on one occasion he was chased by no fewer than ten American privateers during a voyage from Nova Scotia to his home port. Maritime insurance rates soared, and by late 1813, few companies were prepared to insure vessels bound for Canadian ports.

The war also produced its own privateering heroes. In the summer of 1812, Captain Thomas Boyle commanded

the privateer *Comet*—a converted merchant schooner of 16 guns. On her first cruise she captured three British merchantmen, carrying a lucrative cargo of sugar from the Caribbean to Britain. On Boyle's second cruise, the *Comet* captured five more merchantmen, and on his return to Baltimore he was rewarded with a new ship—the *Chasseur*. He captured 19 more ships before the war ended.

The happy hunting period for the Americans came to an end in late 1813. That winter the British managed to reinforce the blockade of American ports, and by the spring of 1814 it had become almost impossible for a privateer to evade capture. Some simply avoided their home ports altogether and established new bases in France, the Caribbean, or South America. But many were eventually captured. By the late summer of 1814, British maritime insurance rates had almost returned to their pre-war level.

It wasn't only American privateers who had suffered from the blockade. American commerce was brought to a standstill, and by mid-1814 ports such as Baltimore, Boston, Charleston Newport, New York, and Salem all faced economic ruin. Denied American prizes, many British and Canadian privateers were converted back into merchant vessels. The merchants clamored for an end to the conflict, and so in January 1815 the futile war was finally brought to a close.

The Super-Privateers

As soon as the war began, several American shipowners commissioned the building of large purpose-built privateers, designed for endurance and speed. Some of these were so successful that larger versions were ordered. Baltimore soon developed into America's premier privateer building port. One of her products was the 350-ton, 20-gun privateer *America*, which carried a crew of 120 men; she captured 40 British prizes during the war, earning her owners a profit of more than $600,000. However, the most successful privateer of the war was the Boston brig *Yankee*, which took 40 prizes with a total value of over $3,000,000. Other purpose-built super-privateers also proved highly successful, and vessels such as the large privateering schooners *Chasseur* and *Lyon* added to the growing tally of British merchantmen. The best of these specialist schooners were so fast and well designed that they became the model for a later generation of Baltimore clipper ships and transatlantic racing yachts.

Below: In April 1812, the American privateering schooner *Gypsy* was captured by the frigate HMS *Belle Poule* (36 guns) after a dramatic three-day chase across the Atlantic.

The Last of the Privateers

While other major maritime powers outlawed privateering in the mid-19th century, the United States still favored this kind of warfare.

During the American Civil War both privateering and commerce raiding, whereby an enemy's supplies were destroyed, enjoyed a last swan song.

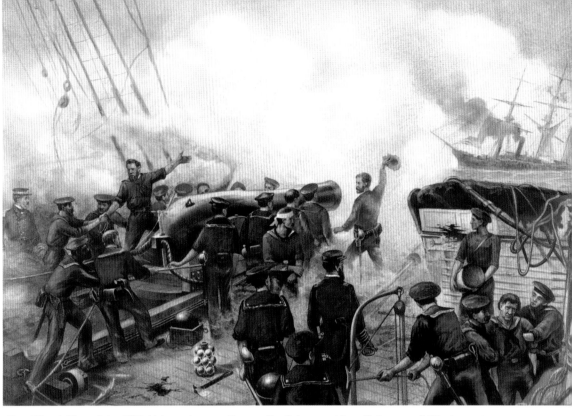

Above: The sinking of the CSS *Alabama*, the most famous Confederate raider, off the port of Cherbourg in Normandy, France in June 1864, as seen from the decks of the USS *Kearsarge*.

THE CONFEDERATE PRIVATEERS

When the American Civil War began in 1861 the U.S. Navy remained loyal to the Union, and consequently the Confederate States of America had to create their own fleet. In the meantime, a blockade was established that effectively sealed off all southern ports.

At first, this blockade was relatively easy to evade, and during the first year of the war a number of Confederate privateers put to sea. In all, some 56 Confederate letters of marque were issued, the majority to the captains and owners of small sailing vessels based in New Orleans, Savannah, and Charleston. They were relatively unsuccessful, mainly due to the problems of returning to port with

a prize. Unable to run the blockade, it was easier to simply destroy enemy ships rather than capture them. Many Confederates soon turned their attention to commerce raiding.

THE COMMERCE RAIDERS

The Confederate Secretary of the Navy, Stephen Mallory, rejected privateering in favor of commerce raiders. Several vessels were converted to this purpose, the first being the CSS *Sumter*, which sailed from New Orleans in June 1861 and destroyed 18 U.S. ships during a six-month cruise. Others followed, including the highly successful CSS *Alabama*, which captured or destroyed more than 60 U.S. vessels. Ultimately, though, these raids had no impact on the course of the war.

The Declaration of Paris

In 1856, the major maritime powers met in Paris to discuss the conduct of naval warfare. The result was the Declaration of Paris, which established international laws governing blockades, the nature of contraband, and the position of neutrality. It also abolished privateering as a legitimate weapon of naval warfare. The United States refused to sign the Declaration, arguing that it relied on privateering to make up for its lack of a powerful navy in times of war. This meant that when the American Civil War broke out five years later, American shipowners were once again able to send ships to sea as privateers.

The Last of the Pirates

In the century following the end of the Golden Age of Piracy, privateering became the legal alternative to piracy. But the end of the Napoleonic Wars saw a handful of the privateers returning to piracy as a means of employment.

Above: A man-of-war chasing a pirate lugger, from an early 19th-century painting by an unknown British artist.

At the end of the Napoleonic Wars in 1815, many French, Spanish, British, and American privateers found themselves out of work. While most found regular employment, a few turned to piracy—and helped to usher in a new wave of crime on the high seas, particularly in the Caribbean.

Another reason for the increase was the start of the Latin American wars of liberation in 1808, as many of the Spanish colonies in the Americas declared independence. Many of the breakaway states such as Colombia, Venezuela, Mexico, and Peru issued letters of marque and were less than stringent about regulating their privateering fleet. This led to many former privateers taking up these letters of marque and using them as a cover for their own piratical activities.

Many of these new pirates were small-time, content to attack ships that carried little in the way of plunder. Captain Lander of the American brig *Washington* reported that during an attack in 1822, Latin American pirates stole $16, food, cooking equipment, clothing, and a compass. While this was not exactly robbery on a grand scale, these pirates frequently murdered their victims in order to prevent anyone identifying them later.

By this time the United States was a growing commercial power in the region, which meant that American shipping was particularly vulnerable to attack. During the decade after the end of the War of 1812, more than 400 American ships were attacked and plundered in the Caribbean; reports of brutality and murder outraged the American public. As a result, the U.S. navy joined forces with the British navy to eradicate piracy in the Caribbean. Aggressive action gradually brought the situation under control—pirates like Jean Lafitte were driven from the seas, and although a few remained at large, attacks were reduced to a handful per year.

Jean Lafitte

The pirate Jean Lafitte was a rarity—a pirate and smuggler who briefly gave up his piratical activities to help defend a city from attack.

In defending New Orleans, Jean Lafitte became known for his patriotic heroism as well as his piracy. In the process, however, he sacrificed his own pirate empire.

Obscure Origins

We know little about the origins of Jean Lafitte, save that he was born in France around 1780; in most accounts his birthplace is given as Bayonne on the Bay of Biscay. A recent study suggested he was born in Saint Dominique (now Haiti). By 1809, Jean and his brother Pierre were living in New Orleans in French Louisiana, which had recently been purchased from France by the United States.

The Kingdom of Barataria

The perfect pirate haven was one that was safely out of reach of the authorities yet close to a major marketplace, where the pirates could sell their stolen goods—Barataria was just such a place. Barataria Bay was an inlet, just to the west of the Mississippi Delta, and linked to the river by a network of hidden bayous, lagoons, and backwaters. Jean Lafitte used the island of Grand Terre at the head of Barataria Bay as a base. These waterways offered a means of escape if attacked, but they also provided him with access to the city of New Orleans.

Reputedly, they ran a blacksmith's shop. If this business ever existed it was a front—their real trade was smuggling.

As early as 1810, Jean Lafitte was named as the leader of a group of smugglers and pirates who operated from the so-called "Kingdom of Barataria," on the island of Grand Terre, just a few miles from New Orleans but hidden in the bayous to the west of the Mississippi Delta. Two years later, the brothers were arrested for smuggling, but the charges were eventually dropped for lack of evidence. They were clearly involved in piracy as well as smuggling, as during this period they were linked to several attacks on shipping in the Gulf of Mexico. One of the main cargoes to pass through Barataria was slaves, captured from Spanish slave trading vessels and sold to the Louisiana plantation owners by auction.

The authorities raided the island in September 1814. Jean escaped but Pierre was captured and their base destroyed.

Above: A contemporary American woodcut, showing Jean Lafitte's pirate crew boarding a prize. In fact, most of his victims were much smaller vessels.

The Hero of New Orleans

Three months later, the British arrived and attempted to capture New Orleans—the last act of the War of 1812. Lafitte turned down British offers of money in exchange for guides and information, choosing instead to inform the Louisiana authorities of the impending British assault in exchange for the release of his brother. He then offered his services to General Jackson whose troops defended the city. The British assault was repulsed on

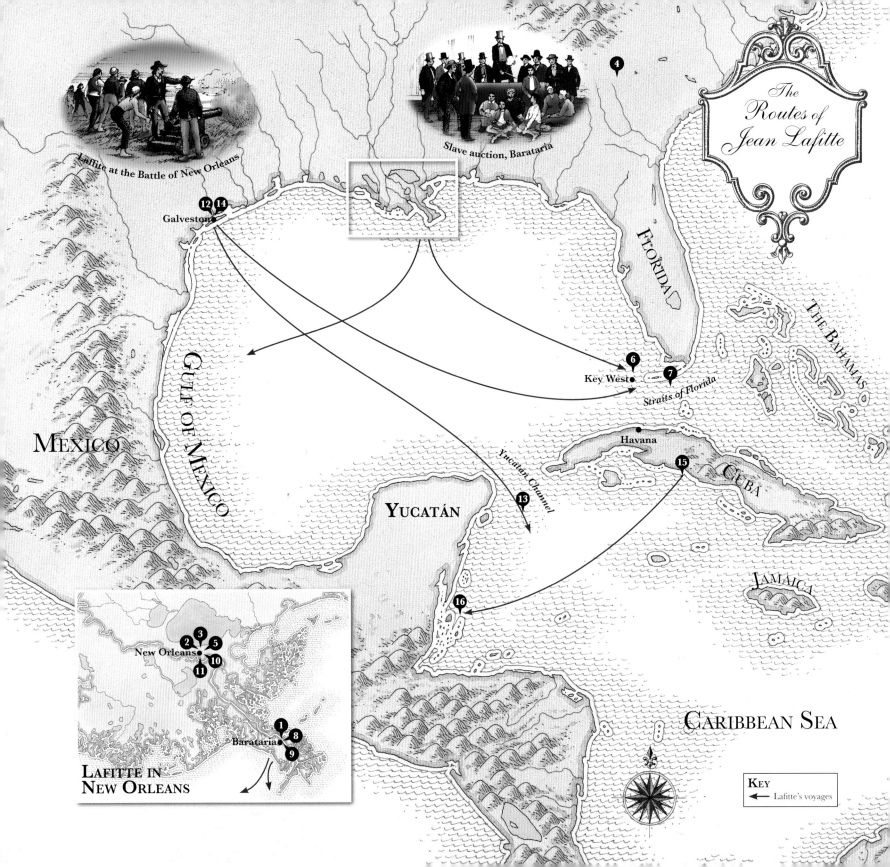

The Routes of
Jean Lafitte

Lafitte at the Battle of New Orleans

Slave auction, Barataria

4

FLORIDA

THE BAHAMAS

6
Key West
7
Straits of Florida

MEXICO

GULF OF MEXICO

12 14
Galveston

Havana

CUBA

15

Yucatán Channel

YUCATÁN

13

JAMAICA

16

LAFITTE IN
NEW ORLEANS

2 3 5
New Orleans
11 10

1 8
Barataria
9

CARIBBEAN SEA

KEY
← Lafitte's voyages

The Pirate Hero of New Orleans, 1811–23

1811

1 **Jean Lafitte** is named as the leader of a group of pirates and smugglers who operate from a secret base known as the "Kingdom of Barataria"(Grand Terre), in the bayous south of New Orleans.

2 **Summer** Smuggling operations into New Orleans are attributed to Lafitte.

1812–13

3 **1812** The Lafitte brothers (Jean and Pierre) are linked to a large-scale illegal slave-trading operation.

4 **June 1812** Start of the War of 1812 between Britain and the United States.

5 **October 1812** Lafitte's application for a privateering license is rejected.

6 **Early 1813** Jean Lafitte is linked to his first pirate attack—the capture of a Spanish slave trader off Key West, Florida.

7 **Summer 1813** More attacks follow in the Florida Strait and the Gulf of Mexico.

1814–15

8 **September 1814** The Governor of Louisiana attacks and destroys the Barataria pirate den. Although his brother Pierre is captured, Lafitte escapes to sea.

9 **September 1814** Lafitte rejects a British appeal for help in an attack on New Orleans when he meets British officers in Barataria Bay.

10 **January 1815** Lafitte and his men come to the aid of the city and help repulse the British assault in the Battle of New Orleans.

11 **February 1815** The Lafitte brothers are granted a full pardon.

1817–23

12 **1817** Lafitte establishes a new base at Galveston (now in Texas)—then part of Mexico.

13 **1818** He forges letters of marque, and his ships begin attacking vessels of all countries in the Gulf of Mexico, and the Yucatán Channel.

14 **May 1821** The USS *Enterprise* attacks and destroys the pirate den at Galveston. Lafitte flees.

15 **Lafitte** may be operating from a base on the southern coast of Cuba.

16 **February 1823** Lafitte is reputedly killed during an attack on Spanish merchantman in the Gulf of Honduras.

January 8, 1815, during an engagement known as the Battle of New Orleans, in which Lafitte and his pirate gunners played a major part. In retrospect, Lafitte probably backed the wrong side—New Orleans was now too well policed to permit the sale of stolen goods to continue.

GALVESTON ISLAND

Within two years, the Lafitte brothers had left Louisiana for good. They established themselves on Galveston (then known as Campeche), on the coast of what was then Mexican-owned Texas. Galveston was already used as a base for Latin American privateers, and was

According to New Orleans folklore, in 1813, the Louisiana governor William Claiborne offered a reward of $500 for the head of Jean Lafitte. The pirate responded by offering a ransom ten times as large for the head of the governor. Although this is a great story, there is no evidence the incident ever took place!

Left: William Claiborne (1775–1817), the first Governor of Louisiana (1812–16), who strongly disapproved of Lafitte's criminal activities.

known as a lawless place. Lafitte had little trouble turning it into a new Barataria. Pirates, smugglers, criminals, and rogue merchants flocked to the port, which soon developed

Above: Early 19th-century Hispanic pirates disguise themselves as innocent passengers, in an attempt to lure an American merchant ship close enough to board her. From a painting by Auguste François Biard.

into a small hive of criminal activity. The slave trading continued: one slave trader who reputedly dealt with Lafitte was Jim Bowie, inventor of the Bowie Knife and later a hero of the war for Texan independence. By 1818 it was claimed that 20 pirate schooners operated out of Galveston, including Lafitte's own vessel the *Pride*. However, in September of that year a hurricane struck, sinking several ships, flattening most of the settlement, and severely disrupting Lafitte's enterprise.

It was at that point that Lafitte made the mistake of attacking and plundering two American ships. The authorities responded by sending in the U.S. Navy, and in May 1814, Lieutenant Kearney arrived in the 14-gun brig USS *Enterprise*. He ordered the pirates to disperse or risk a bombardment. The pirates responded to the order by setting fire to the port and then escaping in the resulting confusion. What happened to Jean Lafitte after that is something of a mystery.

Recently, an author claimed that Lafitte escaped from Galveston before the arrival

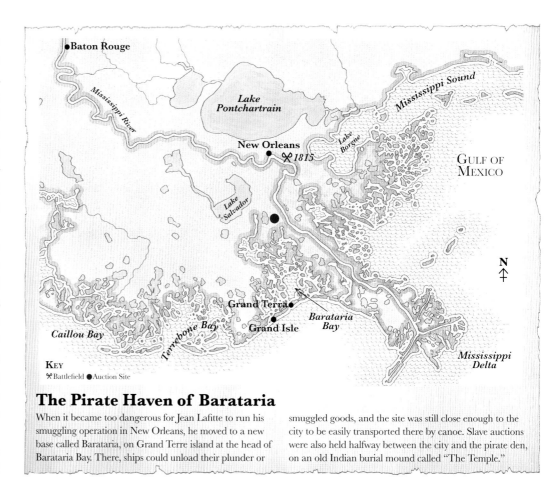

The Pirate Haven of Barataria

When it became too dangerous for Jean Lafitte to run his smuggling operation in New Orleans, he moved to a new base called Barataria, on Grand Terre island at the head of Barataria Bay. There, ships could unload their plunder or smuggled goods, and the site was still close enough to the city to be easily transported there by canoe. Slave auctions were also held halfway between the city and the pirate den, on an old Indian burial mound called "The Temple."

of the navy, and in 1821 he established a new base on the Cuban coast. The following year he was given a privateering letter of marque by the Venezuelan government, and authorized to attack Spanish shipping. It is also claimed that in February 1823, he was killed during a fight with two Spanish warships and was subsequently buried at sea in the Gulf of Honduras. In truth, we will probably never resolve what happened to the pirate and his brother Pierre. Their ultimate fate may never be known.

Left: The brig USS *Enterprise* commanded by Lieutenant Commander Kearney, in action against the pirate fleet of Charles Gibbs, off Cuba in 1821.

Above: Benito de Soto's pirate sloop the *Black Joke*, sailing away from her prey, which he has left to sink.

Benito de Soto and "Don" Pedro

During eighteen years of small-time piracy in Atlantic waters, two cut-throats stand out for their brutal inhumanity.

Benito de Soto and Don Pedro Gilbert were among the most bloodthirsty of the last generation of pirates. Their ruthless crimes caused a sensation in the world's press.

BENITO DE SOTO

In 1827, Benito de Soto was a Spanish sailor serving on board an Argentinian slave ship. He led a mutiny off the coast of Angola, and those who refused to join him were cast loose in an open boat. Then, to remove any threat to his captaincy, he shot the Mate in an engineered argument, leaving him in unchallenged command of the ship. De Soto renamed her *Burla Negra* (Black Joke) and set off in search of prey.

First, de Soto crossed to the Caribbean, where he sold his cargo of slaves. He then headed south through the West Indies, attacking any ships he met. In each case he murdered the crew, plundered the ship, and sank it to hide the evidence of his crime.

The only clue to his progress was a trail of missing ships. He had less success on the South American coast so headed out into the Atlantic, to intercept the busy shipping lanes between Europe and the Cape of Good Hope. Here the prizes were bigger, and once again the insurers were puzzled by the seemingly inexplicable loss of ships.

DE SOTO'S RAMPAGE

In February 1832, the pirates came upon the British bark *Morning Star*, homeward bound from Ceylon to London. de Soto ordered his prize to heave to, and ordered the British captain to come aboard the *Burla Negra*. When he appeared slow to comply, de Soto cut him down with his sword, reputedly exclaiming, "This is how Benito de Soto rewards those who disobey him!" The pirates then began ransacking the *Morning Star*, randomly killing some of her crew and raping the women

passengers. After locking the survivors in the hold they blew a hole in the hull of the British ship, and left her to sink.

This time the pirates were unlucky. The crew managed to escape, and manned the pumps. A passing ship rescued them the following day, becoming the first survivors of De Soto's rampage. News of the attack caused outrage around the world. The pirates knew nothing of this. After selling their plunder on the Spanish coast, the *Burla Negra* ran aground near Cádiz, and was abandoned. De Soto and his men made their way to Gibraltar, hoping to find a ship to steal. Instead they were spotted by one of the survivors—a wounded soldier. The notorious pirate was duly taken to Cádiz where he was tried and executed for his crimes in 1830.

Left: After his execution, Benito de Soto's head was displayed on the waterfront at the port of Cádiz.

"DON" PEDRO GIBERT

Pedro Gibert was born around 1800, probably in Latin America. He became a seaman and spent some time as a Colombian privateer. At some stage he adopted the title of "Don," suggesting a noble lineage to which he had no claim. By 1830, he was a smuggler and illegal slave trader, in command of the schooner *Panda,* which he operated from a base near St. Lucie Inlet in northern Florida. In 1832, he decided to try his hand at piracy.

On September 20, he encountered the brig *Mexican* in the Florida Straits, bound for Argentina. Captain Butman of the *Mexican* was wary of the stranger and turned away, but Gibert gave chase and the *Panda* soon overhauled the American vessel. Just before the pirates boarded, the captain hid the $20,000 in coins he was carrying. Gibert's men ransacked the ship. When they couldn't find any money, they tortured the captain and his crew until the hiding place was revealed.

As Gibert was taking the money back to the *Panda,* one of his men asked him what to do with the prisoners. Gibert replied, "Dead

Above: The crew of the Spanish slave ship *L'Antonio* turned to piracy, but were captured off the West African coast.

Left: Pedro Gilbert's pirate schooner *Panda,* pictured during his attack on the American merchantman the *Mexican,* 1832. She was designed for smuggling rather than piracy, and was therefore unarmed.

cats don't mew—you know what to do!" Rather than kill the prisoners in cold blood, the pirates locked them below decks, then set fire to the ship. They then returned to the *Panda,* leaving the Americans to burn alive, but somehow one of them escaped and freed his shipmates. They managed to control the blaze but left a part still burning to prevent the pirates from becoming suspicious. When the *Panda* disappeared over the horizon, the crew doused the fire, repaired the ship, and sailed it back to a friendly port.

A JUST REWARD

As for Gibert, he resumed his smuggling and slave-trading activities. In March 1833, he arrived off the West African coast, hoping to find a cargo of slaves. Instead he ran into a Royal Navy warship. Gibert and his crew were captured and shipped to Britain. Once their identities were revealed they were extradited to Boston where they stood trial. In the courtroom, Captain Butman was on hand to identify them. Two pirates were acquitted, six went to prison, and Gibert and two others were hanged. These three had the dubious honor of being the last people executed for piracy in the United States.

David Porter:
pirate hunter

By the start of the 1820s, mounting losses to pirates forced the U.S. government to take forceful action to suppress piracy, which led to one of the great pirate-hunting success stories.

The government's solution to the growing problem of piracy in the West Indies was to establish an anti-piracy squadron. It was put under the command of one of the most able officers in the U.S. Navy.

During 1820, a total of 27 American ships were attacked by pirates in the Caribbean, and insurance rates doubled. Both shipowners and the public demanded action be taken, so early the following year the president, James Monroe, authorized the creation of an anti-pirate squadron. It was to be commanded by Commodore David Porter USN.

Born in 1780 in Illinois, the 42-year-old captain had been at sea since his early teens, and had fought the French, the British, and the Barbary states. He now commanded the largest peacetime collection of American ships that had ever been assembled. Due to their small size, which allowed them to be maneuvered over the shallow areas and reefs in the Keys, these warships were collectively known as the "Mosquito Fleet." Key West in the Florida Keys was chosen as a base because of its central location in pirate waters. Soon, this island township was to boast the busiest naval base in the United States.

Above: David Porter was a determined and gifted naval commander—the perfect pirate hunter.

ROOTING OUT THE PIRATES

Offensive patrolling began early in 1823. Porter's fleet scoured the Caribbean, the Bahamas, and the Gulf of Mexico, hitting hard at pirate bases, escorting American ships, and capturing pirate ships. One problem he had to deal with was the elusiveness of the pirates, who disguised themselves as fishermen or local traders. He concentrated his efforts around the known pirate havens of Puerto Rico, the Cuban coast, and the Yucatán Peninsula, seeking out and destroying pirate vessels and bases.

The Ships of the Mosquito Fleet

The Mosquito Fleet consisted of 16 assorted vessels: naval brigs, fast converted Baltimore schooners, an early paddle steamer, and even a decoy merchant ship armed with hidden guns. All the ships were chosen for their shallow draft, making them ideal for coastal operations.

Left: Both the British and the Americans used fast, well-armed schooners as their main pirate-hunters.

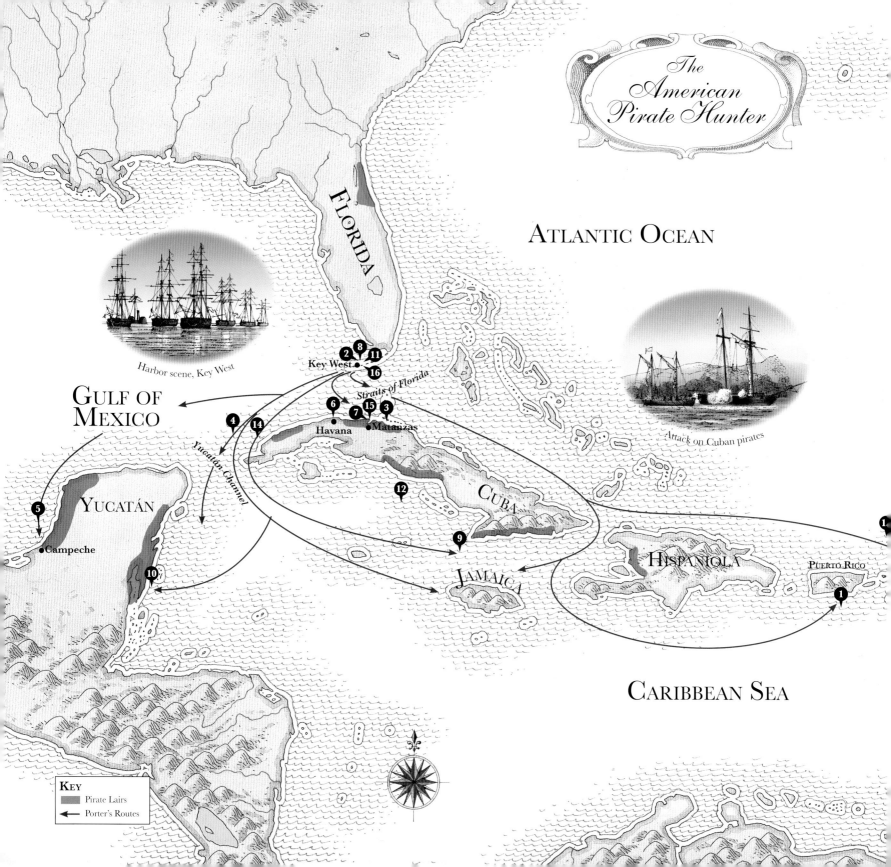

The
American
Pirate Hunter

ATLANTIC OCEAN

FLORIDA

Harbor scene, Key West

GULF OF
MEXICO

Key West

Straits of Florida

Attack on Cuban pirates

Yucatán Channel

Havana

Matanzas

YUCATÁN

CUBA

Campeche

HISPANIOLA

PUERTO RICO

JAMAICA

CARIBBEAN SEA

1 **March 1823** On his way to Key West, Commodore Porter's squadron is fired upon as it tries to enter the Spanish port of San Juan, Puerto Rico.

2 **April** Establishes a base in Key West, Florida.

3 **April** Two U.S. schooners attack and capture a pirate known as "Domingo" off the Cuban port of Matanzas. This is Porter's first success.

4 **May** Porter sends the steamer USS *Seagull* to patrol the Yucatán Channel, and the waters as far as Jamaica.

5 **June** The USS *Grampus* captures a Cuban pirate off the Mexican port of Campeche. The sailors then land and destroy the pirate den.

6 **July** As violent pirate attacks are still continuing to take place around Cuba, Porter sends a delegation to Havana to urge the Spanish to cooperate with him.

7 **July** American small boats are used to attack another pirate lair near the Cuban port of Matanzas. Several pirate ships belonging to the notorious pirate "Diabolito" are captured.

8 **Late July** A British warship arrives in Key West to discuss a joint anti-piracy strategy. Porter's squadron is also reinforced.

9 Another pirate ship is captured off Cape Cruz, on the southern coast of Cuba.

10 **August** The Yucatán Peninsula is declared free of pirates following American operations there.

11 **Late August** Yellow fever strikes Key West, and hampers anti-piracy operations.

12 **January 1824** Porter sends ships to patrol the southern coast of Cuba.

13 **April** These are extended as far as the Windward Islands, as Cuba is deemed virtually pirate free.

14 **May** Diabolito is reported to have re-appeared off the western tip of Cuba, but Porter hunts for him in vain.

15 **May** Porter visits Matanzas in Cuba, and he declares the island free of pirates

16 **June** The operation is officially declared to have been completed.

THE CUBAN PROBLEM

Cuba was a particularly difficult area to deal with, as the Spanish resented the American presence and some local governors even seemed to support pirate activities. This meant that Porter was constantly having to deal with diplomatic affairs in the Caribbean. However, nothing spoke louder than success, and the benefits of his actions and those of a smaller British Royal Naval squadron based in Jamaica soon became apparent.

One of his greatest achievements was the defeat of the notorious Cuban pirate "Diabolito" (Little Devil) in April 1823. The Mosquito Fleet surprised the pirates off the northern coast of Cuba, forcing them to abandon their ship and flee inland.

The careers of other pirates such as Charles Gibbs and Jean Lafitte were also cut short by Porter's fleet. By 1825, very few instances of attacks by pirates occurred and safe maritime trade was restored.

AFTER THE PIRATE HUNTING

In 1825, Porter seized the town of Fajardo in Puerto Rico following the arrest of an American sailor by Spanish authorities. Porter was court-martialed over the incident, and so resigned from the navy in protest in 1826. He went on to command the fledgling Mexican navy for three years, before becoming a diplomat, and ending his days as U.S. Ambassador to the court of the Ottoman Turkish Sultan.

Above: Small-oared barges from Porter's "Mosquito Fleet" attacking a pirate schooner near Matanzas Bay, Cuba, in July 1823. The vessel was commanded by the notorious "Diabolito," who abandoned his men and fled ashore.

Pirates in Eastern Seas

Piracy as a form of criminal activity wasn't only a transatlantic problem. In fact, piracy in the Caribbean was a short-lived phenomenon compared to the longevity it enjoyed in the Far East.

Left: Malaysian pirates beating British prisoners after capturing their ship. The wounded captive is Mr. Sharp, chief mate of the brig *Admiral Trowbridge*.

Throughout history piracy ebbed and flowed around the globe. It flourished at times of weak central government or naval power when coastlines were not policed, and it favored areas where there was a suitably large selection of victims.

In Chinese waters, however, the threat of piracy remained constant for seafarers for more than a thousand years. The first recorded incident of piracy took place in AD 589, around the time Emperor Wen first unified China. In all probability, piracy was flourishing long before that. For much of Chinese history the line between ruler, merchant, and pirate was blurred, as minor warlords used piracy as a means of gaining power and revenue.

Piracy would continue to plague the region until the early 19th century and the arrival of the European powers and western navies. European traders also came into contact with other smaller pirate communities in the Philippines, the Indonesian waters of the East Indies, and along the coastline of South-East Asia. In these areas, piracy was often conducted along tribal lines, where primitive maritime communities were as likely to attack each other as they were to prey on foreign trading ships or settlements.

Probably the worst of these were the tribes who inhabited Indonesia, such as the Dyaks of Borneo. Spanish, Dutch, and then British traders and colonists all vouched for the ferocity of these pirate raiders. From the mid-19th century onward a concerted effort was made to subdue piracy in the region. The problem was greatly reduced, but it never completely went away.

Piracy in the Far East

The first recorded instance of piracy in the Far East was more than 14 centuries ago, and within living memory the Chinese coast was a haven for opium smugglers and pirates.

To this day, the waters of the East Indies remain a pirate hot spot, making the region one of the most continually troublesome areas in maritime history.

While the first recorded instance of a pirate attack in Chinese waters took place in the 6th century AD, in all probability the lawlessness that preceded the foundation of Emperor Wen's Sui dynasty in AD 581 would have played into the hands of pirates. From as far back as the collapse of the Han dynasty in AD 220, the Chinese coast was rules by minor warlords, whose ships would have been as likely to raid their neighbors as to trade with them. While central control was re-established in China, the emperors were unable to wrest control of the coastal regions from these warlords. As a result, imperial power was limited to dry land.

THE ROOT OF THE PROBLEM

While maritime trade flourished during the 13th and 14th centuries, and Chinese merchants ventured as far afield as India, Persia, and even East Africa, little was done to protect these traders from attack. It was not until the 15th century that the emperors of the Ming dynasty managed to take control of Chinese waters from the petty warlords and pirates who infested them. Even then,

A Boatload of Piratical Rascals

imperial control was often illusory—the Emperor frequently resorted to paying these local rulers to suppress piracy. In effect, he was asking them to police themselves! This strange and inefficient Chinese policy would remain unchanged for five centuries.

Another problem was that piracy in China was a highly organized business. In Europe or America, pirates tended to hunt alone, or in small groups. In the South China Sea, pirates often hunted in fleets. Instead of operating from isolated pirate dens, they enjoyed the use of major ports; pirate confederations or local warlords controlled whole coastal provinces. As a result, piracy went largely

East Meets West

From the mid-19th century onward the European naval powers enjoyed an immense technological advantage over the Chinese pirates. While the pirates used the war junks and primitive cannon that had been the mainstay of their fleets for centuries, the Royal Navy, the French Navy, and other Western maritime powers were able to deploy steam-powered ships, armed with shell-firing ordnance. More than anything else, these were the tools that brought a thousand years of piracy to an end in the Eastern seas.

Above: A watercolor sketch by British naval surgeon Edward Cree, which he entitled *A Boatload of Piratical Rascals*. In 1848, he took part in the campaign against Shap-'ng-Tsai, and made several sketched studies of Chinese pirates.

unchecked, as both the honest local rulers and the Chinese Emperor lacked the naval power needed to counter such an immense problem. It was only when the Europeans established themselves on the Chinese coast that things began to change. By the early 19th century, these traders enjoyed the protection of the major maritime powers, who finally had the force and firepower needed to deal with the pirate problem.

PAYING FOR PROTECTION

Chinese pirates rarely made substantial sums of money from attacks on shipping. They relied instead on the payment of protection money. Often their ships flew the flag of a local warlord, and officially they patrolled the seas to safeguard trade. Of course, they only safeguarded the ships whose owners paid for the service; others were plundered. Occasionally the pirate fleets would hire themselves out for use as a makeshift navy, but for the most part these

Chinese pirates tended to keep themselves aloof from politics. An exception was Cheng Chi-Lung (1604–61), who, together with his son Cheng Sen ("Koxinga") expanded their piratical operations until they ruled the most powerful maritime empire in the region.

PIRACY IN THE FAR EAST

Naturally, the Chinese didn't enjoy a monopoly on piracy in the Far East. Piracy also flourished in Japanese waters until the 16th century, when the Emperor's fleet finally managed to deal with the problem. Piracy was also endemic in the waters of the Philippines, in the Malay Archipelago, and indeed throughout the islands of the East Indies. During the 18th and 19th centuries the coast of Vietnam was also a pirate haven, as local rulers used piracy as a tool, much like the Chinese warlords were doing. It was

Right: China didn't have a monopoly on Far Eastern pirates—this 19th-century print depicts a Japanese pirate, armed with a revolver.

only when the European powers intervened in Vietnamese affairs that piracy along their coast was brought under control.

At first, the Europeans had little impact on piracy in the Far East. Indeed, many European merchants encouraged the semi-legal opium trade, which benefited the local warlords, smugglers, and pirates as much as it did the western visitors. However, this trade also led to the Opium Wars of the early and mid-19th century, which in turn involved the use of Western military force to support the European trading enclaves on the Chinese coast. That meant the arrival of powerful naval flotillas. When the gunboats arrived, the days of the Chinese pirates were numbered.

Kuo Hsing Yeh

During the 17th century a pirate dynasty emerged in China. Its leaders combined the roles of warlord, local ruler, merchant, and pirate.

The founder of this dynasty—which led to the creation of the largest maritime empire in Chinese history—was Cheng Chi-Lung, but it was his son Kuo Hsing Yeh who expanded its dominion.

THE PIRATE ADMIRAL

Chi-Lung's early days had been spent as an apprentice in Japan. In 1623, his mentor died, leaving Chi-Lung his business, which included a fleet of merchant junks and a handful of war junks. At first, he operated from ports in Taiwan, but the growing power of the Dutch forced him to move to the Amoy islands and the nearby ports in the Fukien province. By this time he had begun to use his war junks as pirate vessels, and over the next decade he expanded his influence until his fleet dominated the southern Chinese coast. However, he was careful to limit his attacks to Oriental ships, leaving the Dutch well alone.

In 1641, the Chinese Ming Emperor appointed Chi-Lung his "Admiral of Coastal Waters," a post he held for three years, until

Kuo Hsing Yeh (Koxinga) is depicted at his desk, dealing with the business of running a pirate empire as well as a war against the Manchu, in this 17th-century Chinese engraving.

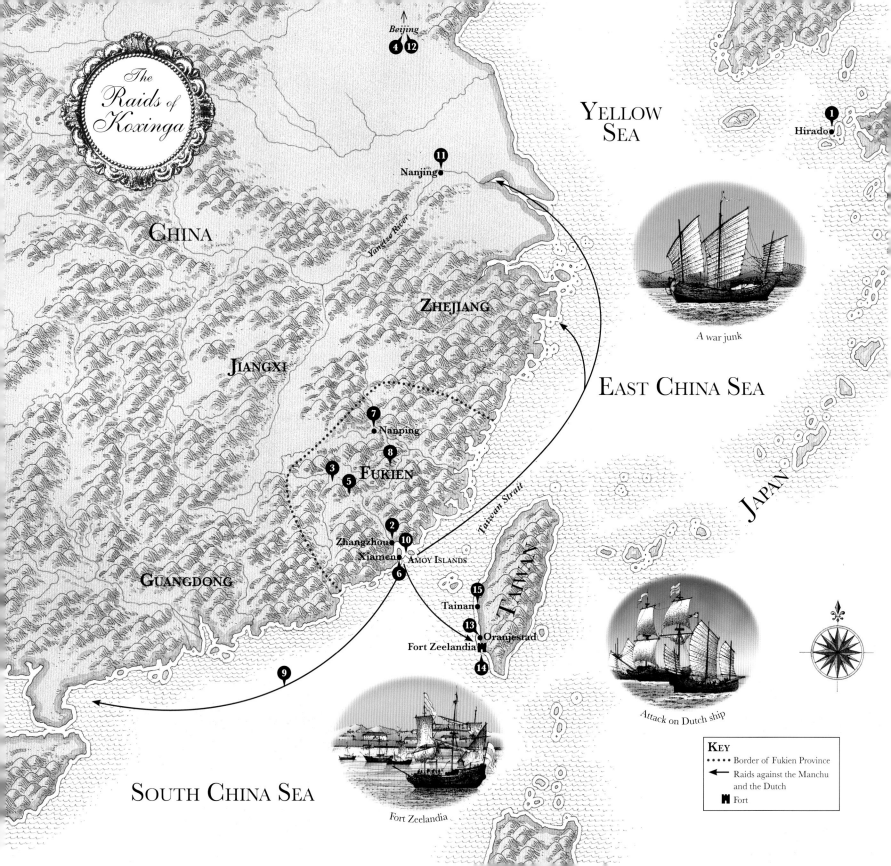

The Raids of Koxinga

CHINA

YELLOW SEA

Beijing
4 12

Hirado 1

Nanjing 11

ZHEJIANG

Yangtze River

JIANGXI

A war junk

EAST CHINA SEA

7
Nanping

8

3 **FUKIEN**
5

Taiwan Strait

JAPAN

2
Zhangzhou 10
Xiamen **AMOY ISLANDS**
6

GUANGDONG

15
Tainan

TAIWAN

13
Oranjestad
Fort Zeelandia
14

Attack on Dutch ship

9

SOUTH CHINA SEA

Fort Zeelandia

KEY
•••• Border of Fukien Province
→ Raids against the Manchu and the Dutch
🏰 Fort

Koxinga, the Chinese Pirate King, 1624–62

1 **1624** Kuo Hsing Yeh (Koxinga) is born in Hirado, Japan.

2 **c.1631** His father relocates his business to Fukien province, where the young Koxinga learns the trades of maritime commerce and smuggling.

3 **1641** Koxinga's father, Cheng Chi-Lung, is appointed Admiral by the Emperor.

4 **1644** Manchu invaders capture Beijing (Peking), and depose the Ming Emperor. Cheng Chi-Lung remains loyal to the Ming Dynasty.

5 **1646** The Manchu conquer Fukien province, forcing Cheng Chi-Lung to make peace with the invaders.

6 **1647** Koxinga refuses to surrender, and establishes himself in Xiamen, in Fukien's Amoy Islands. He also begins attacking Manchu ports and ships.

7 **Late 1647** Koxinga's mother commits suicide in Nanping, rather than surrender to the Manchu.

8 **1650** Koxinga takes over his father's empire, and concentrates on developing its smuggling and piratical activities.

9 **1651** The pirate junks of Koxinga's fleet are now extorting protection money throughout the South China Sea basin. The only groups who refuse to pay are cities held by the Manchu, and the Dutch, based in their island colony of Taiwan.

10 **1656** A Manchu invasion force is decisively defeated by Koxinga at Jinmen, in the Amoy Islands. Koxinga's base is now considered virtually invulnerable.

11 **1659** Launches an abortive attack on Nanjing (Nanking), but is repulsed by the Manchu.

12 **1661** By way of retaliation, Cheng Chi-Lung is called to Beijing, where he is executed.

13 **April 1661** Koxinga besieges the Dutch settlement of Oranjestad on Taiwan.

14 **February 1662** The Dutch stronghold of Fort Zeelandia, protecting Oranjestad, surrenders after a ten-month siege, and the Dutch colony is captured by the pirates. Koxinga is now the master of Taiwan.

15 **July** Koxinga dies in Tainan, after contracting malaria during a tour of Taiwan.

---

the collapse of the Ming dynasty at the hands of the Manchu rebels. Ironically, one of his tasks was to suppress piracy in Chinese waters. He remained loyal to the Ming cause—at least for a while—and ruled Fukien province in the name of the Ming dynasty. Then in 1649 he was paid handsomely to change sides, and so declared himself a supporter of the new Manchu rulers. For a decade Chi-Lung continued to rule his province, leaving his son, Koxinga, to command his fleet. Then in 1661 he was called to meet the Emperor in Beijing's Forbidden City. There he was held to account for the rebel activities of his son,

and was duly executed. But the Emperor had made a grave miscalculation, as by then the real threat to his power came from the son.

THE RISE OF KOXINGA

Chi-Lung's son Cheng Sen (1624–62) was nicknamed Fukumatsu, which translated as "Lucky Pine." However, the Matsu were an aristocratic family from Hirado in Japan, and soon after the death of his father Cheng Sen came to be known as Kuo Hsing Yeh (or Koxinga), which meant "Lord with the Imperial Surname." He was born in Japan, probably during his father's sojourn in

Above: Kuo Hsing Yeh established a safe base of operations in the Amoy Islands, off the coast of Fukien province.

Left: The remains of Fort Zeelandia, now called Anping Fort, built by the Dutch in 1624 to protect their trading colony on Taiwan. It was their administrative center as well as military headquarters.

being repulsed with heavy losses, the pirate leader demonstrated he had the power to strike where he liked. Unable to retaliate, the Manchu emperor Yongzheng took revenge against Koxinga's father. Inevitably, the son swore to avenge the death of his father.

WAR WITH THE DUTCH

Since 1650, Koxinga had continued his father's policy of offering protection to those who paid for his services. By 1661, his pirate fleets had almost complete control of the South China Sea and its hinterland, from the southern tip of Vietnam up to the Gulf of Tonkin, then along the Chinese coast past Fukien as far as the mouth of the Yangtze River. The only maritime power of any note that could oppose him were the Dutch, based on Taiwan (an island they called Formosa). To these Dutch merchants, Koxinga was less of a rebel than a pirate—unlike his father, Koxinga was willing to attack their ships.

Before turning his attention to the Manchu, Koxinga decided to attack Taiwan and drive the Dutch from Chinese waters, which would consolidate his grip on the South China

Sea. In April 1661, he blockaded the main settlement of Oranjestad with 400 pirate junks and a 25,000-man army. The settlement was protected by the powerful stronghold of Fort Zeelandia, but rather than risk an all-out assault, Koxinga was prepared to starve out the enemy. Sure enough, after a ten-month siege the Dutch surrendered, and the pirate assumed control of Taiwan on behalf of the Ming dynasty.

Unfortunately, the pirate leader didn't live long enough to take advantage of his triumph, dying of malaria less than six months later. His pirate empire passed into the hands of his son Cheng Ching (1642–81), who continued to rule Taiwan for another two decades, until his death at the hands of the Manchu, who finally conquered Taiwan in 1681.

Nagasaki, but he was raised in Fukien province, and trained in the family businesses of trade, administration, and piracy. From 1650, he ran the family empire, leaving his father free to concentrate on his political responsibilities. However, Koxinga preferred piracy to his other responsibilities, and as his fleet grew in strength, so too did his audacity.

Koxinga began to raid Manchu shipping and coastal towns, as unlike his father he retained his loyalty to the old Ming dynasty. The Emperor retaliated by sending an army to Fukien province, driving Koxinga from his mainland bases, and forcing him to retreat to the Amoy Islands, just off the coast. His chief refuge became the port of Chinmen, where his pirate fleet was able to protect him. Safe from Manchu attack, he continued his raids for the best part of a decade. A particularly daring venture was his attack on the Manchu city of Nanjing (Nanking) in 1659. Despite

Koxinga the Chinese Hero

Since his death, Koxinga has been portrayed as a pirate king, the defender of a lost Chinese civilization, a semi-mythical deity, a Taiwanese hero, and even a sort of Chinese Robin Hood.

Right: In some regions, Koxinga is worshiped as a god. In Tainan City, Taiwan, a temple has been dedicated to the pirate chief.

The Great Pirate Confederation

During the early 19th century a new pirate empire arose in China, ruled first by a pirate king, Cheng Yih, and then by his wife who became a daring and powerful pirate leader.

Although its heyday only lasted a decade, at its height this pirate confederation rivaled Koxinga's maritime empire in both size and power. By 1807, it was a formidable force, and one of the most powerful pirate fleets in China.

Cheng Yih was born in 1765, as the son of a Chinese pirate leader operating in Vietnamese waters. He followed in his father's footsteps, and by 1801 had inherited his father's pirate business. A civil war was then reaching its conclusion in Vietnam, and rather than wait for the re-establishment of central power, Cheng Yih opted to move his operation along the coast to the Chinese province of Guangdong (Kwangtung), where he set up headquarters in Canton (now Guangzhou). In the process, he took control of any smaller pirate fleets he encountered along the way.

RAPID EXPANSION

Over the next four years, Cheng Yih expanded even further, joining forces with other Chinese pirate fleets to create a large pirate confederation. His first real test came in 1804, when he blockaded the Portuguese trading post of Macao when the traders refused to pay him protection money. He then defeated a Portuguese squadron sent

Above: Pirates under the command of Cheng Yih depicted attacking a Western longboat in the Perfume River in 1806. Its crew of Lascar (Indian) seamen were accompanied by John Turner, First Mate of the British merchant ship *Tay*. Turner was captured and held by the pirates for five months while a ransom was negotiated.

to its relief. His success encouraged others to join the confederation, and by 1805 its numbers had increased so much that the British in Hong Kong demanded extra protection from the Royal Navy. However, Cheng Yih had no wish to encourage the Europeans to send large fleets into Chinese waters and so generally discouraged attacks on European ships.

By 1805, Cheng Yih commanded more than 600 pirate junks, and 30,000 men. His own Red Flag Fleet alone had grown to include over 300 vessels. He could also draw on men from the coastal communities under

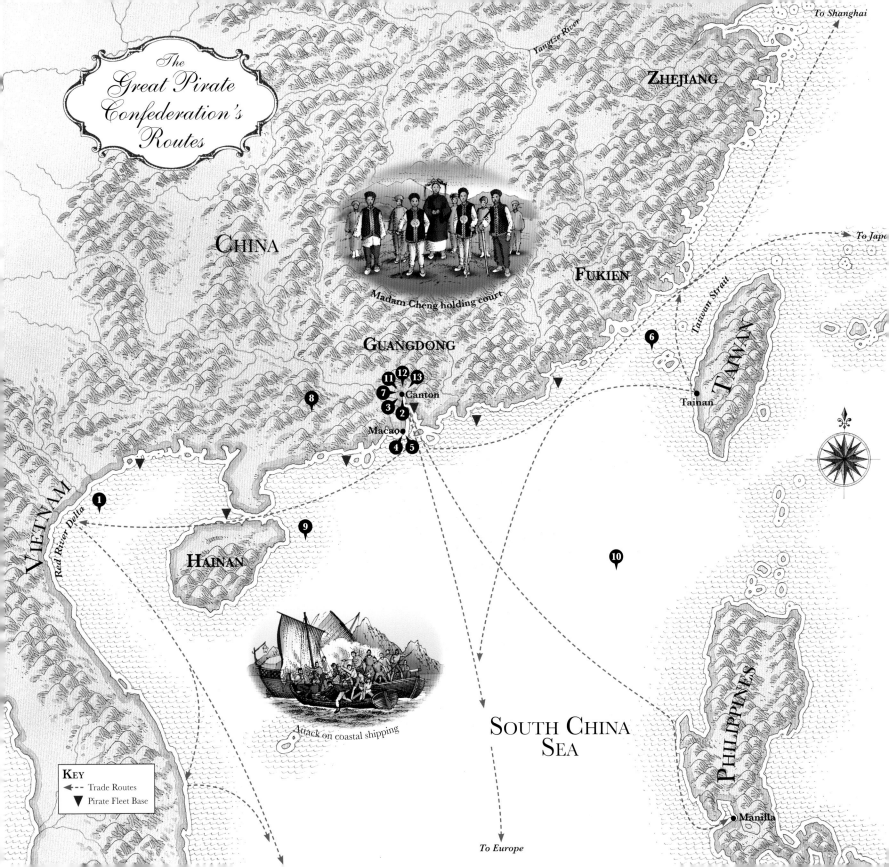

The Great Pirate Confederation's Routes

CHINA

ZHEJIANG

FUKIEN

GUANGDONG

Madam Cheng holding court

Canton

Macao

TAIWAN

Tainan

VIETNAM

Red River Delta

HAINAN

Attack on coastal shipping

SOUTH CHINA SEA

PHILIPPINES

Manilla

Yangtze River

Taiwan Strait

To Shanghai

To Japan

To Europe

KEY
→ Trade Routes
▼ Pirate Fleet Base

Cheng Yih, Madam Cheng, and their Pirate Confederation, 1801–10

1 **Early 1801** The pirate Cheng Yih inherits his father's pirate fleet, which was then based on Vietnam's Red River Delta.

2 **Summer 1801** Moves his pirate fleet to Guangdong province (Kwangtung), and establishes his base in Canton (Guangzhou). By joining forces with other pirate groups he encounters on the way, Cheng Yih establishes a nascent pirate confederation.

3 **Late 1801** Cheng Yih marries Cheng Shi, who was then working in a Canton brothel.

4 **March 1804** The pirates of the confederation blockade the Portuguese port of Macao.

5 **September 1804** Cheng Yih's pirate fleet drives off a squadron of Portuguese warships sent to raise the pirate blockade of Macao. The Portuguese therefore capitulate, agreeing to Cheng Yih's demands for protection money.

6 Cheng Yih extends his control eastward to encompass Fukien province and Taiwan. He now controls the entire Chinese coast south of the Yangtze River.

7 **1805** Cheng Yih's great Pirate Confederation is now composed of six fleets, the largest of which is his own Red Flag Fleet, based in Canton.

8 **1806** The pirates attack coastal villages between Macao and Canton, in order to establish control over Guangdong province.

9 **1807** Cheng Yih is lost at sea off Hainan, and his wife Cheng Shi becomes the new ruler of the pirate confederation. She becomes known as "Madam Cheng."

10 **1808-09** Madam Cheng re-establishes direct control over the other pirate fleets after they tried to secede. She proves a highly disciplined and efficient pirate leader.

11 **September 1809** Madam Cheng's men kidnap a group of British seamen in Canton, causing a diplomatic incident.

12 **Summer 1810** A Western naval force attacks and destroys the bulk of the pirate Red Flag Fleet.

13 **October 1810** The Emperor offers the pirates an amnesty and Madam Cheng acceptes. From then on she becomes the leader of a major opium smuggling ring.

his control, which meant that in time of need he could call on over 150,000 men to fight for him. This made him the commander of what was probably the largest pirate confederation in history.

The Chinese Emperor had been slow to react to these developments. He also lacked the naval muscle. After all, if one pirate fleet was threatened, the rest could sail to its aid, and even the Emperor lacked the power to fight so many ships at once. This made the pirates invulnerable to attack—Cheng Yih's pirate junks were able to roam at will, attacking ships or demanding payment with impunity.

THE PIRATE WIDOW

Cheng Yih was at the height of his power when he died in late 1807, probably by being washed overboard during a storm. His wife Cheng Shi maneuvered her way into a position of power and assumed command of the Red Flag Fleet. Through sheer willpower she managed to hold her husband's pirate confederation together and within three years, had assumed her husband's position as its overall leader. Cheng Yih's forceful widow, a former prostitute on a floating brothel in Canton, became known

The Red Flag Fleet: One of Six

By 1805, Cheng Yih commanded a mighty pirate empire, consisting of more than 600 pirate junks, crewed by around 30,000 men. It was also highly organized. He divided this force into six fleets, each known by the color of its flag—black, white, red, blue, yellow, and green. Each fleet was also given a particular area to operate in, which helped ensure that the fleets would not fight each other, or interfere in one another's operations. Cheng Yih maintained a loose control over the pirate confederation, although each fleet was given latitude to operate as it saw fit. He also retained direct command of the largest of these forces—the Red Flag Fleet—which contained more than 300 pirate junks.

Above: An attack on pirate junks by Western warships, during the mid-19th century. After the collapse of the great Pirate Confederation these large pirate fleets became a rare sight in Chinese waters. A fleet of pirate junks were no match for a single Western steam-powered gunboat.

Right: A 19th century Chinese pirate, wearing a mask designed to intimidate his victims.

as "Madame Cheng." By 1810, she ruled a pirate empire and proved to be a natural leader. She developed a reputation for daring and, unlike her husband, was willing to attack European ships if the opportunity arose. However, her empire was soon to unravel.

Unable to defeat the pirates by using force, the Emperor used guile. He started by forcibly resettling the coastal communities of Guangdong province, to deny the pirates the provisions they needed. Next he forged an alliance with the European powers, and during 1810 a joint naval expedition found and destroyed much of the Red Flag Fleet in harbors and hidden inlets around Canton. Finally, in late 1810, the Emperor offered a pirate amnesty. Madame Cheng's deputy, Cheung Po Tsai, was one of the first to accept, and he surrendered the remains of the Red Flag Fleet. He then

Madame Cheng's Law

In September 1809, Madame Cheng kidnapped seven seamen from a British ship anchored off Canton, and returned them only after the East India Company had paid their ransom. One of them later wrote about his experience.

He described the code of laws under which Madame Cheng governed, in which theft, disobedience, or rape was punishable by death, and lesser crimes such as desertion involved the cutting off of an ear, a thumb, or a limb. The effect was to create a pirate brotherhood that was disciplined, resolute, and united.

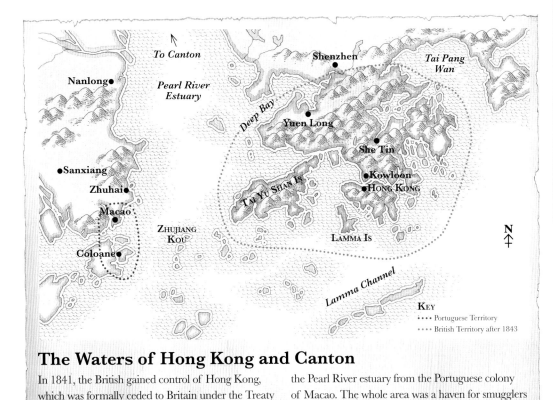

Madam Cheng (right), leader of the Pirate Confederation that dominated Chinese waters during the 1800s. At the height of her career she commanded about 2,000 ships.

The Waters of Hong Kong and Canton

In 1841, the British gained control of Hong Kong, which was formally ceded to Britain under the Treaty of Nanking in 1842. It lay close to Canton and across the Pearl River estuary from the Portuguese colony of Macao. The whole area was a haven for smugglers and pirates throughout the early 19th century.

became a pirate hunter and imperial admiral. The remaining pirates began fighting among themselves. Eventually, Madam Cheng bowed to the inevitable and accepted the pardon. She was allowed to retain a small trading fleet and remained in Canton, where for the next three decades she operated the largest opium-smuggling business in China.

Map labels:
To Canton, Nanlong, Pearl River Estuary, Shenzhen, Tai Pang Wan, Deep Bay, Yuen Long, She Tin, Sanxiang, Zhuhai, Tai Yu Shan Is, Kowloon, Hong Kong, Macao, Zhujiang Kou, Lamma Is, Coloane, Lamma Channel, N

KEY
•••• Portuguese Territory
•••• British Territory after 1843

Shap-'ng-Tsai

A former opium smuggler turned pirate, Shap-'ng-Tsai became one of the last of the Chinese pirates to pose a serious threat to trade in the South China Sea.

The Chinese pirate also provided the Western powers with the chance to demonstrate just how effective their warships really were.

TROUBLE IN CHINA

The end of the great pirate confederation in 1810 meant that the problem of piracy was greatly reduced in Chinese waters, but it never completely went away. The policy that had worked against Madame Cheng relied on the control of China's coastal provinces, and a joint resolve between the Chinese Emperor and the European powers. Unfortunately, trade restrictions imposed by the Emperor led to tensions between China and the Europeans, and these came to a head in 1839, over the right of the Europeans to import opium into China.

When the Chinese authorities began to seize ships carrying the drug, the British

Above: This elaborate silken flag was once flown from the pirate flagship sailed by Shap-'ng-Tsai, which was captured in October 1849.

reacted with military force, so beginning the First Opium War (1839–42). It ended in British victory, and the Emperor was forced to sign a humiliating trade agreement that permitted the trade and opened up parts of its coast to European merchants. Hong Kong Island was formally ceded to Britain in 1842, and the following year Canton became a "treaty port" (effectively, a port open to Western trade). Thanks to Madame Cheng the port was also a thriving center for the opium-smuggling trade; and thanks to the British, Westerners now controlled the business.

FROM SMUGGLER TO PIRATE

The problem was that there was a very thin line between a smuggler and a pirate. Both were operating outside the law, and both were prepared to take risks to preserve their

Opium Smuggling

By Chinese law, European merchants were forced to pay with silver for Chinese products such as porcelain, silk, tea, or spices. As silver was in short supply, traders preferred to import opium into China from India. The drug was then sold for cash, which was used to buy Chinese goods. The East India Company devised a complicated system of payment and semi-legal smuggling, while maintaining a monopoly over the trade. In effect, it relied on smugglers like Madam Cheng to take the risks, while it gathered the profits. By 1838, China was importing more than 1,400 tons of opium a year, despite the imperial ban.

Above: A British squadron depicted attacking the defenses of Canton from the Pearl River, during the Anglo-Chinese war known as the First Opium War (1839–42).

The Emperor then resorted to military means to enforce the ban—forcing the British into the strange position of having to fight for the right to smuggle drugs into a foreign country.

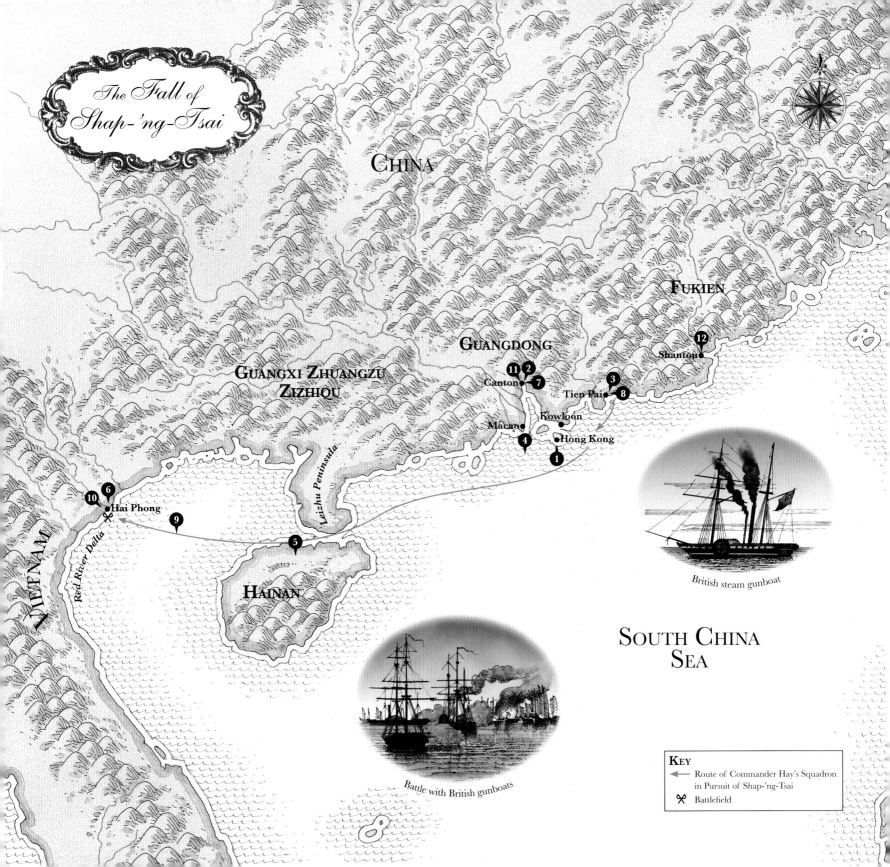

The Fall of Shap-'ng-Tsai

CHINA

FUKIEN

GUANGDONG

GUANGXI ZHUANGZU ZIZHIQU

Shantou

Canton

Tien Pai

Kowloon

Macao

Hong Kong

Leizhu Peninsula

Hai Phong

Red River Delta

VIETNAM

HAINAN

SOUTH CHINA SEA

British steam gunboat

Battle with British gunboats

KEY

Route of Commander Hay's Squadron in Pursuit of Shap-'ng-Tsai

Battlefield

From Opium Smuggling to Piracy, 1842–49

1 **1842** Hong Kong island is ceded to the British as part of the Treaty of Nanking, which brings the First Opium War to an end.

A war junk

2 **1842** Canton is declared an "open port," and Western merchants begin shipping goods there, including opium. In effect this puts local opium smugglers like Shap-'ng-Tsai out of business.

3 **August 1843** Shap-'ng-Tsai leaves Canton, and establishes a smuggling and pirate den at Tien Pai, approximately 100 miles (160km) east of Hong Kong.

4 **1846** The pirate empire of Shap-'ng-Tsai grows steadily, and he now charges protection money to all non-Western ships entering the waters around Hong Kong, Macao, and Canton.

5 **1848** His influence extends as far as Hainan Island, and the coast of Guangxi province.

6 **February 1849** Extends his influence into the northern coast of Vietnam, including the port of Hai Phong. He now extorts protection money from all local shipping operating in the Chinese ports of the South China Sea, with the exception of the Western "treaty ports."

7 **March 1849** Captures several Western trading ships in the Pearl River (Zhu Jiang), just below Canton. He is now considered a dangerous pirate by the British.

8 **September 1849** A British naval squadron attacks the pirate den at Tien Pai, but Shap-'ng-Tsai has already fled. More than 100 captured junks are re-captured.

9 **October 18** Commander Hay's Royal Navy Hong Kong squadron arrives off Hai Phong on the Red River Delta, and begins searching for Shap-'ng-Tsai's pirate fleet.

10 **October 20** The pirate fleet is located and trapped on the Red River. Hay attacks, and the pirate fleet is destroyed. Local villagers massacre the survivors as they struggle ashore.

11 **December 1849** Shap-'ng-Tsai manages to escape and returns to Canton.

12 He is offered a pardon and becomes an Imperial Chinese naval officer, based in Shantou, to the east of Guangdong province.

business. The opening up of markets to the British cut into the profits enjoyed by these smugglers. As a result, many turned to piracy. In theory, the Chinese fleet should have been able to limit the activities of both smugglers and pirates. Unfortunately, it had suffered badly during the war with the British, and so by 1841, it was in no position to patrol its own coastal waters.

SHAP-'NG-TSAI

One of these former opium smugglers was Shap-'ng-Tsai, who operated from the fishing village of Tien-pai in Guangdong province to the west of Hong Kong. He began by running a local protection racket, protecting small-time opium smugglers who wanted to avoid the Imperial patrols. During the 1840s, his business expanded significantly, until by 1848 he commanded a fleet of 70 pirate junks and his area of protection extended as far as Hainan Island, more than 500 miles (805km) to the west. The following year, his reach extended into the Gulf of Tonkin and the northern coast of Vietnam.

Then he made his big mistake. His pirates captured one American and three British clipper ships, all carrying opium into the "treaty port" of Canton. This led to a widespread panic in Canton, Hong Kong, and Macao, and many ships refused to leave port without a naval escort. It was clear that something would have to be done. If Shap-'ng-Tsai had limited his attacks to Chinese ships, then the Westerners would

The British steam sidewheel gunboat, HMS *Medea*, attacking a fleet of pirate junks near Hong Kong in March 1850. The Chinese were unable to counter the superior firepower of these Western warships.

Indian opium was smuggled into China by illegal Chinese traders like these depicted in Macao in a late 18th-century painting by John Webber. Their activities were supported by European merchants, who traded with them until the Chinese Emperor signed a treaty with Britain at the end of The First Opium War in 1842.

have left him alone. However, Shap-'ng-Tsai had now become a threat to trade.

In September 1849, Commander Hay of the Royal Navy's Hong Kong squadron led a fleet of steam warships to Tien-pai, but found that Shap-'ng-Tsai had fled. The pirate had fled west to Vietnam. Pausing only to destroy the base and recapture more than 100 junks, Hay then set off in pursuit. In late October, he reached the mouth of the Red River Delta (now the Hong Ha), just north of Haiphong. The pirates were trapped upstream. After

blockading the entrance, Hay led three steam warships up the river, supported by a squadron of imperial junks. The pirates were taken completely by surprise.

AN END TO THE THREAT

What followed was little short of a massacre. In a one-sided battle the shell guns of the warships made short work of the pirates, sinking or capturing 58 of their junks. More than 1,800 pirates were killed in the battle,

either by naval gunfire or by the local Cochin villagers. Shap-'ng-Tsai managed to survive the battle and fled back to China, where he was offered a pardon. Strangely, he then became an officer in the Imperial fleet, where his main task was the hunting down of pirates and smugglers. Although there were continued incidents of piracy throughout the rest of the 19th century, the superior technology of Western warships meant that pirates would never again become a serious threat in the South China Sea.

The Chinese Pirate Junk

The Chinese junk was the standard sailing vessel of the Far East. Suitable for sailing both the high seas and inland waterways, it was a design that suited the pirates' needs.

To Western eyes the efficient and sturdy Chinese junk looked unusual and ungainly, but by the 19th century its design had been perfected over several centuries.

The first Westerner to ever see a junk was Marco Polo in the late 13th century. He regarded the vessel as superior to anything he had seen in his native Venice. His description of it—single-decked, with a single rudder, and a double layer of underwater planking—also applied to junks five centuries later. The design was almost timeless.

Before the 17th century, Chinese junks had ventured as far as Persia and Africa, but the insular policy of the Manchu emperors meant that from the mid-17th century onward, voyages were limited to within the bounds of the South China Sea. Most junks were fitted with two or three masts, and gaff-rigged sails.

The pirate junks of the 17th to 19th centuries were similar to these merchant vessels; in fact many were simply converted from merchantmen. These were armed with broadside-firing guns, and smaller *lantaka* guns that were designed to be fired at point-blank range. Some of the largest pirate junks were more than 100 feet (30.5m) long, but most were significantly smaller—often half that size. Many pirates sailed with their families on board, and while the captain lived in the stern cabin, his crew and their families were housed in cabins inside the main hold. Pirate crews could vary in number from a few dozen on small craft to almost 200 men on larger junks.

The seagoing junk was roomy, it handled well under sail, and it was well-suited to the region's weather conditions. Although Western sailors might have regarded them as primitive, in reality they were the perfect sailing vessel for Chinese waters—and the ideal type of ship for pirates.

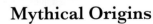

Mythical Origins

The name "junk" was first applied to Chinese sailing ships by the Portuguese, who based the term on the word *djong*, which they first heard in the East Indies. It was also claimed that this in turn derived from an old Chinese word—*jun*—meaning ship or large vessel.

According to Chinese legend it was the Emperor Fu Hsi, the son of a sea nymph, who taught the Chinese how to build the craft, around 2,800 BC. If this were true, it would mean that the junk was the oldest type of sailing vessel in history.

Left: Model of an ocean-going junk, identical to a pirate junk and typical of the 19th-century merchant vessels that plied the waters of the South China Sea.

The Indonesian Pirates

For centuries, piracy and warfare were endemic in Indonesian waters, and the arrival of the Europeans only presented these fierce people with a new and lucrative prey.

It was not until the late 19th century, when the Europeans set up anti-piracy patrols to protect their interests, that the Indonesian pirates were finally brought under control.

THE COMING OF THE EUROPEANS

The first Europeans arrived in Indonesia in the 16th century in search of spices. They found the Spice Islands, but they also encountered the local tribes, to whom piracy was a favored pursuit. The thousands of islands that made up Indonesian and Philippine archipelago were perfect pirate havens, and for centuries local tribes attacked each other and the boats stocked with goods that sailed between the islands. Now they could prey on the Europeans.

During the 18th and 19th centuries, with the exception of the settlements controlled by Europeans, most of this vast region was divided into small tribal areas. Warfare was endemic but no single power was powerful enough to dominate the rest. The establishment of permanent Spanish settlements in the Philippines and Dutch settlements in Indonesia did little to bring stability to the region. The Europeans were largely powerless to control the tribes that operated beyond the borders of their settlements.

Generally, the Europeans were distrusted by the local tribes, and their ships were singled out for pirate attack. Particularly vulnerable were ships sailing between Europe and China, as these had to pass through the Malacca Strait between the Malay peninsula and the island of Sumatra. Then, as now, it was considered a hotbed of pirate activity. From there the ships had to sail through the South China Sea, running the gauntlet of the numerous pirate havens bordering its shores—Borneo, Malaya, the Sulu Archipelago, and the Philippines. The most feared pirates in Indonesian waters were the Balanini, the Ilanun, and the Dyaks, whose boats were small and swift.

Below: Dyak tribesmen, ambushing Western canoes with poisoned arrows, during Rajah Brooke's expedition of 1846. Brooke and his well-armed Europeans had a vital technological advantage over their native adversaries.

THE BALANINI

The Balanini pirates lived in the Sulu Archipelago, with their main settlement on the island of Jolo. This meant they were well placed to raid Spanish settlements in the Philippines, and to intercept Spanish coastal shipping. They operated in small craft known as *Corocoros*—fast sailing vessels fitted with outriggers, which could be powered by sail or oar. Some of the larger *Corocoros* weighed up to 100 tons and could carry as many as 60 pirates. Other pirate groups of the area included the Bugis of Sulawesi, who combined trading with piracy depending on economic conditions, and were described by Europeans who encountered them as a mercenary, bloodthirsty, inhuman race.

THE ILANUN

The Ilanun pirates from Mindanao plagued the waters of the Philippines, but they also raided far out into the South China Sea, where they came into contact with European ships bound for China. During the late 17th century, English and Spanish sailors who came into contact with them described the Ilanun as being a peaceable people, but within a century that had changed. They became known as slavers, who raided throughout the Philippines and Indonesia, and sold their captives in the slave markets in Java and Sumatra. Like the Balanini, they

Left: An Ilanun pirate, one of the fiercest seagoing tribes in the waters of Southeast Asia.

also preyed on Spanish coastal shipping in and around the Philippines. Like other Indonesian peoples they used *prahus* or *praus* —Malayan sailboats with a single outrigger, which in their case were rowed by slaves.

THE DYAKS

The head-hunting Dyaks of Borneo and the Malay peninsula were generally acknowledged to be the fiercest pirates in the region. They ranged throughout the area and developed a reputation for attacking the European ships that sailed between Borneo and Singapore. The Iban, or "Sea Dyaks" of Borneo used a variant of the *prahu*, the lighter, faster *bangkong*. Further to the south, the Atjeh (Achin) and Riau pirates of Sumatra specialized in attacking ships in the Malacca Strait.

During the 1850s, the British naturalist Alfred Russel Wallace described the way these pirates operated: "Their long well-manned praus escape from the pursuit of a sailing vessel by pulling away right into the wind's eye, and the warning smoke of a steamer generally enables them to hide in some shallow bay or narrow river or forest-covered inlet until the danger is past."

Right: The native peoples of Sarawak, whose number included several tribes known to indulge in piracy.

RAFFLES OF SINGAPORE

In 1819, the British colonial official Stamford Raffles founded Singapore as a British colony. It was ideally placed to protect British interests in the area, and to safeguard the Malacca strait. From 1836 onward, a combined Royal naval and East India Company squadron was based there, and it conducted regular anti-piracy patrols. It proved successful and the British began launching punitive expeditions against the Dyaks and other Malay pirates. Gradually the area was made safer for European shipping. By the 1860s, the power of the pirates had been destroyed by a combination of Spanish military expeditions and British naval patrolling. Although piracy was never eradicated completely, the region was made considerably safer for Europeans than it had been before.

Frau.   Dajak's (Borneo). Krieger.   Vornehmes Mädchen.

The White Rajah

The most celebrated British pirate-hunter of the mid-1800s was Sir James Brooke—the first "White Rajah" of Sarawak—who was highly successful at suppressing piracy in the area.

Above: Sir James Brooke, the British Rajah of Sarawak. During his 26-year reign (1842–68), he cleansed his Borneo fiefdom of piratical tribes.

The Dutch generally tolerated piracy as long as it didn't interfere with their trade, but the British were less tolerant and sought to eradicate it.

James Brooke was born in India in 1803, the son of British parents, but he was schooled in England. At 19, he joined the army of the East India Company as an ensign, and in 1825 he saw action during the Burma campaign. He eventually left the army and turned his hand to trade. In 1833, the young Brooke bought the schooner *Royalist,* and spent five years as a less-than-successful merchant captain, trading in the Far East. He arrived in Borneo in late 1838, where he found an uprising in progress against the local ruler, the Sultan of Brunei. He helped to quell the revolt peaceably and as a reward (having threatened the Sultan with military force) he was given the title of Rajah of Sarawak in 1841. Brooke ran the province, then a province of the sultanate, as his own personal fiefdom from his headquarters in Kuching.

THE PIRATE-HUNTING RAJAH

Brooke took his duties seriously. He reformed the administration of his domain, applied judicial rule, and waged an unremitting war against the Iban and Dyak pirates that preyed on his coast. These pirates were based in the coastal and riverside villages of northern Borneo, and it was there that Brooke went in search of them. He gathered together a group of fellow British adventurers, which included Henry Keppel, a young naval officer.

In July 1843, Brooke entered the Saribas River to the east of Kuching with five small boats, crewed by 80 British sailors and

The Pirate-Hunting Activities of James Brooke, 1838–49

1 **August 1838** James Brooke arrives in Kuching, on the coast of Borneo, in time to help quell an uprising against the Sultan of Brunei.

2 **September 1842** A grateful (and heavily coerced) Sultan grants Brooke the title of the Rajah of Sarawak, effectively giving him independent control over the 48,000-square-mile (124sq km) province, on the western coast of Borneo.

3 **May 1843** Reports reach Brooke in Kuching that Iban, Malay, and Dyak pirates have been attacking the coast of Sarawak. However, the biggest threat is posed by the Iban pirates of the Saribas River, within Sarawak itself.

Dyak prahus

4 **July** Brooke leads an expedition up the Saribas River, and reaches the Iban village of Boling.

5 **Late July** The expedition attacks an Iban force at Padeh, and forces the villagers to accept Brooke's authority. He continues up the river to destroy the last pockets of Iban resistance.

6 **March 1844** Brooke commands a joint force of Royal Navy seamen and his own gentlemen adventurers, and attacks a Dyak lair at Patusan, 50 miles (80km) up the Batang Lupar River. However, the pirates are too numerous and Brooke retires.

7 **August** A second attack is launched, and this time the fortifications of Patusan are captured. Brooke goes on to destroy the remaining Dyak strongholds further up the river and its tributary.

8 **March 1849** A joint force of Iban and Dyak pirates appear on the Sarawak coast, at the mouth of the Sadong River.

9 **May** Brooke leaves Kuching to give battle, leading another joint Royal Naval and local adventurer force, supported by Sarawak Malay auxiliaries. The pirates retreat up the Batang Lupar River.

10 **July 31, 1849** In an engagement known as the Battle of Bantung Maru, Brooke inflicts a crushing defeat on the pirates, effectively ending the pirate threat to Sarawak.

SOUTH CHINA SEA

The
White Rajah
and the *Pirates*

Mindanao•

Jolo•

SULU ARCHIPELAGO

Pirates defend their den

Seria• **2**

BRUNEI

SARAWAK

9

✂

10 *Batang Lupar River* **6** **7**
                              ✂
1 **3** **8**   •Patusan

Kuching **4**

Saribas R. ✂ **5**

SINGAPORE

Malacca Strait

SUMATRA

BORNEO

THE WATERS OF THE EAST INDIES

THAILAND

VIETNAM

CAMBODIA

SOUTH CHINA
SEA

PHILIPPINES

PACIFIC
OCEAN

MALAYSIA

SARAWAK

BORNEO

SUMATRA

JAVA SEA

INDONESIA

JAVA SEA

INDONESIA

KEY
• • • Sarawak's Borders
✂ Battlefield

Above: James Brooke used technology and firepower to win his victories over the Borneo pirates, as demonstrated in the attack pictured here, which was conducted in 1843 with the help of HMS *Dido*.

volunteers, accompanied by 180 local allies. They fought their way up river, demolishing the stockades of the Iban pirates as they went. The expedition was a complete success.

WAR AGAINST THE DYAKS

Brooke then attacked the Dyak stronghold of Patusan, 50 miles (80km) up the Batang Lupar River. This time he was helped by the East India Company as well as the navy, and together they destroyed the bases of more than 5,000 pirates. Brooke went on to crush the last pockets of Dyak resistance.

In 1848, the Iban resumed their attacks, and even raided Sarawak. This time, Brooke had steamers at his disposal and, escorted by canoes, they chased the Saribas' pirates, trapping them at Bantung Maru in the mouth of the Batang Lupar. In the ensuing battle, the pirates were crushed.

BROOKE THE MAN

Despite his success, Brooke was criticized for his actions. He was accused of the needless massacre of natives, criticized for accepting "head money" from the Admiralty for each pirate he killed, and castigated for his penchant for teenage youths. Nonetheless, he continued to rule Sarawak until his death in 1868.

Right: The "White Rajah" James Brooke, pictured negotiating a treaty with a powerful tribal chieftain within his Sarawak dominion.

Sending a Gunboat

By the end of the 19th century piracy had been largely eradicated in the eastern seas, the main reason being the powerful Western warships that patrolled these waters and kept them safe.

Pirate activity was never completely eradicated in the East. Different areas became flashpoints from time to time, and were swiftly dealt with.

In most cases, when an outbreak of piracy occurred, Western forces were sent to quell the flare-up. This happened in the Persian Gulf during the early 19th century, when Persian pirate dens were destroyed by punitive expeditions. Forces were also sent in

The Hong Kong Squadron

Following the First Opium War of 1839, the Royal Navy maintained a permanent squadron in the Far East, based in Hong Kong. While its main job was to safeguard British trade, it also made regular punitive attacks against pirates bases, often working in conjunction with the Chinese. In one form or other it remained in almost continual existence until 1997.

Below: British sailors depicted being sent ashore to deal with Dyak pirates during Rajah Brooke's campaign against the pirates of Borneo in the 1840s.

along the coast of Vietnam in the 1880s, during which time the French cleared the region of pirates. However, after World War I it was sometimes felt that the need to "send in a gunboat" to deal with pirates was an action of the past.

But in the 1920s, the specter of piracy raised its head once again in the waters of the South China Sea.

THE SUNNING INCIDENT

In November 1926, some 40 pirates disguised themselves as passengers and took passage on the British streamer *Sunning*, bound from Shanghai to Canton. They came on board at Amoy, more than halfway through the voyage, hijacked the ship, threw four crewmen overboard, and ordered the rest to sail the steamer to a remote anchorage. Amazingly, the crew broke free, and arming themselves with revolvers seized the bridge and held it against all-comers. Unable to recapture the bridge, the pirates set fire to the ship.

Fortunately, the gunboat HMS *Bluebell* came to the rescue, and a boarding party was sent on board. The fire was put out,

Above: Chinese pirates, photographed on board the Hong Kong Squadron flagship HMS *Vindictive* in 1926. These men were captured on board the *Sunning*, the British steamer they attacked and set fire to.

many of the pirates were captured, and the *Sunning* was towed to a safe port. *The Illustrated London News* of December 18, 1926 called it "the most sensational instance of piracy for more than twelve years." Nineteen pirates were sentenced and later hanged in Hong Kong.

The incident was part of a miniature pirate crime wave that plagued the Chinese coast from 1926 onward. To counter it the Royal Navy deployed extra gunboats in Chinese waters and spearheaded the international community's war against the pirates. The crime wave lasted until 1935, when the navy finally managed to eradicate the last of them.

Piracy Today

While piracy has existed for many years, most thought it had been relegated to the pages of history, but anyone following the news will know that piracy isn't a thing of the past. It still happens today and, worse still, it is on the increase.

Above: Armed militants or pirates (depending on your viewpoint) from the Movement for the Emancipation of the Niger Delta, pictured in 2006 after destroying a Nigerian army outpost that guarded oil installations in the Delta.

One of the most dramatic of recent attacks took place in November 2008, when the bulk super tanker *Sirius Star* from Saudi Arabia was captured by Somali pirates off the East African coast. Its cargo of crude oil was worth more than $100 million.

For the owners this was a major financial disaster. For the crew, it was worse, as they then spent two weeks at gunpoint. The crisis was eventually resolved when a ransom was paid. Since then, the number of attacks has grown, as the success of these pirates encouraged others to follow their example.

The new wave of piracy isn't limited to the Indian Ocean. Over the past decade other areas have been labeled pirate hotspots. In recent years, the Malacca Strait, beween Malaysia and Sumatra, has been the most dangerous trouble spot in the world—until the focus of attention turned to Somalia. Elsewhere in the East Indies and the Far East pirates have been equally busy, while pirate attacks have also been regularly reported along the coast of West Africa. Minor incidents also occur off the coast of Latin America, and no doubt the specter of piracy will reappear elsewhere in the future.

In the past, piracy flourished in areas where there was no strong government, or where waters were poorly policed. This is exactly the situation in Somalia, the East Indies, and other regions. International organizations have also reported links between piracy and terrorism, and where once plunder was the objective, a growing number of attacks are now carried out for political or religious motives. Just as they did in the days of Blackbeard, the navies of the world need to maintain their vigilance, and the international community needs to pull together, to combat this growing threat.

The New Pirates

A new breed of pirates is on the rise—men motivated by politics, by desperation, by religion, and by greed. The threat they pose is real, and highly dangerous.

As the statistics all too clearly show, in recent years there has been an unprecedented rise in piracy, and in maritime hijacking.

Each year, the International Maritime Bureau (IMB) produces a report on piracy around the world, and the one they published in early 2009 made grim reading. The organization—part of the International Chamber of Commerce—first began reporting instances of pirate attacks back in 1991. They started compiling reports because they saw piracy as a growing problem, particularly in the Far East. As a result, the international community began to take the problem seriously.

While the number of instances grew fairly steadily, by 2005 it was felt that the problem was under control. The worst-hit area was the Malacca Strait, and a combination of

Above: A young Somali militiaman guards a captured ship held in a Somali port. The fishermen supply the boats for piratical attacks, while the militiamen supply the weapons, technology, and manpower.

naval patrolling and better policing in the neighboring coastal communities went a long way toward solving the problem.

A GLOBAL PROBLEM

Clearly, the world community was being over-optimistic. Since 2005, the IMB has been warning shipping companies that piracy is on the rise in the Red Sea. In 2007, it issued its starkest warning yet: "There has been a marked increase in attacks and hijackings off the southern part of Somalia, particularly off Mogadishu. The attacks are mainly targeted toward vessels with cargo for Somali ports. Vessels are advised to steer well clear of Somalian waters at all times." However, much of the Somali coastline is on the southern coast of the Red Sea. Thanks to the Suez

Somalia and the Gulf of Aden

Since 2002, piracy has become a serious problem along the coastline of war-torn Somalia—it is now the world's leading pirate hotspot.

A growing number of ships have been attacked in the Gulf of Aden or the Indian Ocean, and the ships, crew, and cargo held for ransom.

KEY
⚓ Major Pirate Base
⚓ Ransom Anchorage
● Pirate Port
••• Country Borders

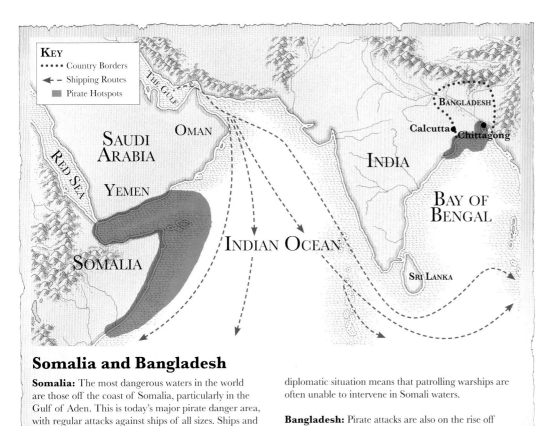

Somalia and Bangladesh

Somalia: The most dangerous waters in the world are those off the coast of Somalia, particularly in the Gulf of Aden. This is today's major pirate danger area, with regular attacks against ships of all sizes. Ships and their crew are regularly held for ransom, and a hazy diplomatic situation means that patrolling warships are often unable to intervene in Somali waters.

Bangladesh: Pirate attacks are also on the rise off Bangladesh, particularly in the busy port of Chittagong.

The West African Coast

Over the past decade, regular attacks have been conducted against offshore oil installations and oil-related shipping off the Niger Delta. While these attacks have abated due to military and naval pressure, other piratical attacks still take place against ships anchored in busy West African harbors such as Lagos in Nigeria and Tema in Ghana.

Above: Large container ships are vulnerable to attack, as they lack the speed to escape and have relatively small crews. When traveling through pirate waters most ship captains are particularly vigilant, and take precautions to guard against pirate attacks. Similarly, the navies of the world maintain non-stop patrols in these dangerous waters.

Canal, it is one of the busiest shipping lanes in the world. Despite increased naval patrols, the problem has become steadily worse.

The IMB report of early 2009 claimed that during 2007, a total of 18 ships had been hijacked around the world—the majority of them off Somalia. During 2008, that figure almost trebled to 49 ships. Around the world 293 pirate incidents were reported in 2008—some 11 percent more than the previous year. In Somali waters the number of incidents had doubled—with 19 attacks in September 2008 alone.

PIRATE "HOTSPOTS"

Since 1991, the waters of Indonesia, Somalia, India, Sri Lanka, Bangladesh, Burma, West Africa (especially Nigeria), the Philippines,

Brazil, Colombia, and Venezuela have all been identified as high-risk areas. This increase corresponds with changes in the international political climate. The end of the Cold War and the collapse of the Soviet Union dramatically influenced the role of the world's navies. Then the growth of Al Qaeda and the September 11, 2001, attack introduced the world to the notion of a long-term war against terrorism. All this has had an effect on the way piracy is perceived, and how it is countered.

Above: Captured Indonesian pirates. Many claim they are driven to piracy by poverty and hunger.

Malaysia and the Philippines

Malacca Strait: Before 2005, the Malacca Strait was plagued by pirates, but a determined international naval effort has paid off, and the threat posed by local pirates has greatly diminished.

Malaysia: The small island groups of Natuna and Anambas on the southern edge of the South China Sea, between the Malaysian peninsula and Borneo, are known as pirate lairs, and regular attacks are made against passing ships. Even Tioman, off the Malay Peninsula, has been linked to pirate attacks, despite being a major tourist attraction.

The Philippines: For more than a decade the presence of rebel groups has made the waters of the Philippines a dangerous place, and vessel crews and yachtsmen have been kidnapped and held for ransom. Since 2008, attacks have been reported on ships anchored in Manila harbor, one of the busiest anchorages in Asia.

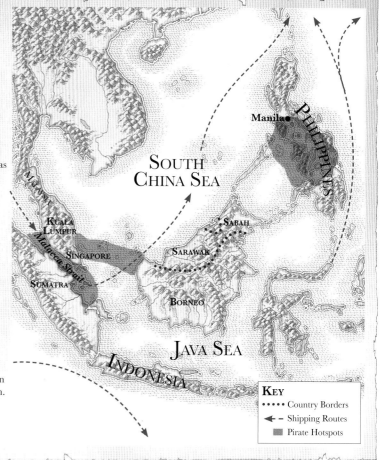

KEY
- ••••• Country Borders
- ◄ – Shipping Routes
- ▨ Pirate Hotspots

Brazilian Waters

Since 1990, a number of attacks have been reported off the Brazilian coast, particularly around the port of Santos, just south of Rio de Janeiro on the Atlantic coast.

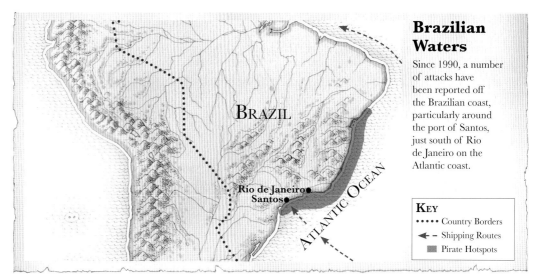

KEY
- ••••• Country Borders
- ◄ – Shipping Routes
- ▨ Pirate Hotspots

Hotspot: Eastern Waters

For centuries, the Far East was plagued by pirates, from the South China Sea down to the islands of the East Indies. Today, it still remains a troubled region.

Despite a major international effort to protect shipping and to curb piracy, attacks against commercial ships continue to plague the area and interfere with world trade.

THE MALACCA STRAIT

Until fairly recently, the most dangerous stretch of water in the world outside a war zone was the Malacca Strait, a 550 mile (885km) long waterway running between the coast of Malaysia and the island of Sumatra. It is one of the busiest stretches of water in the world—as many as 50,000 ships pass through this maritime bottleneck every year. Around a quarter of all the oil produced in the world is shipped through the Strait, carried in some of the largest supertankers in existence. Bulk carriers transport the goods of China and Japan to markets in Europe, Africa and America, and liners carry cruise passengers to Singapore, Bali, and other exotic destinations.

All this traffic in a narrow waterway means that the ships have to slow down as they pass through the Strait, which leaves them vulnerable to attack. Pirates use fast speedboats or inflatables to attack passing ships, and to return to the safety of the coast before the alarm can be raised. Others disguise themselves as local fishing boats or other coastal craft. The number of pirate attacks in the region climbed steadily during the 1990s, until by 2004 there were more than 80 pirate attacks a year—some 40 percent of the world total.

All of this prompted the introduction of international anti-piracy patrols, backed by satellite intelligence gathering and raids

Above: Malaysian or Indonesian pirates, caught while attacking a merchant ship in the Malacca Strait, 2006.

Anti-Piracy Measures

The International Maritime Bureau (IMB) recommends that ship captains take certain precautions when sailing through pirate-infested waters. These include keeping all deck lights on, rigging water hoses over the side to deter boarders, posting lookouts around the ship, keeping emergency radio channels open, and, above all, being very vigilant. If attacked, they suggest increasing speed, taking evasive action and heading toward rough, open water. Most merchant ships don't carry any weapons, which leaves them vulnerable, so preventing the pirates from boarding is still the safest course of action.

Above: Recently, patrols by the international maritime community have reduced the pirate threat in Eastern waters.

on the ground. As a result, since 2005 the number of attacks has fallen steadily, but the International Maritime Bureau (IMB) still warns crews to maintain a strict anti-piracy watch while transiting the Strait. In 2008, a fresh crop of attacks took place beyond the Strait, near Tioman Island off the east coast of the Malay Peninsula, as a consequence of which the authorities have extended their patrols to cover this new threat.

INDONESIA AND THE PHILIPPINES

During the 1980s, pirate attacks began to be reported in Indonesia. One vulnerable group of victims were the Vietnamese boat people, fleeing their country in often unseaworthy craft that were were frequently attacked as they passed through the islands. Guerrilla movements both in Indonesia and the Philippines have added to the problem because many of these groups see piracy as a way of raising funds. In 2006, more than 79 attacks were reported in these waters, mainly in the Celebes Sea off the eastern coast of Borneo, but also around Java and Sumatra. There the pirates are local fishermen, armed with guns, knives, and machetes. Since then the same areas have remained a problem, but pirate attacks have also been reported in the Sulu Archipelago and the Philippines, including Manila Bay, one of the busiest anchorages in Asia.

THE INDIAN SUBCONTINENT

During the first years of the 21st century, Bangladesh became another trouble spot, and the port of Chittagong was listed as the most dangerous anchorage in the world. No

fewer than 47 attacks were reported there in 2005 alone, but a clampdown by the authorities has greatly reduced the problem. Attacks still take place, though, mainly conducted by small-time opportunist pirates armed with knives and metal pipes. Since then other attacks have been reported off Mumbai, Cochin (Kochi), and Sri Lanka.

THE SOUTH CHINA SEA

In recent years, the Chinese coast guard has been involved in a number of incidents, although these might well represent the actions of real pirates who sometimes use

Left: A group of well-armed pirates, operating from a secret island base off the Malay Peninsula. They use fast speedboats to attack their prey.

the coast guard as a cover. For example, in June 1995, a Chinese customs cutter stopped the Panamanian-registered freighter MV *Hye Mieko* in international waters. The freighter had sailed from Singapore two days before, bound for Cambodia. A dozen men in Chinese uniforms seized the vessel, and sailed it more than 900 miles (1,448km) through international waters, until it reached the Chinese port of Shanwei. There the vessel was impounded on "suspicion of smuggling." The ship was later released.

The most recent incident of this kind was in 2006, when fake customs officials ransacked a container ship in Huangpu. Attacks have also taken place in Haiphong, in northern Vietnam and off the southern coast of Vietnam. Fortunately, such incidents are rare, and at the moment the South China Sea is a relatively safe place.

Below: Anti-piracy patrols in the Malacca Strait are a deterrent and reduce the risk of opportunistic attacks.

Hotspot: Somalia

The Red Sea was once the favorite hunting ground of pirates like Thomas Tew, William Kidd, and Henry Every.

Piracy in these waters is not a new phenomenon, and continues today. However, this new generation of pirates uses speedboats and automatic weapons.

In the early 19th century, the waters of the Red Sea and the Persian Gulf were plagued by pirates, and it took a major initiative by the British East India Company to stamp out the coastal enclaves of these small-time criminals. Today, the Persian Gulf is too well policed to permit any such activity. On the Red Sea, however, piracy is enjoying a dramatic renaissance, and unless major action is taken the problem will continue to increase.

Below: The luxury German cruise liner *Seabourn Spirit,* which was attacked by well-armed Somali pirates in November 2005.

THE BACKGROUND

Somalia is a thin, L-shaped country that encases the Horn of Africa, bordering the Gulf of Aden and the Indian Ocean. The Gulf of Aden leads directly to the Red Sea, through the narrow Bab el Mandeb (Gate of Tears), which was once the haunt of the late 17th-century "Red Sea Roundsmen." From the 1970s, Somalia was ruled by a military dictatorship led by General Siad Barre, who enjoyed limited support from the Soviet Union. However, by 1990, the regime had become deeply unpopular and opposition groups led an armed insurrection against the dictator, supported by the neighboring government of Ethiopia.

General Barre was ousted from power in 1991, at which point the northern part of the country declared independence, becoming Somaliland. So far, the republic remains unrecognized by the international community. Elsewhere, the various victorious factions fell out with each other, and a civil war was fought to determine which group should control the remainder of the country. In the process, what remained of any national infrastructure was destroyed, and the capital Mogadishu became a war-torn and divided city. The war also caused widespread famine, prompting the launch of a major UN relief effort.

American troops became embroiled in the conflict in 1993, when they tried to

The *Semlow* Incident

A typical attack of the past few years involved the capture of the Kenyan-owned MV *Semlow*. On June 27, 2005, she was transporting a cargo of rice to Somalia as part of a UN food program. Somalian pirates attacked and captured her under cover of darkness just off the port of Harardhere. Her ten-man crew were held hostage for over three months. One of the crewmen later reported:

"These pirates are worse than the pirates we read about in history books … These Somali pirates are better armed, and they want ransom, not just our goods."

The crew were released, after the shipowners paid the pirates a ransom.

The majority of the pirates come from Puntland, the Somali region which forms the tip of the Horn of Africa. The town of Harardhere in central Somalia remains one of the principal pirate lairs on the Somali coast. According to journalists and outside agencies, approximately 1,500 pirates were active in 2009, divided into five or six principal gangs. Their numbers include local fishermen, with the boats and the skills needed to operate the raiding vessels; ex-militiamen, from the factions of the various Somali warlords, who provide the pirate groups with firepower; and technical or financial experts, who deal with the ransom demands and who have access to GPS satellites, radios, and mobile phones. Their success has made them some of the richest men in the region.

Above: A recent trend has been the preference of pirates to take hostages rather than to plunder ships and cargo. These crewmen from the Chinese fishing boat *Tian Yu* were captured by Somali pirates in November 2008 and taken back to a Somali port, where they and their ship were held for ransom.

Above: Somali pirates usually operate in rigid-hulled speedboats, capable of being launched from the beach.

protect fellow UN troops against the warring faction led by General Aidid. By 1995, the UN had pulled out of the country, leaving the warlords to fight amongst themselves. A makeshift government was formed, but it has little power. In 2006, the fighting escalated as a new hard-line Islamic group battled for control of the country. They were defeated, but the legacy of nearly two decades of fighting is apparent. The country is devastated, the economy is in ruins, and rival warlords still control their own sections of the country.

The threat of piracy in this area was first highlighted in November 1989 when the German-built cruise ship *Seabourn Spirit* was attacked 70 miles (113km) off the Somalian coast. At dawn, two speedboats approached the ship and raked it with machine-guns and rockets. Fortunately, the crew were able to prevent the attackers from boarding. Other incidents followed, but the scale of these attacks remained fairly small. However, the numbers of the incidents increased steadily, until in 2005 there were 19 major attacks in Somali waters. Four years later, the numbers are closer to 20 attacks each month.

TYPES OF ATTACK

Sometimes attacks are conducted from single small boats, or operate from a "mother ship," which allows the pirates to range far out to sea. At other times, a group of pirate craft is used. For instance, in February 2009, a bulk carrier was attacked in the Gulf of Aden. The captain used evasive maneuvers to prevent the pirates from boarding, and the arrival

Below: In November 2008, the 162,000-ton super-tanker *Sirius Star* was seized by Somali pirates, and held for ransom until $3 million was paid.

of a Chinese navy helicopter convinced the pirates to give up the attempt. An hour later, a German warship escorted the merchant ship, to make sure she wasn't attacked again. At present, these incidents are an almost daily occurrence off the Somali coast.

THE *SIRIUS STAR*

The lack of central government in Somalia makes it very difficult for the international maritime community to plan any concerted action. After the blood-letting in Mogadishu in 1993, organizations such as the UN have been extremely reluctant to deploy peacekeeping troops to the region. This means that nobody is really in control, and the pirates can continue their business unimpeded by the threat of attack from the land.

Since 2005, the trend has been for the pirates not only to attempt to hijack a ship but also to ransom it. The hijacked *Sirius Star* was released in January 2009, when a ransom of $3 million was paid to the pirates,

Right: Somali militiamen guard relief supplies, which have been unloaded from a captured UN-registered ship in a Somali port.

a development which set a worrying trend. Piracy has now become a highly lucrative business, and the prospect of rewards of this magnitude will only attract hardened criminals to the Somali coast. Therefore, the situation can only get worse.

NEW TERRITORY

While the world's maritime community was well aware of the threat posed by this new wave of pirates, the *Sirius Star* incident was headline news, and the problem suddenly took center stage. The environmental lobby was horrified—the damage done by the vast amount of crude oil it was carrying would have been unimaginable if it had somehow been released into the Indian Ocean. Just as importantly, while earlier attacks had been limited to ships passing through the Red Sea or close to the coast of war-torn Somalia, this attack took place off the coast of Kenya, in the middle of the busy shipping lane between the Persian Gulf and the Cape of Good Hope. This route was used by tankers that were too big to make the shorter voyage through the Suez Canal. Until the *Sirius Star* incident, it was thought these tankers were safe from attack. Clearly these ships—the largest and most valuable in the world—are now sailing through dangerous waters.

Hotspot: West Africa

In West Africa, local separatist movements have turned to piracy as a way to raise funds, and also to inflict damage on the oil companies they blame for their economic and social woes.

Like the Red Sea, the coast of West Africa is no stranger to piracy. Once the haunt of the likes of Bartholomew Roberts and Howell Davis, today the pirates are Africans.

The targets of choice are the foreign oil workers who work in the rich oil fields off the Niger Delta. The oil production is a major source of revenue for the Nigerian government, but the oil lies off the coast of Biafra, a region devastated during the Nigerian Civil War (1967–70) when more than three million Nigerians and Biafrans died, mainly through disease or starvation. Tensions still run high in the region, where the locals feel they have been denied the benefits of the oil money that has boosted the Nigerian economy. This feeling of injustice, coupled with tribal and religious tensions, has created an atmosphere of instability.

Among the Igbo people of the region, a new regional independence group called the Movement for the Emancipation of the Niger Delta (MEND) has emerged, and its objectives are to right these wrongs through armed struggle. This includes piratical attacks, and the kidnapping of foreign oil workers. The locals blame the oil industry for polluting the water and the coastal land, making legitimate fishing and farming all but impossible.

There were 20 pirate attacks on or just off the Nigerian coast in 2005, before MEND

Pirates, Freedom Fighters, or Terrorists?

In early 2006, MEND sent a message to Shell officials, saying, "It must be clear that the Nigerian government cannot protect your workers or assets. Leave our land while you can or die in it … Our aim is to totally destroy the capacity of the Nigerian government to export oil." As a prelude to an attack on an oil facility in late 2008, the group declared they were fighting a war against the oil industry, a war that they called Operation "Hurricane Barbarossa."

Members of MEND operate as pirates, using speedboats with well-armed crews to overpower their victims—be they offshore installations, oil vessels, or shore stations. However, their objectives are clearly political and military. This may represent a new form of piracy, whereby the crime is the same but the motive has changed. It also raises the specter of terrorist-related piracy. While MEND's activities are relatively low scale, other more powerful groups may also attempt to use piracy as a terrorist weapon.

Top: A speedboat carrying pirates from MEND (Movement for the Emancipation of the Niger Delta). They claim to be freedom fighters, using piracy as a weapon in their war against the oil companies operating in the region, and against the Nigerian government.

Above: A Western oil worker, captured and held captive by the Niger Delta pirates. Kidnapping has now become an integral part of piracy.

claimed responsibility for these assaults. Some of these incidents might have been politically inspired, but most appear to have been simple acts of piracy that involved robbery and some destruction. There were 17 attacks the following year and, as before, most were genuine acts of robbery, involving both tankers and cargo ships lying off Lagos and Port Harcourt. However, in 2007 a total of 34 attacks were reported, and at least half of these were clearly aimed at disrupting oil production or intimidating oil workers.

Shell and other oil companies responded by drafting in outside security consultants, while Nigerian soldiers were brought in to protect oil facilities. A combination of these measures, as well as increased Nigerian naval patrols, saw the number of incidents fall to 17 in 2008. Once again, many of these incidents were financially inspired. The first attack of 2009 was typical. In January 2009, pirates operating from a speedboat attacked a tanker in the Bonny Oil Terminal. Grenades

and automatic weapons were thrown, and the pirates sped away after seizing whatever valuables they could find on board.

POLITICAL AIMS

However, the prospect of politically motivated piracy has not gone away. During 2006, MEND concentrated on attacking land targets, destroying up to 25 percent of Nigeria's oil production in the process. Then they moved from destruction to kidnapping as a means of raising funds. Fourteen oil workers were kidnapped in 2007, and in June 2008, the pirates raided and damaged a major oil platform operated by Shell, located about 70 miles (113km) offshore. Three months later, MEND launched its all-out offensive using land and maritime forces.

However, by that time the oil installations had been heavily reinforced and the attacks were repulsed, with heavy casualties. Many of MEND's speedboats were destroyed in the operation and the offensive power of the group was shattered. Since then MEND has been quiet, and the only attacks in the region are the regular instances of low-level opportunistic piracy that has plagued the West African coast for decades.

Above: The growth of piracy in the Niger Delta is linked to resentment felt by the local population, at what they see as exploitation by the oil companies, who maintain large offshore platforms (top) in the area.

Hotspot: Latin America

Not all modern pirates attack cruise ships, hijack supertankers, or assault oil platforms. Many, particularly in the waters around Latin America, are more opportunistic.

The local criminals operating along the coastlines of Latin America see yachtsmen, fishermen, or coastal craft as easy pickings.

In 2001, the yachtsman Sir Peter Blake took part in an environmental exploration trip to South America. The 53-year old New Zealander had twice won the America's Cup for his country and in 1995 was knighted for his services to yachting.

On December 6, his 130-foot (40m) yacht *Seamaster* lay off the Brazilian port of Macapá, at the mouth of the Amazon. That evening, six to eight armed and masked men clambered on board; Sir Peter was shot and killed as he tried to fire a shotgun at his assailants, and two other crewmen were injured. All the pirates had to show for their attack was a small outboard motor and a few wristwatches. They were subsequently caught and the murderer, 23-year-old Ricardo Tavares, given a 36-year sentence.

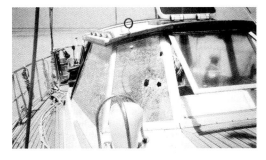

Above: The deckhouse of the German yacht *Jan Wilhelm III*, after she was attacked by pirates in 2001.

A Lucky Escape

This incident is typical of dozens of similar attacks that have taken place in the Caribbean and in South American waters over the past decade. A less dramatic story was told by the German couple Rudolf and Isolde Nuss, whose yacht *Jan Wilhelm III* was attacked off the Isla de la Tortuga in Venezuela in March 2001. The couple anchored for the night off the island and went to bed at 10pm. Four hours later they were woken by footsteps on the deck. Rudolf Nuss turned on the deck light but refused to open the hatches. The pirates fired into the cabin. As they did so, he opened a porthole and fired back at the intruders, who ran off. Nobody was hurt, but the yacht was riddled with bullet holes. The couple had been extremely lucky.

According to the IMB, 28 such attacks have taken place during the past three years, with the main trouble spots being the coasts of Venezuela, Haiti, Peru, and Brazil.

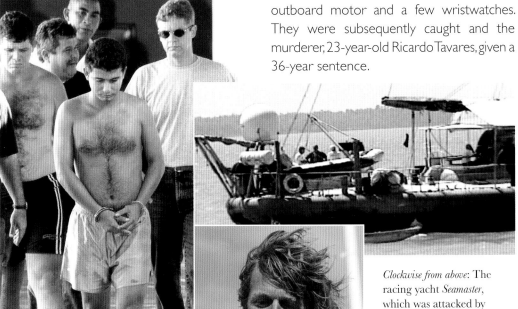

Clockwise from above: The racing yacht *Seamaster*, which was attacked by opportunistic pirates in a Brazilian harbor in December 1995; her captain Sir Peter, who was shot and killed during the attack; and police with two of the seven suspects, who were all arrested in 2001.

Piracy: Fact versus Fiction

This book is an account of the real pirates of history, shown warts and all—without all the romantic trappings that have come to encompass our notions of piracy, which for the past three centuries have been colored by fiction.

Above: The reality of 18th-century piracy—*Blackbeard in Smoke and Flames*, by Frank Schoonover, c.1922.

The modern-day perception of a pirate now owes more to Johnny Depp in *Pirates of the Caribbean*, or to Robert Louis Stevenson than it does to the pirates of history.

This whole process of romanticizing piracy began when they were at their most active. Alexandre Exquemelin wrote *The Buccaneers of America* in 1678. It was meant to be an eyewitness account of buccaneering activities, but it was highly colored, probably to make the book more sensational than it already was. It became a bestseller.

Then in 1724, the mysterious Captain Johnson published *A General History of the Robberies and Murders of the Most Notorious Pyrates*. It was clearly written by an informed and erudite mariner, who had either interviewed pirates or was one himself. For the most part, his collection of pirate biographies was accurate and informed, and it has stood the test of historical scrutiny. However, even Johnson wasn't able to avoid embellishing his

tale with a few clearly invented passages, in order to make his tale more colorful.

The public lapped it up—the first edition sold out in a matter of days, and the book has remained in print ever since. From that day, pirates have been the subject of novels, histories, stage productions, and films. Unfortunately, most of these have helped to obscure the reality of piracy behind a tightly woven screen of romantic myth.

Who Was Captain Johnson?

Nobody has been able to prove who Charles Johnson really was and no trace of a real Captain Johnson has ever been found. Candidates have included the head of the publishing house that produced the book, and Charles Johnson the London playwright. However, neither had the maritime knowledge that pervades the text. A more likely candidate was Daniel Defoe (1661–1731), who wrote *Robinson Crusoe*. Recently, scholars have rejected the possibility that he could have been the author, but he certainly had enough maritime knowledge to be a contender.

Truth and Myth

The later book and stage or screen versions of pirates are largely embellishment, but many details are based on fact.

What we know about piracy comes from a whole range of sources. A good starting point—at least for the buccaneers and pirates of the 17th and early 18th centuries—are two pirate histories written by people who knew what they were talking about.

Left: Robert Newton, who played Long John Silver in *Treasure Island* (1950), created our perception of pirate speech, based on his native West Country accent.

PIRATE TRUTH

Alexandre Exquemelin's *Buccaneers of America* of 1678, and Captain Charles Johnson's *A General History of the Robberies and Murders of the Most Notorious Pyrates* written in 1724 are great sources of information. Exquemelin was a real buccaneer, while at the very least Johnson interviewed surviving pirates, and had read all the details he could of their lives. What is surprising is that while both books contain inaccuracies, much of what the two authors wrote has stood the test of historical scrutiny.

Today, the world inhabited by Henry Morgan or Blackbeard can be revealed through the newspapers of the day, by reading the reports of colonial governors or merchants and the testimonies of pirate victims, or by looking up shipping logs and manifests. Naval officers also wrote accounts of their dealings with pirates. For instance, the details of Lieutenant Maynard's battle with Blackbeard off North Carolina's Ocracoke Island was recorded in official letters, written by the principal officers involved.

One of the best sources of true pirate life are the trial records of the many pirates who were caught and held to account for their crimes. In most cases, the course of

Above: For decades, children's stories portrayed a wholesome, swashbuckling version of piracy, in which the pirate heroes were honorable and chivalrous.

these trials was eagerly followed by the public, and this appetite for information was fed by newspapermen and pamphleteers, who circulated stories about the pirates and their victims. They also circulated the latest statements made in the courtroom, and when a pirate was executed, the same pamphleteers often produced accounts of dramatic gallows' confessions or accusations of injustice—even if the pirates themselves were too rum-befuddled to say a word. All this evidence adds to the very real collection of pirate information available to anyone with the patience to look for it.

Left: Errol Flynn, playing the pirate in the title role of the swashbuckler *Captain Blood* (1935).

Other of these fictional pirate devices are nothing more than hokum. The only pirate known to have actually buried any treasure was Captain William Kidd, and that was only as an insurance measure before he sailed home to New York. And he did it on an inhabited island off the Long Island coast and not a deserted tropical one. That means no pirate ever had need of a treasure map. Even if they did, they wouldn't be rash enough to mark its location with a big X.

The black spot from *Treasure Island*, a pirate curse, was simply a good way of adding drama to the story. And the accent so beloved of pretend pirates is based on the English West Country dialect spoken by Robert Newton, the actor who played Long John Silver in Walt Disney's screen adaptation of *Treasure Island* (1950).

Below: The dastardly Captain Hook in J.M. Barrie's *Peter Pan* was a bumbling yet civilized pirate.

Based on Truth

Like all good myths, pirate myths are grounded in reality. Parrots were in fact popular among seamen during the age of the sailing ship. Seamen brought them home from foreign climes, either to be used as pets or as exotic creatures they could sell. And wooden legs were far from uncommon during the 18th century, but a seaman with a wooden leg was a liability. For this reason, sailors with one leg were relegated to non-active roles, such as cooks—Robert Louis Stevenson made the one-legged Long John Silver the ship's cook on board the *Hispaniola*. Eye patches, however, were more common at sea, as a one-eyed seaman could still swab the decks, man a gun, or climb the rigging.

PIRATE MYTH

The source of some pirate myths are easier to track down than others. For instance, treasure maps, buried treasure, parrots on shoulders, wooden legs, black spots, and the singing of "Yo Ho Ho" all come from *Treasure Island* and the imagination of Robert Louis Stevenson. Eye patches, and hooks instead of hands all come from J.M. Barrie's *Peter Pan*. The same children's book later accounted for pirates wearing hats with the skull and crossbones on the front.

Walking the plank was also an artifice from *Peter Pan*, used to introduce a new character— a crocodile. In reality, there was no need to go to all that trouble. Pirates of the Golden Age would simply have stabbed a victim, and then thrown the body over the side.

The Pirates of Fiction

The first works of pirate fiction appeared while the Golden Age of Piracy was still underway, their realism replaced in the 19th century by the enduring romantic figures we still know today.

Above: Robinson Crusoe by Daniel Defoe, as illustrated here, was based on the experiences of a real shipwrecked buccaneer—Alexander Selkirk—who spent five years as a castaway on a Pacific island.

Some argue that Captain Johnson, who first recorded the exploits of these pirates, was also Daniel Defoe, the man responsible for the first appearance of pirates in fiction in the 18th century. Pirates continued to be the subject of novelists, poets, and artists well into the 19th century.

DANIEL DEFOE'S PIRATES

One of the first practitioners of the novel was Daniel Defoe whose *Robinson Crusoe* (1719) was a runaway success. In the work, the hero was captured by Barbary pirates—probably the first mention of pirates in a work of fiction. He escaped, only to be shipwrecked on a desert island. The novel was based on the story of the Scottish buccaneer Alexander Selkirk, who was rescued from a Pacific island by Woodes Rogers in 1709.

While most people are familiar with *Robinson Crusoe*, few know that Defoe also wrote novels about pirates. The first was *The King of Pirates*, published in 1719. The book was a fictional biography of Henry Every, whom Defoe portrayed as a buccaneer as well as a successful "Red Sea Roundsman." Next came *Captain Singleton* (1720), a novel about a fictional pirate, presented as an autobiography. Like Every, the pirate hero lived to tell the tale and to enjoy his plunder.

Another fictional autobiography attributed to Defoe was *The Four Years' Voyages of Captain George Roberts* (1726). In it the hero, Captain Roberts, falls victim to three pirates, one of which is the infamous Edward Low. As the book was written less than two years after Low's demise, this meant that at the very least, Defoe followed pirate activity very closely indeed. A similar book was *Madagascar: or Robert Drury's Journal* (1729). In it, the author—presumed to be Defoe—told the story of a sailor stranded on Madagascar who fell in with the island's pirates. In this case, Defoe may well have based his book on an existing account and used his own artistic license to embellish it. In both of these works, Defoe wove fantasy

Treasure Island

Over the past three centuries, numerous works of pirate fiction have appeared, but none of them have had a greater impact than that of *Treasure Island*, published in 1883.

Treasure Island is one of the most influential children's books ever published, and it first appeared as a serial under the title *The Sea Cook* in a children's magazine called *Young Folks* between 1881 and 1882. This choice of title showed that to the author Robert Louis Stevenson (1850–93) the real hero was the pirate Long John Silver. Stevenson's hero was not a romantic figure, but a frightening symbol of pirate reality. In creating him he invented the ultimate pirate—the figure that everyone envisaged when they shut their eyes and tried to imagine what a pirate would look like.

The Treasure Map

In fact, the modest Stevenson later claimed that the real inventor of the world of *Treasure Island* was Lloyd Osbourne, the author's 13-year-old stepson. In 1881, Stevenson and his family spent a holiday in Braemar, in the Scottish Highlands. It turned out to be a miserably wet summer and the children spent much of their holiday indoors. Stevenson claims that one rainy day he came across his American stepson coloring in a map he'd drawn—the map of an island.

As Lloyd Osbourne later recalled: "Stevenson came in as I was finishing it, and with his affectionate interest in everything I was doing, leaned over my shoulder, and was soon elaborating the map and naming it. I shall never forget the thrill of Skeleton Island, Spyglass Hill, nor the heart-stirring climax of the three red crosses! And the greater climax still when he wrote down the words 'Treasure Island' at the top right-hand corner!"

Within three days, Stevenson had written the first three chapters, and within two years *Treasure Island* appeared in print. The book has never been out of print and remains one of the best-loved books of all time.

Above: It was Robert Louis Stevenson who invented our idea of treasure maps, where "X" marks the location of the treasure.

Right: An early copy of Stevenson's classic tale, which is popular to this day.

Top right & right: Two illustrations by N.C. Wyeth from a 1911 edition of *Treasure Island*. Stevenson's book may have tinkered with pirate fact, but it remains a great adventure story.

with fiction, and he was clearly familiar with piracy. Whether or not he was also Captain Johnson is another matter entirely.

THE ROMANCE OF PIRATE FICTION

In the 19th century, novelists, poets, and the writers of the first adventure novels all found inspiration in the world of piracy. For them, pirates evoked a world of exotic locations, magnificent galleons, and heroic villains—thanks to them, real pirates were submerged by their literary counterparts.

Lord Byron's poem *The Corsair* (1814) was one of the first of these works, where the pirate was a romantic but tragic figure. The poem was so popular that its publishers sold 10,000 copies on its first day in print, a success that inspired others to follow suit. Sir Walter Scott's novel *The Pirate* (1821) was more down-to-earth and told readers a story about a Scottish pirate, based on the life of a real character—the Orkney pirate John Gow.

Giuseppi Verdi's 1848 opera *Il Corsaro* (The Corsair) was based on Byron's poem. A ballet version called *Le Corsaire* also appeared, while pirates featured in a host of lesser melodramatic novels, plays, and poems. In almost all of these cases, the pirate was cast as the hero, rebelling against injustice and heavy-handed authority. These pirates were noble creatures, reduced to villainy by circumstance. It is hard to imagine what Blackbeard would have made of *The Corsair*!

Left: Verdi's romantic opera *Il Corsaro* was performed in Drury Lane, London, in 1844. The hero was a Barbary pirate.

It was Robert Louis Stevenson who established pirates as a group who appealed to children. While Stevenson's pirates were honest portrayals of the real thing, other pirates in late 19th- and early 20th-century children's fiction were far less real. These pirates were either villainous, bearded creatures, who killed people for amusement, or they were true heroes—youthful, quick-witted, honorable, and clean-cut. These *Boys Own* pirate heroes fought to right wrongs or to rescue damsels in distress.

The Original Swashbuckler

The man responsible for the new type of pirate novel was Rafael Sabatini (1875–1950), an Anglo-Italian author who single-handedly invented the "swashbuckler" as a genre in adventure fiction. However outlandish his sorties, he still based his tale firmly in the realities portrayed by Exquemelin and Johnson.

His first successful novel, was *Scaramouche* (1921), set in the French Revolution, but in 1922 he wrote *Captain Blood*, which proved hugely popular. It also set the standard for the pirate books that followed. His later novels included *The Sea Hawk* and *The Black Swan*. His work also inspired film-makers to produce some of the classic swashbucklers of the silver screen.

Below: Dancers from the Kirov Ballet perform *Le Corsaire*—a far cry from the realities of piracy! Based loosely on Byron's poem, the ballet tells the story of Conrad, a Barbary pirate.

Captain Hook
and pirates of the stage

Long before pirates became the subject of literary fiction, they provided inspiration for playwrights and theatrical entertainers—they made the perfect villain.

Above: In Gilbert and Sullivan's opera *The Pirates of Penzance*, the pirates are portrayed as incompetent figures of fun, rather than violent criminals.

In 1712, the playwright Charles Johnson staged a production in Drury Lane, London, called *The Successful Pyrate*, celebrating the life and love of pirate king Captain Every.

Johnson's character bore little relation to the real pirate, but then nobody really cared. In 1798, James Cross produced a ballet called *Blackbeard*, or *The Captive Princess*, which was loosely based on Captain Johnson's portrayal

of Blackbeard, with a heroine added for good measure.

During the early 19th century, pirates regularly appeared in melodramas, along with smugglers, highwaymen, and bandits—all stock villains of the Georgian popular stage. Gilbert and Sullivan's *The Pirates of Penzance* (1880) drew on this tradition of the pirate as a stage villain, but turned it around, so that in their comic opera the pirates were lovable, soft-hearted

villains. It was clear that by this time pirates were seen as figures of fun, far removed from the reality. The comic opera has been performed ever since, each time reinforcing the notion that pirates are somehow inept, harmless, and lovable.

PETER PAN'S PIRATE

One of the great works of pirate fiction was *Peter Pan*, written by J.M. Barrie (1860–1937). He first wrote the play as a novel, *The Little White Bird* in 1902, and then adapted it for the stage. However, it was as a captivating children's play that it enjoyed its greatest popularity. *Peter Pan* was first performed in London in December 1904, and was an overnight success. A Broadway version appeared the following year. The story of the boy who refused to grow up entranced audiences, and Captain Hook became an instantly recognizable pirate villain.

Captain Hook

In *Peter Pan*, Captain James Hook and his crew of the *Jolly Roger* were portrayed as villainous but inept, thereby following the lead shown by Gilbert and Sullivan. Even more amusingly, J.M. Barrie's pirate captain was schooled at Eton in England, and was described in the original play as "a genteel pirate," obsessed with "good form." It was harder to think of a character more at odds with the reality of pirate captains of the Golden Age of Piracy. Captain Hook resembled more an Edwardian gentleman in a pirate costume.

Left: J.M. Barrie gave us the myth that pirates make their prisoners walk the plank. Real pirates would simply have thrown their captives overboard.

The Pirates of Hollywood

Once upon a time it seemed as if the sword-wielding, flamboyant pirate hero and the cinema were made for each other. For more than three decades, audiences were thrilled by the pirate swashbuckler, after which the genre was replaced by less escapist fare.

During the first decades of cinema, directors in Hollywood struggled to find the right combination of subject matter and actor that would thrill their audiences.

THE SWASHBUCKLER

The original film version of *Treasure Island* was released in 1908, the first of at least a dozen versions of the book to make it to the big screen. However, it was not until 1924 that they hit on the right formula. In 1922, Rafael Sabatini wrote *Captain Blood*, and Hollywood produces bought the script as they felt it would make a good movie. The silent movie *Captain Blood* appeared on the

Above: Douglas Fairbanks (right) in *The Black Pirate*, the 1924 silent movie that established the swashbuckling genre. This film was also one of the first to be shot in Technicolor, using a two-color palette.

What Was a Swashbuckler?

In the 16th century, a "swashbuckler" was a swordsman and a braggart, eager to boast about his prowess with the blade. "Swash" described the sound a sword made as it was wielded, while a "buckler" was a form of small shield favored by Spanish swordsmen. In effect, the word meant someone who made a noise like a sword striking a shield—a noisy display of bravado. It fell into disuse, only to be re-invented by Sabatini, who used it in his novel to describe a new and more heroic breed of swordsman. It also came to refer to the novels in which these heroes featured. In movies, the word embraced those featuring the same sword-fighting heroes.

silver screen two years later, with Warren Kerrigan playing the title role. While the film itself was uninspiring, it led to two more—*The Sea Hawk* (1924) starring Milton Sills, and—more memorably—*The Black Pirate* (1926) with Douglas Fairbanks playing the swashbuckling hero.

The Black Pirate was the first true cinematic pirate classic. Fairbanks was the first screen hero to stick a knife in a sail and slide down to the deck, and he also walked the plank, killed a pirate captain in a sword fight, and rescued the beautiful princess. That was the start of the love affair between Hollywood and the swashbuckler. Of course, Douglas Fairbanks wouldn't have been anything without Rafael Sabatini. The gifted author of adventure novels invented the "swashbuckler" as a fictional genre; indeed, his work seemed to have been written for Hollywood's new breed of romantic action heroes.

THE GOLDEN AGE OF THE SWASHBUCKLER

It was felt that the introduction of sound would kill off the swashbuckler, which relied on excitement rather than dialogue. The producers needn't have worried.

The 1930s and 1940s saw a profusion of talking-picture swashbucklers, many of which were based on the novels of Rafael Sabatini (see page 239). The best of these was probably the remake of *Captain Blood* (1935), which launched the career of the unknown Errol Flynn as the rebellious pirate hero. He returned to piracy in *The Sea Hawk* (1940), a wartime patriotic romp that owed little to Sabatini's original book and a lot to Hollywood's support of Britain's war effort. Another piratical classic of the period was *The Black Swan* (1942), in which Tyrone Power played a fictional pirate serving alongside a bombastic Sir Henry Morgan. Another notable pirate film was the 1934 version of *Treasure Island,* starring Wallace Beery as Long John Silver.

SELF-PARODY

While the pirate genre continued into the early 1950s, tastes were changing, and the tendency was for these later pirate films to parody the swashbucklers that had come before. For example, in the *Crimson Pirate* (1952) Burt Lancaster reprised Fairbanks' earlier role in *The Black Pirate,* but as a former circus acrobat he outdid Fairbanks' physical

In *Captain Blood* (1935), Errol Flynn plays a doctor sentenced to slavery in Jamaica, who escapes and becomes a pirate. The swashbuckling hero ends up thwarting a Spanish invasion and saving the colony.

performance, swinging from ropes and sliding down sails. There was one last piratical spree, with Robert Newton appearing in both *Blackbeard the Pirate* and *Long John Silver*, and the aging Errol Flynn and Maureen O'Hara enjoying one last pirate romp in *Under All Flags*. However, these were the last of their kind—for two decades at least one or two swashbucklers had come out every year, but from the late 1950s they became a rarity.

PORTRAYING THE REAL THING

While most swashbuckling heroes were fictional, to help give the stories some meaning they sometimes had to fight "real" pirates. For the most part these historical figures were portrayed as villains. In *Blackbeard the Pirate* (1952) Robert Newton played history's most famous pirate as a black villain. Strangely, real names from Blackbeard's world were given to characters, including Robert Maynard and Sam Bellamy but, unlike in real life, he also crossed paths with Sir Henry Morgan. As usual, Hollywood was playing fast and loose with history. In fact, Sir Henry Morgan appears in several pirate films, including *The Black Swan* (1942), and the *Pirates of Tortuga* (1961), usually as an early 18th-century villain rather than a mid-17th-century hero.

Another example where Hollywood didn't stick to pirate reality is found in *Captain Kidd* (1945), where the unfortunate privateer turned pirate was played by Charles Laughton. Inevitably, he portrayed him as a chilling villain. One of the few films to show a real pirate in a heroic role was *The Buccaneer*, which featured Jean Lafitte as the hero. He was played by Fredric March in the 1938 version, and by Yul Brynner in the 1958 remake. Even then, the pirate was a hero in the traditional swashbuckling mold, which was probably a far cry from the real Jean Lafitte.

A DROUGHT OF PIRATES

For almost half a century piracy was never properly considered a box office draw. A few pirate films were made during the late 20th century, including *Swashbuckler* (1976) with Robert Shaw, *Yellowbeard* (1983) starring Peter Cook, Roman Polanski's *Pirates* (1986), played with great aplomb by Walter Matthau, and the less memorable *Cutthroat Island* (1995), featuring Gina Davis as a pirate heroine. There was also a film adaptation of Peter Pan—*Hook* (1991)—where Dustin Hoffman played the title role, and no less than four versions of *Treasure Island*, not including *Muppet Treasure Island* (1996), the muppets twist on the classic tale, with Tim Curry playing the role of Long John Silver.

While some of these films were entertaining, none of them really took the box office by storm, or managed to lift the pirate film from the doldrums. Then came the *Pirates of the Caribbean* trilogy. The films resurrected the genre, and once again pirates have box office potential. Plans are afoot for a fourth *Pirates of the Caribbean* film, while reports suggest that a major film about Blackbeard is also being planned. The long-running love affair between pirates and the big screen has never been stronger.

Below: Walter Matthau as Captain Red, in *Pirates* (1986). Matthau was unable to avoid following Robert Newton's piratical example and mimicked both his accent and his exaggerated mannerisms.

The Jack Sparrow Phenomenon

At the start of the 21st century, it seemed that the era of the Hollywood pirate was over. Then along came Johnny Depp, as the fictional Captain Jack Sparrow…

Pirates of the Caribbean ushered in a new age of cinematic piracy, bringing the pirate genre back to the movie-going public.

The idea of basing a film on a Walt Disney theme park ride was certainly unusual. For a decade, writers struggled with a script until they completed one that both Walt Disney and the producer Jerry Bruckheimer were happy with. Rather than sticking to a classic format, they introduced a supernatural element that was part of the original Disney ride.

In 2002, leading Hollywood actor Johnny Depp was signed up to play the leading character, Captain Jack Sparrow. His portrayal of the pirate, with his foppish swagger, slurred speech, and camp mannerisms, alarmed the Disney executives, but they trusted Bruckheimer's judgment and the skills of the director, Gore Verbinski. The rest is box office legend. *Pirates of the Caribbean: The Curse of the Black Pearl* (2003) proved to be a smash hit and grossed millions at the box office. The major cast members were signed up for two sequels.

One of the problems with the trilogy is that the sequels were filmed in quick succession, before a coherent script had been written. The result is a triumph for special effects but the sequels strayed even further from the realities of piracy. Despite this, there can be no doubt that the popularity of the films has added significantly to pirate myth, and Depp has become the pirate role model for a new generation.

Above and right: The sinister Davy Jones (Bill Nighy), above, and the heroic Will Turner (Orlando Bloom), from *Pirates of the Caribbean: Dead Man's Chest* (2006).

Rock Star Approach

Johnny Depp was hailed as having reinvented the screen pirate—a combination of Errol Flynn, Robert Newton, and Douglas Fairbanks. When asked who had been his inspiration, Depp cited the Rolling Stones' Keith Richards, combined with Iggy Pop and Errol Flynn. He added that pirates were "like the rock stars of their time." Just about the only person he didn't mention was a real pirate.

Nevertheless, Jack Sparrow owed more than a passing nod to Blackbeard. In fact, Johnny Depp looked comparatively mundane compared with the real Blackbeard, with his wild beard, blazing eyes, and a burning slowmatch stuck in his hat. This is one of the charms of the subject—real pirates will always be just as colorful as the fictional kind.

Top: Johnny Depp's screen portrayal of a pirate is probably more accurate than many earlier attempts, as consciously or otherwise it encompassed many of the traits ascribed by Captain Johnson to the real pirates of "the Golden Age."

Pirate Perceptions

The gap between real piracy and its modern perception is virtually unbridgeable, but it is worth knowing about the reality.

The modern perception of piracy is more about enjoyment and partygoing than the reality of robbery and murder on the high seas.

For most people, the word "pirate" conjures up a stereotypical image based on three centuries of pirate fiction. In fact, that can really be boiled down to *Treasure Island, Pirates of the Caribbean, Peter Pan*, and a string of Saturday matinee pirate films. Most people are happy to imagine pirates as people who walk planks, wear hats emblazoned with a skull and crossbones, and speak like Robert Newton. This notion of piracy is fueled by pirate toys, theme park rides, pirate Halloween costumes, and pirate parties for adults. Frankly, there's very little harm in it.

PIRATE FESTIVALS

There are several pirate festivals around the world. One of the largest is Pirates in Paradise—an annual event held in Key West, Florida, during late November. This festival, and other events like it, attract pirate enthusiasts, historians, re-enactors, and the simply curious, and involve a range of events from pirate parties to the

Above: Pirates have been used to promote lavish themed hotels and casinos in Las Vegas.

re-enactment of pirate history—and an awful lot of carousing.

What we need to do is remember that there is a difference between pirate fact and pirate fiction. We all have an understanding of pirate fiction. Readers of this book will have learned about pirate fact. Those who follow the news well know that there is a harsh pirate reality, exemplified by the modern pirates of Somalia, Indonesia, and West Africa. These pirates don't wear comedy eye patches or plastic swords. They wear hoods over their faces and wield AK-47 assault rifles. In reality, piracy is a vicious and sometimes deadly business.

International Talk Like a Pirate Day

In 2002, two friends from Portland, Oregon—John Baur and Mark Summers—contacted a journalist, seeking to promote a new festival they had dreamed up—International Talk Like a Pirate Day (ITLAPD), to be celebrated each September 19.

The press found the notion amusing and the idea soon spread. Today ITLAPD is celebrated in several countries, and receives significant press and media coverage. People are actively encouraged to talk like the pirate characters created by Robert Newton, Johnny Depp, or simply to indulge in the whole whimsical nonsense of it all.

Left: Pirates appeal to children because they represent freedom, adventure, and a carefree existence.

The Pirate Legacy

After struggling to wrest pirate fact from pirate fiction, perhaps our one lasting legacy from the days of Blackbeard and his compatriots is the elusive notion of freedom.

Above: Perhaps the greatest pirate artist is Howard Pyle, who captured much of the reality of 18th-century piracy in his children's book illustrations.

Long John Silver as a Role Model

In *Treasure Island*, Long John Silver describes the pirate life to the cabin boy Jim Hawkins: "Here it is about gentlemen of fortune. They live rough, and they risk swinging, but they eat and drink like fighting cocks, and when a cruise is done, why it's hundreds of pounds instead of hundreds of farthings in their pockets. Now the most goes for rum and a good fling, and to sea again in their shirts."

It is little wonder that readers of the time might have felt slightly envious of Long John Silver's piratical freedom.

Whether we like it or not, piracy is seen as much as a lifestyle as it is a real crime. For most people, today and throughout history, piracy represents a form of escapism.

For three centuries, piracy has gripped the popular imagination. In 1724, people read Captain Johnson's bestseller as a form of escapism—it portrayed a world far removed from their safe but unexciting daily lives. This explains the popularity of *Treasure Island*, the Hollywood swashbucklers, and *Pirates of the Caribbean*. Piracy represents a vision of freedom from the constraints of society.

Pirates represent a group of individuals that defy the rules, with a freedom of action denied to those of us who pay taxes, hold down jobs, or take the kids to school. It is a bit like the holidaymaker who envies those that can spend all year lying on a tropical beach, but who has to return home in order to maintain a standard of living that allows these vacations in the first place.

The word "pirate" now has several meanings it didn't have in the early 18th century, and it is also applied in areas that have little to do with robbery on the high seas. Describing someone as a pirate isn't a good thing, but it isn't wholly bad either. The word generally has a romantic, roguish quality

Above: In Howard Pyle's *The Flying Dutchman*, the artist portrayed the mariner, who was damned by Satan in the popular legend, as a piratical figure.

A New Definition

More recently, the term "piracy" has been used in new ways. Whenever you rent a DVD you are warned that "Piracy is a crime." It certainly is—and it involves robbery on the high seas. Film and music companies have used the word "piracy" in a new and inappropriate way—or have they? In 1703, Daniel Defoe complained that his novel *The True-Born Englishman* was being "printed again and again, by pyrates." Clearly the word has always been a flexible one. Of course, Defoe made his statement six years before the first copyright laws were laid down, so he may well have been struggling to find an appropriate description of the rogue publishers.

Above: Two Chinese policemen sift through a haul of pirate DVDs seized in a raid on a bogus distributer.

to it, which has little to do with the reality of piracy. It can be compared to the romance associated with gangsters—devolved from the realities of mob violence or intimidation. It is as though piracy is an acceptable face of criminal activity because the reality of piracy is divorced from the perception of it.

Pirates as Advertisers

Pirates are also used in advertising. Captain Morgan Rum quite sensibly anchors its product on a pirate. Any self-respecting pirate of the Golden Age would have considered the association to be an appropriate one. Piracy has also been used to sell real estate—oceanfront properties with names like "Pirate Cove" or "Treasure Island." However, pirates have sometimes been appropriated to sell children's food, drugs, travel packages, clothing, beer, and even car insurance. Surely a real pirate wouldn't insure his car! This all stems from the lifestyle of the pirate. The association the advertisers want you to make is of a carefree existence and an independence of spirit.

Freedom and Escape

Much has been written about the motivation of pirates. Some pirates of the Golden Age were simply incapable of living in polite society, those like the men who one young captive described in 1722 as being, "A vile crew of miscreants to whom it was a sport to do mischief." Many claimed they took to piracy because they were coerced. Far more claimed the system forced them do it. In other words, they turned to piracy to escape the economic situation in their countries and the injustices of society—to improve their lot. Many of these men (and some women) knew their chances of survival were slim, but for a short time they had the opportunity to chart their own course and to make their own mistakes.

Above and right: Pirates are now used to sell a range of popular products, from Captain Morgan rum—named after the famous buccaneer—to romantic holidays in the Caribbean.

Perhaps that is their greatest legacy—a fleeting illusion of freedom, the notion of grasping the moment, of living life to the full, and escaping from the straitjackets imposed on us by society. Perhaps there are the makings of a pirate in all of us.

Index

Bold page numbers denote a main entry; italicized page numbers denote an illustration (including maps).

Picture Credits

CHAPTER 12

174, 175, 176 ©National Maritime Museum, Greenwich, London; 177 ©The Bridgeman Art Library; 179© National Maritime Museum, Greenwich, London; 180(t&b) ©Bettmann/Corbis; 181 ©National Maritime Museum, Greenwich, London; 183(t) ©Gianni Dagli Orti/Corbis; 183(b) © National Maritime Museum, Greenwich, London; 184 ©Giraudon/The Bridgeman Art Library; 186(t) ©National Maritime Museum, Greenwich, London; 186(bl) ©Archives Charmet/The Bridgeman Art Library; 186(br) ©Philippe Giraud/Corbis; 187 ©Peaboy Essex Museum, Salem, Massachusetts, USA/The Bridgeman Art Library; 188(t) ©The Mariners'Museum, Newport News,VA; 188(b) ©National Maritime Museum, Greenwich, London; 189© The Granger Collection/ TopFoto

CHAPTER 13

190 ©National Maritime Museum, Greenwich, London; 191 ©Stratford Archives; 193(t) ©Mary Evans Picture Library/Rue des Archives; 193(b) ©Stratford Archives; 194 © The Mariners'Museum, Newport News,VA; 195(t&b) ©Stratford Archives; 196(t) ©National Maritime Museum, Greenwich, London; 196(b) ©Stratford Archives; p197(t) courtesy of the U.S. Naval Academy Museum;197(b) ©National Maritime Museum, Greenwich, London; 199 ©The Mariners'Museum, Newport, News,VA

Below: HMS *Aurora* guarding a convoy attacked by Barbary pirates, 1812, by Thomas Buttersworth.

CHAPTER 14

200, 201, 202(t) ©National Maritime Museum, Greenwich, London; 202(b) ©Asian Art & Archaeology, Inc./Corbis; 203, 205 ©Stratford Archives; 206(t&b) ©akg-images/Mark De Fraeye; 207 ©National Maritime Museum, Greenwich, London; 209 ©TopFoto; 210(r) ©Stratford Archives; 210(tl) ©Bettmann/Corbis; 211(t) ©National Maritime Museum, Greenwich, London; 211(b) ©The Granger Collection/TopFoto; 213, 214, 215(t&b) ©National Maritime Museum, Greenwich, London; 216, 217(t) ©Stratford Archives; 217(b) ©Mary Evans Picture Library; 218 ©National Portrait Gallery, London, UK/The Bridgeman Art Library; 220(t) ©Bettmann/Corbis; 220(b) ©Mary Evans Picture Library/Illustrated London News; 221(t) ©TopFoto; 221(b) ©National Maritime Museum, Greenwich, London

CHAPTER 15

222 ©Ed Kashi/Corbis; 223 ©Peter Turnley/Corbis; 225(t&b) ©Reuters/Corbis; 226(t) ©Supri/Reuters/Corbis; 226(b), 227(t) ©Reuters/Corbis; 227(b) ©Ahmad Yusni/epa/Corbis; 228(l) ©George Thande/Reuters/Corbis; 228(r) ©Badri Media/epa/Corbis; 229(t) ©Jason R. Zalasky/epa/Corbis; 229(b) ©Handout/Reuters/Corbis; 230(t) ©Shabelle Media/Reuters/Corbis; 230(b) ©Abdiqani Hassan/Reuters/Corbis; 231 ©epa/Corbis; 232(tl) ©epa/Corbis; 232(c) ©Ed Kashi/Corbis; 232(b) ©George Steinmetz/Corbis; 233(l) ©AFP/Getty Images;233(tc) ©Della Zuana Pascal/Corbis Sygma; 233(c)©Sipa Press/Rex Features; 233(br) ©Stratford Archives;

CHAPTER 16

234© Stratford Archives; 235(l) ©Mary Evans Picture Library/Interfoto; 235(r) ©Bettmann/Corbis; 236(t) ©John Springer Collection/Corbis; 236(c) ©Tom Brakefield/Corbis; 236(b) ©Blue Lantern Studio/Corbis; 237 ©Look and Learn/The Bridgeman Art Library; 238(tr), 238(br) ©The Stapleton Collection/The Bridgeman Art Library; 238(tl), 238(bl) ©Mary Evans Picture Library; 239(t) ©Mary Evans Picture Library/Illustrated London News; 239(b) ©Linda Rich/ArenaPAL/TopFoto; 240(t) ©Lee Snider/Photo Images/Corbis; 240(b) ©Hugo Philpott/epa/Corbis; 241©John Springer Collection/Corbis; 242 ©Sunset Boulevard/Corbis; 243 ©JP Laffont/Sygma/Corbis; 244 (tr, br&bl) ©Peter Mountain/Industrial Light & Magic/Bureau L.A. Collection/Corbis; 245(t) ©Atlantide Phototravel/Corbis; 245(b) ©Awilli/zefa/Corbis; 246(r) © Delaware Art Museum, Wilmington, USA/ Museum Purchase/The Bridgeman Art Library; 246(l) ©Mary Evans Picture Library; 247(l) ©Sipa Press/Rex Features; 247(tr) ©image courtesy of The Advertising Archives; 247(br) ©Swim Ink 2, LLC/Corbis.

Every effort has been made to trace the copyright holders, and we apologise in advance for any accidental errors. We would be happy to apply the corrections in the following edition of this publication.

Creative Team

Author: Angus Konstam

AA Media Ltd:
Managing Editor: Paul Mitchell

Hunkydory Publishing Ltd:
Project Editor: Rebecca Fry
Copy Editor: Nicky Gyopari
Designer: Kelly-Anne Levey
Picture Researcher: Shelley Noronha
Illustrator: Brian Delf
Colorist: Samantha Emms
Indexer: Sarah Hilton